New Directions in Mission and Evangelization 2

New Directions in Mission and Evangelization
Edited by
James A. Scherer
Stephen B. Bevans, S.V.D.

New Directions in Mission and Evangelization is an Orbis Series which offers collections of important articles and papers, all previously published but not easily available to students and scholars of mission. Selections included in each volume represent examples of mission theology and theological reflection which deal creatively with issues affecting the church's mission and the postmodern world.

Volumes in the series will appear periodically and will include Roman Catholic, Orthodox, Conciliar Protestant, Evangelical, Pentecostal, and other points of view. Each volume focuses on a theme such as
  • The Theological Foundations of Mission
  • Contextualization of Theology
  • Mission Spirituality
  • Theology of Religion and Dialogue Between Persons of Living Faiths
  • Ecology and Mission
  • Social Justice and Mission

NEW DIRECTIONS
IN MISSION
AND EVANGELIZATION 2

Theological Foundations

Editors
James A. Scherer
Stephen B. Bevans

ORBIS BOOKS

Maryknoll, New York 10545

The Catholic Foreign Mission Society of America (Maryknoll) recruits and trains people for overseas missionary service. Through Orbis Books, Maryknoll aims to foster the international dialogue that is essential to mission. The books published, however, reflect the opinions of their authors and are not meant to represent the official position of the society.

Introductions and comments copyright © 1994 by James A. Scherer and Stephen B. Bevans. Permission is gratefully acknowledged to the holders of copyrights on articles and papers presented in the book and mentioned in the acknowledgments for permission to reproduce their materials.
Published by Orbis Books, Maryknoll, New York 10545, U.S.A.
Manufactured in the United States of America.

Library of Congress Cataloging-in-Publication Data
(Revised for vol. 2)

New directions in mission and evangelization.

  Includes bibliographical references and index.
  Contents: 1. Basic statements 1974–1991
—2. Theological foundations.
  1. Missions.   2. Evangelistic work.   I. Scherer,
James A.   II. Bevans, Stephen B., 1944–   .
BV2030.N42   1992   266.'001   92-1273
ISBN 0-88344-792-4 (v. 1)
ISBN 0-88344-953-6 (v. 2)

To
David J. Bosch
1929–1992

friend and colleague

Contents

Part III
Missionary Praxis

Part IV
The Study of Mission

Part V
Documentation

A Word on Style

The articles and papers that make up *New Directions 2* come from a variety of sources. Together they say a great deal about the plurality of voices and points of view that comprise world Christianity. They also testify to the immense variety of usages of English worldwide. While we have corrected typographical errors and actual "mistakes" we have found in articles and papers selected for this volume, we have made no attempt to standardize such things as reference styles, spelling, and punctuation. While this will no doubt annoy purists, it has the advantage of retaining the linguistic and stylistic varieties of the original sources.

Introduction

James A. Scherer and Stephen B. Bevans

New Directions in Mission and Evangelization 2: Theological Foundations is the second volume in Orbis Books' "New Directions" series. It was conceived by the editors to continue the pattern of the earlier *Mission Trends* (Anderson and Stransky, 1974–1981) series so as to make available significant and rather recently published missiological literature in an accessible and relatively economical form. The immediate predecessor of this present volume was *New Directions in Mission and Evangelization 1: Basic Statements, 1974–1991* (Scherer and Bevans, 1992), a collection consisting exclusively of basic statements on mission from conciliar ecumenical, Roman Catholic, Eastern Orthodox and evangelical Protestant sources, and one which was intended to serve as a preface to the entire *New Directions* series. *New Directions 2: Theological Foundations*, as the subtitle indicates, is an attempt to gather together articles and statements which, in one way or another, reflect efforts of missiologists and churchpersons to explore the various theological foundations on which the church's missionary efforts are based.

As we observed in our earlier volume, Christian mission today is in search of a postmodern, ecumenical paradigm, a paradigm which is being determined by a number of epochal changes in our world: (1) we now live in a pluricentric, rather than Western-dominated world, despite the fact that the Cold War is now over; (2) structures of oppression and exploitation are today being challenged as never before; (3) a profound feeling of ambiguity exists about the value of Western technology and development, and the older idea of "progress"; (4) we inhabit a shrinking global village with finite resources, and this calls for growing mutual interdependence; (5) humans are for the first time aware of their capacity to destroy the earth and make it uninhabitable for future generations; (6) societies everywhere now seek their own local cultural identities and reject slavish imitation of Western models; (7) freedom of religion and greater awareness of other faiths force Christians to re-evaluate their own earlier attitudes toward other faiths (Bosch, 188–89; *See* Scherer and Bevans, 1992, ix). As David Bosch insisted, "quite literally, we live in a world fundamentally different from that of the nineteenth century, let alone earlier times" (Bosch, 189).

At the same time, and in response to the challenge of the paradigm that is still developing but nevertheless ineluctably emerging, Christian mission is undergoing what Robert Schreiter calls in this volume a "new birth,"—or, as Anthony Gittins puts it in his essay, mission is developing a new "myth"—and such "new directions" in search of a new paradigm is what this series attempts to trace. This volume, as we have said, focuses on the theological foundations of mission in today's post-modern, post-Cold War, and—as some might even claim—post-Christian world. Subsequent volumes will offer collections of articles which explore such issues as the theology of religions and interreligious dialogue, the interaction of faith and culture and the challenge of developing contextual theologies, and the missionary implications of the churches' call to be signs and instruments of justice in the world.

The Fifth World Conference on Faith and Order, meeting in Santiago de Compostela, Spain, in August of 1993 (See *Koinonia*, 1993) underscored the intimate relationship between the unity of the church as *koinonia* in Christ: the common *confession* of the apostolic faith, the *sharing* of a common life in Christ, and the call to a *common witness* in mission and evangelism. The close link between unity in Our Lord Jesus Christ and our common calling as Christians to witness to the faith of the apostles is now being more widely recognized, despite the inevitable tensions. As the Compostela document points out:

> The unity of the Church to which we are called is a *koinonia* given and expressed in the common confession of apostolic faith; a common sacramental life entered by the one baptism and celebrated together in one eucharistic fellowship; a common life in which members and ministries are mutually recognized and reconciled; and a common mission witnessing to all people to the gospel of God's grace and serving the whole creation (*Koinonia*, 5/85 [par. 18.2.1]).

The essays and statements in *New Directions 2* are intended to support and contribute to a close and growing communion between local churches in all aspects of their life: confessing the one faith, coming together in worship and witness, and reaching out in mission and evangelization for a renewed and reconciled humanity. As such, this volume is offered as the fruit of *koinonia* in faith and witness. As editors who come from the Lutheran and Roman Catholic traditions, we have put together a collection of articles and statements that come from a number of "Christian families in mission" (See Phillips and Coote, 1993). Our contributors write out of our own conciliar and Roman traditions, but also from evangelical, Orthodox, and Mennonite traditions as well.

The fourteen essays and two regional statements included in this volume have all been previously published in journals and books dealing with mission, but many are not easily accessible to nonspecialists. Each contribution is introduced with a short summary of its content, and information is provided about its original publication and the background (where relevant) of the author. Besides representing a wide spectrum of confessional viewpoints, we have made efforts to include articles by women missiologists, and have tried to include as well perspectives other than those of our North Atlantic, Western world. While the views presented are very diverse, and possibly contradictory, what they have in common is that they each represent a search for new theological foundations of missionary reflection. Not every contribution is, strictly speaking, theological; yet each one, in our judgement, provides an important perspective from which to view the entire panorama of theological synthesis. More complete scrutiny of related issues (theology of religions, contextualization, justice, and liberation) will, as we have said, be forthcoming in subsequent numbers of the "New Directions" series, but these issues are so closely intertwined with the theological reflections in this second volume that some of these perspectives are necessarily included (e.g., the contributions of Orlando Costas, George Brunk, and Jacob Kavunkal).

One of the most frustrating aspects of editing a volume of this kind is that we could not include all the articles or statements that might have merited reprinting in a collection of this type—our "short list" was really quite long, and some difficult decisions had to be made. However, we do think that the essays and statements which appear here represent the very best of missiological literature that has been published within the last decade and a half.

We have grouped the essays or statements that appear in this volume under five general categories. Part I deals with the properly theological question of what mission is in a six-continent era of global interdependence and mutual partnership. This is the largest section of our collection, and contains reflections by some of the best missiological minds of our day: Orlando Costas links mission to the church's commitment to the world's poor and oppressed; Lesslie Newbigin sees mission as the participation of the church in God's own mission; Anastasios of Androussa provides an Orthodox perspective, while George Brunk writes out of his convictions as a Mennonite. Other essays by Charles Van Engen, Michael Amaladoss, David Bosch, and Jacob Kavunkal explore the ecclesiological, biblical, and Christological foundations of mission in today's world. Since mission theology is done within the context of various ecclesial traditions, a second section of the volume traces the development of mission theology in the evangelical (Utuk), Roman Catholic (Schreiter), and conciliar Protestant (Pope-Levison) "families"; and since mission is not an abstract undertaking but the work of very concrete women and men, a third section is devoted to essays that provide theological foundations for mission by reflecting on the ideas and ideals of missionaries. In this section, Anthony Gittins speaks of the demise and recovery of the "missionary myth," and Stephen Bevans proposes a theology of mission by "seeing through" a number of images of the missionary. A single article constitutes the fourth section of the book: James Scherer presents a reflection on the nature and scope of the discipline that studies the church's mission—missiology. Then, in a final section, we present statements from two regional churches. First, a statement from the Protestant churches of Latin America presents an equal challenge to the church in the midst of poverty; and a statement out of the Caribbean calls for a missiology that is thoroughly inculturated. This last section fits most loosely into the chosen theme for this volume, but we feel that a continual documentation of official statements is a most necessary feature of the series.

Some final observations are in order. First, while this book explores the theological foundations for the church's mission, we must insist that those foundations are not yet fully firmly in place. Today's missiological world is characterized by continuing change and abrupt transition rather than ultimate finality and smooth development. However disconcerting it may be to the beginning student of missiology to learn that we have to build on what is still an uncertain theological foundation, no less a person than the eminent missiologist David Bosch has characterized missiology as "a multi-colored mosaic of complementary and mutually enriching as well as mutually challenging frames of reference" which must be examined critically, one by one, and which at best point in the direction of "the emerging ecumenical paradigm of mission" (Bosch, 8). A second observation is that missiology today is unmistakably becoming more global and universal—*catholic* in the true and best sense of the word—as the international provenance of our authors and the broad scope of their experiences suggests. We can no longer listen only to Western voices, but must be sensitive and open to the pioneering work of a new generation of missiologists from the two-thirds world. On the other hand, the Christian mission has its roots in a long and venerable theological tradition, and those who struggle creatively to cast the gospel in terms of other thought forms, or try to cast new light on the gospel in dialogue with such thought forms, neglect that tradition at their own peril. Third, churches and church theologians—especially in the developed Western world—need to take the discipline of missiology much more seriously if they are to be rescued from provincialism and stagnation and to become faithful once again to their identity as members of the community-in-mission that is the church. As authors such as Lesslie Newbigin and his disciple George Hunsberger have continually reminded us in the last several years, the rediscovery of the missiological dimension of theology and of ecclesial life is essential to the survival of Christianity in today's secularized, privatized, and consumerized world (Hunsberger, 1991). The church is "missionary by its very nature," as Vatican II's Decree on Missionary Activity has reminded us (AG 2). It is this ecclesiological fact that needs to ground all our theological reflection and all our pastoral action. It is this theological reality which assures us in our faith that theological foundations for our mission are indeed possible.

BIBLIOGRAPHY

AG. 1965. *Ad Gentes.* "Vatican Council II. Decree on the Church's Missionary Activity." In A. Flannery, ed. *Vatican Council II: The Conciliar and Post-Conciliar Documents.* Collegeville, MN: The Liturgical Press, 1981, pp. 813–56.

Anderson, Gerald H. and Thomas F. Stransky, eds. 1974–1981. *Mission Trends.* Five Volumes. Grand Rapids, MI: William B. Eerdmans Publishing Company; New York: Paulist Press.

Bosch, David J. 1991. *Transforming Mission: Paradigm Shifts in Theology of Mission.* Maryknoll, NY: Orbis Books.

Hunsberger, George. 1991. "The Newbigin Gauntlet: Developing a Domestic Missiology for North America." *Missiology: An International Review* XIX: 4 (October 1991): 391–408.

Koinonia. 1993. "Towards Koinonia/Communion in Faith, Life and Witness." Revised Discussion Paper for the Fifth World Conference on Faith and Order, Santiago de Compostella, Spain, August 3–14, 1993. *Ecumenical Trends* 22: 6 (June 1993): 2/82–23/104.

Phillips, James M. and Robert T. Coote, eds. 1993. *Toward the 21st Century in Christian Mission.* Grand Rapids, MI: William B. Eerdmans Publishing Company.

Scherer, James A. and Stephen B. Bevans, eds. 1992. *New Directions in Mission and Evangelization 1: Basic Statements 1974–1991.* Maryknoll, NY: Orbis Books.

Part I

THE NATURE OF MISSION

1

Christian Mission in the Americas

Orlando E. Costas *

In "Christian Mission in the Americas," Orlando Costas sets forth a biblical and trinitarian view of the mission of God, one grounded in eschatology and using the Kingdom as its frame of reference. The missiological vision is unique in its simultaneous focus on the Latin American and Caribbean contexts, as well as its discussion of these issues in relation to Canada and the United States. Costas, known for his concern to bridge Evangelical and Conciliar viewpoints, is convinced that the priorities of the Kingdom demand a united approach to mission by Christians of both American continents.

Is a joint Christian mission possible in the Americas? That question should not surprise those of us who represent the peoples south of the Rio Bravo, the Caribbean islands, or the oppressed minorities of North America, for we have been able to observe at close range the great contradictions within the mission work that Christians and their respective churches experience in all the vast American territory. It may come as a surprise to those Christians from both sides who, due to their dedication to the missionary mandate, have been able to see only the strong points and not the weak, the triumphs but not the failures of Christian mission in the Americas. But for those of us who have identified with the realities of these closely related continents and with the missionary practice carried on by Christians and their churches within their respective countries, the issue is eminently relevant and practical.

THE AMERICAS

Let us clarify the question that we want to consider in this chapter. What is it about the Americas that presents a mutual challenge for Christians and their churches? And, further, as followers of Jesus Christ, how are we to understand our mission within that reality?

* Taken from Orlando E. Costas, *Christ Outside the Gate: Mission Beyond Christendom* (Maryknoll, NY: Orbis Books, 1982), pp. 86–99. The late Orlando Costas, Hispanic Evangelical theologian and missiologist, served first as a pastor in his native Puerto Rico and then as dean of the Latin American Biblical Seminary in San José, Costa Rica. He earned his doctorate at the Free University of Amsterdam and later taught at Eastern Baptist Seminary in Philadelphia and at Andover-Newton Seminary in Newton, Massachusetts. In addition to the volume from which the present chapter is taken, his major works include *The Church and Its Mission* (Wheaton, IL: Tyndale, 1974).

To discuss the Americas is to be concerned with a region of great contrasts. These contrasts are not merely geographical, cultural, linguistic, religious, or ethical, but are also sociological, economic, and political in nature.

LATIN AMERICA AND THE CARIBBEAN

Latin America and the Caribbean have been stratified into an exploitable region.[1] Its countries are for the most part ruled by unpopular repressive governments.* The majority of the people do not have access to the goods their countries produce; they lack adequate food and housing; public health and educational services are only minimally available; and their whole culture is at the mercy of the culture of the affluent groups that control the means of social communication. These minority groups enjoy good food, housing, and education. On the whole, it can be said that, with few exceptions, the entire region has been incorporated into the structure of international capitalism as the provider of raw material and cheap labor. Accordingly it finds itself not only in a situation of dependence, but worse yet, of misery, since it gets poorer and poorer as the years go by.

NORTHERN AMERICA

In Northern America (the United States and Canada) with its predominantly Anglo-Saxon culture (though Canada has a strong Francophone minority), the situation is the other way around. Most parts of the society live in relative comfort, with employment that provides high wages, modern schools, hospitals and medical facilities, modern means of transportation, and time for rest and recreation. These groups have a strong economic position combined with political power: they choose—and remove—public leaders; they make the rules of the (political) game and organize society life. Therefore the means of social communication respond to their interests, and North American culture advertises that *modus vivendi*, the "American Way of Life." (Canadian lifestyle differs only in degree from that of the United States.)

To be sure, these sectors of North American society have their problems. They have fallen victim to "consumerism"; they suffer serious psychophysical disturbances and live in a chaotic process of sociocultural disintegration. In short, they are victims of the "technical-managerial dinosaur."[2] But, in contrast with the rest of the world and especially with the oppressed minority ethnic groups, their situation is extremely affluent.

What the majority of people in Latin America and the Caribbean suffer is what certain minorities suffer in North America: in the United States, Blacks, Native Americans, Hispanics, and Asians; in Canada, the Francophones and Native Canadians; in both countries, women and handicapped persons. All of these sectors have been stratified (in various degrees) into exploitable nuclei. Their social, economic, and political marginality responds to the interests of dominant groups, the institutions they control, and the ideology that guides their behavior. Racism,

---

* *Editors' note*: This essay was published in 1982, at which time the political situation throughout Latin America was different from that of today.

sexism, and the indifference that often characterizes both public and private sectors of society toward the handicapped are mechanisms created by order to preserve the economic advantages that go along with the domination of the weak by the strong—to mention some of the most obvious: cheap labor, the expropriation of property without fair compensation, menial jobs in subhuman working conditions, the submission of women to men in all spheres of human production, and the lack of adequate care for the plight of the handicapped.

The reality of this internal conflict helps us to understand, in part, the tremendous military complex and the extensive investigative machinery ("the intelligence community") that exists in the Anglo-Saxon countries of Northern America. One does not need much imagination to understand the great threat to society represented by an oppressed minority whose counterpart in the other America is the majority. "National Security" is the catch-phrase that nourishes both militarism and the "intelligence" complex (in the United States this embraces about ten federal agencies, from the Central Intelligence Agency [CIA] to the Federal Bureau of Investigation [FBI]). "National Security" rises like a war cry in order to protect the economic and political interests of the majority of North Americans from the (potential) revolutionary threat posed by the "wretched" of the Americas, the minority from the North and the majority from the Caribbean and Central and South America. This explains why in the last decades most aid of U.S. origin to Latin America and to the Caribbean nations has been military.[3]

THE MISSION OF GOD

In these circumstances of contrasts and conflicts within these two continents, what can we say about Christian mission?

We must look for the answer to this question in the mission of God. This proceeds from the fact that the mission of Christians can be understood only in the light of the mission of Jesus Christ, which is grounded in the missions of the Father and the Holy Spirit. A basic presupposition of Christian mission is thus the missional dynamic of the Father, the Son, and the Spirit, in and for history. To understand the mission of Christians in any situation we need first and foremost to understand God's mission as it is revealed in his trinitarian history.

A TRINITARIAN MISSION

In referring to the trinitarian history of God, I am dissociating myself from those who conceive of the trinitarian God in metaphysical categories and apart from reality. God's mission is not grounded on metaphysical speculation and theoretical abstractions inspired by classical Greek philosophy, but rather on historical *deeds*. I wish to understand the God of Christian faith in his missionary activity in history, in his relation with the world, and in his plan for humanity. I wish thus to understand God because the faith that Christians profess is derived from the Old and New Testaments, which speak of God as Father, Son, and Holy Spirit, and describe his work in the world historically, as the trinitarian history of God.[4] This is also the reason why I am motivated not by a theoretical but by a practical and pastoral concern. Ultimately I am interested in understanding the implications of God's trinitarian activity for the church's task in the Americas today.

What is therefore the biblical witness about the mission of the triune God in the world? How is that mission related to our situation in the Americas? What are the pastoral implications?

The Bible states that "God is love" (1 Jn. 4:8). God's relationships with the world are based on this affirmation. The psalms especially tell us of love as the foundation of creation (cf. Pss. 33; 74:12–17; 104). Israel is created in love (Deut. 7:7–8), is a priestly people (i.e., a mediator of God's love) in the presence of the nations (Ex. 19:4–6) because of God's love for it (Isa. 42:5-7). If the predominant Old Testament traditions present Yahweh in relationship with Israel, it is because at bottom Yahweh is interested in the well-being of all nations. Surely Yahweh is the shepherd of Israel (Ps. 23:1ff.; Isa. 40:11; Ezek. 34:12), the father and mother of the nation (Ps. 103:13; Isa. 49:15; 66:13), its progenitor, provider, and protector (Isa. 43:1ff.; 44:2ff.). Nevertheless the background of this parenthood is creation (in which Yahweh is revealed as creator of all humanity) and the sovereignty that Yahweh exercises over all peoples. Israel is a prototype of the new humanity that God wants to create. Hence Hosea refers to Israel as both Yahweh's wife (2:1–23) and son (11:1ff.). Israel is the partner whom Yahweh chooses in order to procreate a new race and is also the first offspring of this union.[5] In the New Testament we notice a correspondence between Israel and Jesus of Nazareth. Jesus is the authentic Israelite (Mt. 2:15), the only one who fulfills the mission entrusted to Israel (Mk. 1:8–11; Jn. 1:49ff.; Lk. 1:31–33, 76–77; Heb. 1:1–4) because he is the man in whom God's Eternal Word became flesh (Jn. 1:14). Jesus Christ, Son of God, is the firstborn of the new humanity (Eph. 2:14–18), the head of the new body (Eph. 1:23), the cornerstone of a new temple and leader of a new people (1 Pet. 2:6–8). As a result, those who follow him are born to a new life (Jn. 1:12), are incorporated into the People of God, and are made to be his body. In this way, the Son, because of his death on the cross, finds a wife who, as in the case of the first Adam, is taken from his side, but who, in contrast with the first Eve, must await his return (Mt. 25:1–13), developing (in the fullest sense of the word), and preparing herself for the marriage that will take place in the consummation of the kingdom of God. By his resurrection he has also opened the way for a new people, the emerging new humanity already prefigured and announced in the history of Israel.

At the heart of this great mystery is the Father's love manifested by the Spirit. We are dealing here with the same Spirit that "moved over the face of the waters" at creation (Gen. 1:2); the breath that gave life to Adam's body (Gen. 2:7); the power that rested on Israel and its leaders in times of national crisis and that fertilized the womb of the humble virgin (Lk. 1:35) so that she could be the bearer of the Son of God; that enabled Jesus to offer himself to the Father as a perfect sacrifice for the sins of the world (Heb. 9:14) and by whose power Jesus was raised from the dead (Rom. 1:4). The Spirit spreads God's love to men and women everywhere, shaping them into the body of Christ, comforting, guiding, and teaching them "all the truth" (Jn. 16:7, 13); "convincing" the world of its sin, of justice and righteousness (Jn. 16:8); and nourishing the hope of all creation for its future liberation (Rom. 8:20–23). The Spirit is the agent of love that the Father has revealed in the Son. The focus of the Spirit's work in the world finds its goal precisely in the reconciliation of all created things under the lordship of the Son and for the glory of the Father (Eph. 1:14).

AN ESCHATOLOGICAL MISSION

It goes without saying that the Holy Spirit's special function within the mission of God is eminently eschatological. The Gospels introduce us to Jesus as he begins his ministry in the power of the Spirit (Lk. 4:14ff.; Mk. 1:8, 12, 14–15; Mt. 3:16–17). The content of that ministry is the proclamation of the good news of the kingdom of God. This proclamation is not a mere reminder of God's sovereignty over all creation.[6] On the contrary, something totally new is happening here: the eruption of a new era, a new order of life, the new creation. This messianic "newness" is made possible by the death and resurrection of Jesus. Men and women appropriate this messianic reality by faith in Christ. Thus they are freed from the power of sin, experience a new life with messianic values, become part of the messianic community (which is committed to the cause of freedom, justice, and peace), and share in the hope of new heavens and a new earth. Conversely, faith in Christ is verified in the development of a messianic lifestyle, active involvement in the messianic community, and participation in the struggle for a just and peaceful world in anticipation of the promised new heavens and new earth.

As a messianic community, the church is that fellowship of men and women, both liberated and in the process of liberation, which appears in Acts and in the epistles as the firstfruits of Pentecost (Acts 2:1ff.) brought into being by the power of the Spirit. The Spirit is the earnest of the kingdom, that messianic reality, the new creation and order of life that the Father offers to humanity in Jesus Christ the Son (Eph. 1:14). The Spirit makes possible the acceptance of the promise of the kingdom as ultimate, sure, and genuine. The Spirit creates *faith* where there is no faith, making believers participants in God's *love* and heirs to the *hope* for a new world. This activity turns believers into truly spiritual persons, who are nonconformists within history. They are happy only in the new life they have begun to enjoy and are not satisfied with anything that obscures or eclipses the hope for the final appearance of God's kingdom of freedom, justice, and peace.

A HISTORICAL MISSION

Hence the mission of God is not only eschatological but also historical. The fact that it has as its goal the final consummation of the kingdom and that it is transcendentalized in the hope of new heavens and a new earth does not mean that this mission is either atemporal or beyond history. On the contrary, it is a mission whose stage is history: a redeemed creation; the definitive overcoming of hatred, chaos, and corruption; and the burgeoning of a world of love, justice, freedom, and peace. This hope is adumbrated in the crossroads of life, amid the tensions of history where ideologies and political, economic, social, and religious systems clash. Because of this the New Testament adds the kingdom's present reality to the hope for the future (Lk. 17:20–37). Furthermore, the future hope of the poor (of whom it is said that they are privileged recipients of the good news) is nourished by concrete signs: "the blind see, the lame walk, the lepers are cleansed, the deaf hear, the dead are raised . . . " (Lk. 7:22). Those who own nothing in the world need not await the consummation of the kingdom to recover their rights as creatures of God. Instead they can begin now to anticipate (and appropriate by faith) the kingdom's transforming power. Because of its eschatological nature, the mission of God is historical.

The new order of life is seen most concretely in the small and large transformations that occur within history. To be sure, these historical signs are not easy to discern. Just as wheat and chaff grow together, so signs of the new order appear in the middle of contradictory situations and thus make it very difficult at times to distinguish clearly between a real signal and a short circuit. Nevertheless it is possible to discern the "signs of the times" through the Holy Spirit's guidance and by the orientation of the Word of God. The church, as the community nourished by the Spirit and the Word, has the privilege and the responsibility to interpret history, distinguishing the signs of the kingdom of God from the antisigns produced by the kingdoms of this world. Thus, not every historical change may be identified with the kingdom, but only those that conform to kingdom principles: love, justice, freedom, and messianic peace.

THE FRAME OF REFERENCE: THE KINGDOM OF GOD

The kingdom serves as the frame of reference for the mission of God. His working in history, as we have noted, is made known by the conclusive revelation of his liberating purpose and by the consistent denial of all tendencies that counter his will. The participation of the People of God in his mission will have to be directed, therefore, by the message of the kingdom.[7]

PROCLAIMING THE KINGDOM

To participate in the mission of God is to announce the good news of the kingdom. This is an all-embracing, dynamic activity that is not limited to a predetermined set of verbal propositions, be they doctrinal or homiletical. Surely, proclaiming the kingdom implies an affirmation of faith that is frequently expressed in doctrinal formulations. Thus we have the church's great creeds and "evangelistic sermons." Such sermons and doctrinal affirmations, however, must be part of what I should like to call a "kerygmatic climate." Because of its transcendence and its constant newness, announcing the kingdom is considered a part of the new life and not an isolated occurrence divorced from reality. The proclamation is always contextual, presented in new Spirit-filled words and by means of a dynamic transforming witness.

This becomes clear in Jesus' own life and ministry, where the announcement of the kingdom appears in these impressive words: "And all spoke well of him and wondered at the gracious words which proceeded out of his mouth" (Lk. 4:22; cf. Mk. 1:22). The words are accompanied by prodigious acts. "What is this? A new teaching?" asked the people. "With authority he commands even the unclean spirits, and they obey him" (Mk. 1:27). The apostle Paul continues in the same vein when he testifies to the Romans: "For I will not venture to speak of anything except what Christ has wrought through me to win obedience from the Gentiles, by word and deed, by the power of signs and wonders, by the power of the Holy Spirit, so that from Jerusalem and as far round as Illyricum I have fully preached the gospel of Christ" (Rom. 15:18–19). The proclamation of the kingdom is not a matter of words or deeds, but of words and deeds *empowered* by the liberating presence of the Spirit.

THE DEMANDS OF THE KINGDOM

The kingdom of God is not simply good news but also exigencies. The new order of life demands a radical change. There can be no reconciliation without conversion, just as there can be no resurrection without the cross, much less new life without birthpangs. Hence, Jesus came not only announcing the kingdom, but calling for repentance and faith (Mk. 1:15).

On a personal level this implies a change of attitudes and values, the appropriation of a new relationship with God and neighbors, and a new commitment to the messianic cause. The kingdom demands a transfer from "self" to "other," from an individualistic egocentric consciousness to one communally and fraternally oriented. Zacchaeus is exemplary: "Behold, Lord, the half of my goods I give to the poor, and if I have defrauded anyone of anything, I restore it fourfold" (Lk. 19:8). We are not talking of salvation by works; rather, of works that authenticate salvation by grace. "Today salvation has come to this house" (Lk. 19:9), for Zacchaeus demonstrated what he believed. His works were evidence of a profound change of values and attitudes.

The demands of the kingdom are not limited to personal attitudes or a single historical incident. They are permanent: "If anyone would come after me," Jesus said, "let him deny himself and take up his cross daily and follow me" (Lk. 9:23). The kingdom's demands affect all areas of life: "You are the salt of the earth; but if the salt has lost its taste, how shall its saltiness be restored? . . . You are the light of the world. A city set on a hill cannot be hid. . . . For I tell you, unless your righteousness exceeds that of the scribes and Pharisees, you will never enter the kingdom of heaven" (Mt. 5:13–14, 20).

It is this situation of "permanent change" to which Paul refers when he speaks of the transformation that the Spirit effects in those whose faces are turned to Christ (2 Cor. 3:18). Similarly Paul has this in mind when exhorting the Romans to present their bodies to God "as a living sacrifice, holy and acceptable to God," to live not conformed to the old order and to be renewed in their understanding in order to confirm God's will (Rom. 12:1–2).

The demands of the kingdom do not encompass only personal and ecclesial affairs, but also social and institutional issues. This new order is not limited to the community of faith. Instead it embraces all of history and the universe, and it is the task of the ecclesial community to witness to that all-encompassing reality. As Revelation 11:15 tells us, "The kingdom of the world has become the kingdom of our Lord and of his Christ, and he shall reign forever and ever." Paul adds in

Colossians 2:15 that on the cross Christ "disarmed the principalities and made a public example of them, triumphing over them . . . ";[8] at the very least, this implies that the kingdom of God is to be present among the kingdoms of this world. But how?

The Gospels tell us that the kingdom works in history like yeast, leavening all the dough (Lk. 13:21). Paul tells us that the kingdom manifests itself by limiting evil via political institutions (the "governing authorities") whom God has appointed in order to guarantee order and the commonwealth (Rom. 13:1–5). This authority can, however—in agreement with Revelation—become corrupted and turn into a demonic beast (cf. Rev. 13:1ff.). Above all, the kingdom makes itself felt in the hopeful groanings of creation (Rom. 8:22).

The kingdom makes demands in every one of these instances. For example, for dough to rise there must be yeast. The church is God's yeast; therefore it needs to be present in the world to help and transform it. So that political institutions may be agents of good, their citizens must cooperate. Christians are called to set examples by respecting all public institutions that work for the common good (that is, for the well-being of all, especially the poor and the oppressed). But they are also called to unmask and resist those institutions when they become possessed of the devil and turn into enemies of justice. The children of God are bearers of the hope for universal liberation. They are called to wait patiently not only for their own final liberation, but also for the liberation of all creation, by suffering the birthpangs of the world that is about to be delivered. Their own hope is directly related to the hope for the creation to be freed "from bondage to decay" (Rom. 8:21).

Christians bear a double eschatological burden: their own and that of the rest of creation. It is this to which Paul refers when he says: "likewise the Spirit helps us in our weakness, for we do not know how to pray as we ought, but the Spirit himself intercedes for us with sighs too deep for words" (Rom. 8:26). In other words, the Spirit helps us suffer the birthpangs of that new world that God has promised in the Son, perfecting our intercession until the day of total redemption. That intercession assumes a vicarious form. It is manifested when Christians are willing to bear the suffering of creation, a suffering that we can describe today as hunger and poverty, as persecution and loneliness, environmental pollution, the constant threat of war, racism, exploitation (economic, social, and sexual), political imperialism, and hegemonism that besiege our planet. But it is also evident in a hopeful enthusiasm when we discern and interpret the signs of the kingdom in the middle of this suffering.

PRIORITIES OF THE KINGDOM

The kingdom's demands go hand in hand with its priorities. I am not referring to priorities arranged in order of importance, since all of the kingdom's demands are important. Accepting the kingdom as a point of reference for mission implies acceptance of *all* its demands in the missionary mandate of God's people. Moreover, these priorities are historical; they correspond to the context of mission. Since situations change, particular *emphases* of the kingdom's message also change. This explains, for example, the varying emphases of the New Testament documents, the different kinds of churches that arose very early in Christian missions, and the changes in theme (hermeneutic keys) that we notice throughout the history of Christian theology. The setting of priorities does not mean, however, that other issues are put in "storage." The church is called not only to *accept* all the demands of the kingdom but to *communicate* them. It should do so, however, in order of need and opportunity, a responsibility that requires pastoral wisdom and courage.

THE PASTORAL CHALLENGE:
KINGDOM PRIORITIES IN THE AMERICAS

The question before us now is this: What are the kingdom's priorities in the Americas today? To answer this question we need to turn to the sociohistorical analysis with which we began because it gives us a pastoral focus. Indeed the question is none other than the challenge that the kingdom sets before Christians in the Americas today. This challenge is pastoral, since it assigns us concrete tasks. (By pastoral is meant all those actions whereby God's People announce the good news of the kingdom and make its demands clear.) Our problem, therefore, is to find our bearings in order to direct God's People in general and our respective churches in particular so that all of us may carry out the mission that God has entrusted to us. In other words, we must define the historical priorities for the kingdom in the Americas today.

AFFIRMING LIFE AND DENOUNCING VIOLENCE

During the last decade a dark cloud has surrounded the peoples of the hemisphere. Life has been denied and death exalted through the violent machinery of oppression and repression in the name of law and order, in defense of the Christian tradition, and under the pretext of benevolence and humanitarianism. The first priority of the day is to snatch the kingdom from the agents of death by affirming life and denouncing violence. This affirmation is, of course, with implications.

The first implication is, *the poor's right to life must be defended and the machinery of socioeconomic oppression and repression that contributes to poverty must be fought*. During the Carter administration much attention was paid to the matter of human rights. Interestingly, however, very little was said in the Americas about the rights of the poor. While we should not take lightly the positive impact of President Jimmy Carter on human rights in many repressive Latin American countries, we should not forget that the greatest and severest violations took place against the poor people of the hemisphere and that this policy suffered at times from the old ambiguity of American foreign policy.

In 1976 and 1978, respectively, we saw such an institution as the International Monetary Fund (IMF), under the pressure of the Carter administration, force Jamaica and Peru into inhuman, cruel, and repressive austerity programs that increased the basic cost of living and led to widespread unrest and deaths. In 1977 this same agency, again under the pressure of the United States, helped Argentina, a country with one of the most cruel, repressive records of the 1970s in all Latin

America, to borrow $1.1 billion in Eurocurrency and in United States markets. Then in May 1979, with U.S. support, the IMF granted Somoza a $66 million loan so that he could continue to bomb innocent Nicaraguans.[9]

As Christians we ought to criticize strongly such contradictory behavior. We ought to oppose the inter-American socioeconomic oppression and repression.

In the same way we ought to defend the rights of the poor to enjoy the basic amenities of life by championing more communal structures of social organization, such as an economy that offers genuine possibilities of socialized production and consumption, and a political structure that allows greater participation and guarantees personal rights and public safety. In my opinion this can be achieved only in a socialistically organized society—though, admittedly, there are several models of socialism, none of which could be applied to any one situation without some kind of modification.

In the second place, affirming life and denouncing violence means *condemning torture and championing fair legal procedures*. In less than fifteen years we have made a nearly 180-degree turn in the Americas, regressing hundreds of years in history with the reintroduction of cruel methods of punishment, such as torture, that had been replaced by more humanitarian, civilized procedures. Torture has been employed as a normal repressive method in order to put down any form of opposition and as a police method to obtain information. Its reappearance in the Americas is directly related to the disappearance of constitutional rights, with all their implications, including the right of habeas corpus. But more than anything, it has arisen as a fundamental part of the ideology of "national security" spread by the Pentagon and current regimes. (Where did the repressive governments of Latin America learn to use torture as a political tool, if not in the courses for training in nonconventional warfare that United States military agencies have offered to Latin American police and military?)

The complicity is worldwide or at least nearly so. Certain parts of the Christian church have spoken up in response to this situation whereas others have kept quiet. Those that have kept silent have done so either because of their radical historical isolation or their uncritical acceptance of the idea that this happens only to subversives, propaganda that the torturers themselves spread. Moreover, the majority of the churches that have spoken out against torture have done so only when their members have become victims.

In the third place, to affirm life and denounce violence implies *that human freedoms must be defended and that the arms complex that permits their repression must be attacked*. We Christians in the Americas may not sit by twiddling our thumbs in the face of systematic violation of voting rights that occurs with shameless and impudent prohibition of free elections, with fraudulent elections, or with legal conditions that hinder popular participation in electing officials. We Christians may accept neither the systematic persecution of those whose opinions differ from the majority nor the denial of the rights of free association. At all costs, these and many other freedoms must be defended on every level of society.

At the same time, we Christians of the Americas ought to attack the arms race that the developed countries are carrying on. Not only has the entire planet's well-being been jeopardized by their nuclear arsenals; the doors have also been opened for such poor nations as Brazil to start on the same road. Furthermore, the arms race allows the military-related industries of the United States and Europe to grow wealthy on the sweat and blood of the underdeveloped peoples of the hemisphere. The sales of arms to these peoples enables the systematic violation of the freedoms listed above. (Curiously, that same industry nourishes the national violence that convulses the countries of the North, since the arms industry strongly opposes arms control. Add to this the film industry's support and you have an atmosphere of terror, especially in the streets of major cities in the United States.)

The challenge to denounce this panorama of violence and to affirm life becomes unavoidable for Christians and churches in the Americas. The kingdom of which we are part and whose message we have been called to proclaim demands that we side with love, not with hate; with justice, not with inequality; with peace, not with aggression. Since this is the case, we have no alternative but to marshal our forces to denounce institutionalized violence, to affirm the right of the poor and oppressed to life, and to commit ourselves to programs that place the human being above the state and its institutions. To do anything different would be to turn coward and to deny our duties as firstfruits of God's new order of life.

HUMAN SOLIDARITY AND CHRISTIAN UNITY

That responsibility demands human solidarity, since it is not possible to affirm life without making a commitment of solidarity with all humanity in its struggle for life. The division of peoples into economic classes, ideological blocs, racial groups, religious movements, and sexual chauvinisms reflects the threat of death that besieges the human race. This is especially evident in the Western Hemisphere, where we see such a long history of fratricidal wars; of economic blocs; of antagonism among classes, races, and sexes; of religious conflicts; and of ideological prejudices. At present the hemisphere is, both internally and externally, one of the most divided and broken parts of planet Earth. In order to affirm life, it is necessary to overcome these frictions and to form a united human front.

These hemispheric divisions find their counterpart in the extraordinary divisions among Christians. The conflict among Christians is not simply the traditional Catholic–Protestant controversy. On the contrary, we are speaking here of divisions between Catholics and Catholics, between Protestants and Protestants, between laity and hierarchy, between local organizations and national bodies, between church structures and para-church groups, and between differing theological positions and various pastoral positions. In short, we are dealing here with a compound fracture. Because of this, Christians in the hemisphere find themselves unable to serve as agents of reconciliation among the peoples of the Americas, unable to be the firstfruits of the new humanity.

As Christians of the Americas we cannot evade the ecumenical challenge. It is urgent that we develop an ecumenical pastoral strategy, a combined effort to benefit cooperative Christian programs that aim for a more fraternal life of solidarity among the peoples of our continents. Such programs will have to be of various kinds and degrees—from interconfessional theological meetings to inter-church activities of common witness and socioreligious coalitions in favor of human dignity and the social well-being of all peoples.

COMMITMENT TO EVANGELIZATION
AND CHURCH GROWTH

In order for this to occur we need a deep commitment to an integral evangelization and a healthy church growth. I understand by "commitment to an integral evangelization" a total devotion to the cause of communicating the good news of God's kingdom in word and deed, "in season and out of season," with all available means at our disposal. In my opinion, such a dedication is possible only when a deep conversion experience occurs. (Here we see one of the basic problems of the Christian mission in the Americas: an amorphous community with very shallow roots in the gospel of Christ.) By "healthy growth" I understand a process of holistic development in which the community of faith is fed by new members, expands the participation of its members within its organic life, deepens its understanding of the faith, and becomes an incarnated servant in its social situation.[10]

Such evangelization and growth are imperative among the churches of both continents, because these churches currently are stagnant (and thus subject to obvious deterioration) or getting fatter by the day (thus running the risk of a fatal aneurysm). No wonder the fruits of the kingdom have been so little evidenced in the Americas! Its proclamation has been distorted; its demands have been cheapened! The Americas *still* need to be evangelized.[11]

Therefore, a prophetic mobilization of the People of God for a profound and effective evangelization is urgently needed. This would bring about a new wave of Christians deeply rooted in the gospel, dedicated to proclaiming the kingdom and its demands in all areas of society, and supported by vibrant and healthy churches. Without a mobilization of such magnitude, the churches will remain stagnant and will become more impotent every day. For their part Christians will lose the opportunity to contribute significantly to the transformation of their history by denying their missionary vocation and by allowing themselves to be absorbed by the kingdoms of this world. If we wish to be faithful to the kingdom of God, we ought, therefore, to pool our resources to develop programs that foster a radical commitment to the gospel and that stimulate healthy growth in our respective churches.

We began this chapter by asking if it were possible for Christians of both American continents to develop a united mission. We can conclude that not only is it possible, it is imperative. Such a mission will have to be grounded in the mission of God and will have to be steered by the message of the kingdom. Seen from this perspective, our mission priorities would be, first, to create and take part in programs that affirm life and denounce violence; second, to promote human solidarity and to encourage unity among Christians by using all means within our reach and at all levels; and, third, to cooperate in evangelistic efforts that foster holistic church growth and a deep historical commitment to the gospel. Thus we shall be helping to pour out our churches' energies toward the transformation of the space we occupy on our planet.

NOTES

1. For a historico-anthropological explanation of this process, see Darcy Ribeiro, *The Americas and Civilization*, trans. from Portuguese by Linton Lomas Barrett and Marie McDavid Barrett (New York: E. P. Dutton, 1973). For a historico-economic analysis, see Eduardo Galeano, *Las venas abiertas de América Latina* (Mexico City: Siglo XXI Editores, 1971); English trans.: *Open Veins of Latin America: Five Centuries of the Pillage of a Continent* (New York: Monthly Review Press, 1973). For additional material on the precarious economic history of Latin America, see, further, Celso Furtado, *La economía latinoamericana: Formación histórica y problemas contemporáneos* (Mexico City: Siglo XXI Editores, 1971); and Agustín Cueva, *El desarollo del capitalismo en América Latina* (Mexico City: Siglo XXI Editores, 1977).

2. Cf. Rubem Alves, *Tomorrow's Child* (New York: Harper & Row, 1972).

3. Cf. José Comblin, *The Church and the National Security State* (Maryknoll, NY: Orbis Books, 1980), pp. 64–120; Penny Lernoux, *Cry of the People* (Garden City, NY: Doubleday, 1980), pp. 155ff.

4. Cf. Jürgen Moltmann, *The Church in the Power of the Spirit: A Contribution to Messianic Ecclesiology*, trans. from German by Margaret Kohl (New York: Harper & Row, 1977), pp. 50ff. See also Lesslie Newbigin, *The Open Secret* (Grand Rapids, MI: Wm. B. Eerdmans, 1978), pp. 20ff.; David J. Bosch, *Witness to the World* (London: Marshall, Morgan and Scott; Atlanta: John Knox Press, 1980), pp. 239ff.

5. Cf. H. Berkhof's concept of the history of salvation as God's quest for a faithful covenant partner. *Christian Faith*, trans. from Dutch by Sierd Woudsta (Grand Rapids, MI: Wm. B. Eerdmans, 1979), pp. 225ff.

6. For a further elaboration of the proclamation of the kingdom, see my *The Integrity of Mission* (New York: Harper & Row, 1979), pp. 1ff.

7. Cf. J. Verkuyl, *Contemporary Missiology* (Grand Rapids, MI: Wm. B. Eerdmans, 1978), pp. 197ff.; Carl E. Braaten, *The Flaming Center: A Theology of the Christian Mission* (Philadelphia: Fortress Press, 1977), pp. 39ff.

8. On the theme of principalities and powers, see my *Christ Outside the Gate*, chap. 10.

9. Cf. Washington Office on Latin America, *Update Latin America*, (September/October 1979), p. 2.

10. On this perspective of church growth, see my *Christ Outside the Gate*, chap. 3, and my *Integrity*, pp. 37ff.

11. This is one reality that is readily admitted by Catholics and Protestants alike. Cf. John Eagleson and Philip Scharper, eds., *Puebla and Beyond* (Maryknoll, NY: Orbis Books, 1980), pp. 123ff.; Fraternidad Teológica Latinoamericana, *América Latina y la evangelización en los años 80* (Mexico City: FTL, 1980), passim; Comité Editorial del CLAI, *Oaxtepec 1978: Unidad y misión en América Latina* (San José, Costa Rica: CLAI, 1980), pp. 205ff.

2

The Logic of Mission

LESSLIE NEWBIGIN *

Bishop Lesslie Newbigin's name has become legendary for students of mission theology. The Gospel in a Pluralistic Society *is Newbigin's most compelling and mature statement of conviction. It orginated as a series of lectures at Glasgow University and reflects the author's lifelong effort to grapple with the meaning of mission as missionary, ecumenical theologian, administrator, and finally as evangelist in secular Britain. "The Logic of Mission," to be read in the context of other chapters of the volume, presents Newbigin's view that "the Church is not so much the agent of mission as the locus of [God's] mission." Mission is "not an action of ours, but the presence of a new reality, the presence of the Spirit of God in power." The presence of the Kingdom in the church, Newbigin believes, is not that of a victorious crusade shaping and controlling history but a foretaste, a first-fruit, a pledge of the Spirit in which God's power is forever veiled in the weakness of the cross.*

Perhaps my title, "The Logic of Mission," may seem an odd one, but I am concerned to explore the question of how the mission of the Church is rooted in the gospel itself. There has been a long tradition which sees the mission of the Church primarily as obedience to a command. It has been customary to speak of "the missionary mandate." This way of putting the matter is certainly not without justification, and yet it seems to me that it misses the point. It tends to make mission a burden rather than a joy, to make it part of the law rather than part of the gospel. If one looks at the New Testament evidence one gets another impression. Mission begins with a kind of explosion of joy. The news that the rejected and crucified

---

* Taken from Lesslie Newbigin, *The Gospel in a Pluralistic Society* (Grand Rapids, MI: Eerdmans, 1989, ch. 10, pp. 116–27), and reprinted with permission of the publisher. Lesslie Newbigin went from Cambridge University as a missionary to South India, where he played a key role in the creation of the Church of South India and served as a bishop of that church in Madurai and Madras. During the transition of the International Missionary Council as it was being integrated into the World Council of Churches as the Commission on World Mission and Evangelism, Newbigin was the last general secretary of the IMC and the first director of the new CWME. Prior to the publication of the present work, Newbigin spelled out his theology of mission in *The Open Secret: Sketches for a Missionary Theology* (Grand Rapids, MI: Eerdmans, 1978). His memoirs were published as *Unfinished Agenda: An Autobiography* (Geneva: WCC Publications, 1985).

Jesus is alive is something that cannot possibly be suppressed. It must be told. Who could be silent about such a fact? The mission of the Church in the pages of the New Testament is more like the fallout from a vast explosion, a radioactive fallout which is not lethal but life-giving. One searches in vain through the letters of St. Paul to find any suggestion that he anywhere lays it on the conscience of his readers that they ought to be active in mission. For himself it is inconceivable that he should keep silent. "Woe to me if I do not preach the gospel!" (1 Cor. 9:16). But nowhere do we find him telling his readers that they have a duty to do so.

It is a striking fact, moreover, that almost all the proclamations of the gospel which are described in Acts are in response to questions asked by those outside the Church. This is so in the case of Peter's sermon on the day of Pentecost, of the testimonies given by the apostles and by Stephen under interrogation, of the encounter of Philip with the Ethiopian, of Peter's meeting with the household of Cornelius, and of the preaching of Paul in the synagogue at Antioch of Pisidia. In every case there is something present, a new reality, which calls for explanation and thus prompts the question to which the preaching of the gospel is the answer.

This is clearly so in the first of the cases I have cited, the sermon of Peter on the day of Pentecost. Something is happening which prompts the crowd to come together and ask, "What is going on?" The answer of Peter is in effect a statement that what is going on is that the last day has arrived and the powers of the new age are already at work, and that this is so because of the life, ministry, death, resurrection, and ascension of Jesus. The sermon leads up to a climax in the citing of Psalm 110 (Acts 2:34). Jesus, whom they had crucified, is now seated at the right hand of God until all things are put under his feet. This has to be told to all who will hear simply because it is the truth. This is the reality all human beings must henceforth take into account. The real government of the universe, the final reality which in the end confronts every human being, is the crucified and risen Jesus. And to the question "What, then, are we to do?" the answer is "Repent and be baptized in the name of Jesus." To repent is to do the U-turn of the mind which enables you to believe what is hidden from sight, the reality of the presence of the reign of God in the crucified Jesus. To be baptized is to be identified with, incorporated into that which Jesus did when he went down into the waters of Jordan as one of a company of sin-burdened men and women and so inaugurated a mission that would lead him through his great encounter with the principalities and powers to its victorious climax in the cross. To be baptized is to be incorporated into the dying of Jesus so as to become a participant in his risen life, and so to share his ongoing mission to the world. It is to be baptized into his mission.

His mission. It is of the greatest importance to recognize that it remains his mission. One of the dangers of emphasizing the concept of mission as a mandate given to the Church is that it tempts us to do what we are always tempted to do, namely to see the work of mission as a good work and to seek to justify ourselves by our works. On this view, it is we who must save the unbelievers from perishing. The emphasis of the New Testament, it seems to me, is otherwise. Even Jesus himself speaks of his words and works as not his own but those of the Father. His teaching is the teaching of the Father, and his mighty works are the work of the Father. So also in the Synoptic Gospels, the mighty works of Jesus are the work of

God's kingly power, of his Spirit. So also with the disciples. It is the Spirit who will give them power and the Spirit who will bear witness. It is not that they must speak and act, asking the help of the Spirit to do so. It is rather that in their faithfulness to Jesus they become the place where the Spirit speaks and acts.

This means that their mission will not only be a matter of preaching and teaching but also of learning. When he sends them out on their mission, Jesus tells the disciples that there is much for them yet to learn and he promises that the Spirit who will convict the world will also lead them into the truth in its fullness (John 16:12–15). What does it mean that Jesus is at the right hand of God until all his enemies submit? To believe it is not to arrive at an end of all learning but to arrive at a starting point for learning. All history and all experience have now to be understood in terms of this faith and this promise. But this "understanding" is something the Church has to be learning in the course of its mission. Even the incarnate Lord, according to the Scriptures, had to learn obedience by the things he suffered (Heb. 5:8). Like its Lord, the Church has to renounce any claim to a masterful control of history. By following the way her Lord went, the way of suffering witness, she unmasks the powers which claim this masterful control and confronts each succeeding generation with the ultimate goal of history. What Christ's lordship over the world means, what it means that all authority is given to him, is something the Church has to learn in her journey. The Spirit, the foretaste of the kingdom, who performs the works of power in the midst of human weakness and thus convicts the world in respect of its most fundamental ideas, by the same token leads the Church into the fullness of the truth, a fullness that will be complete only when Christ's lordship is no longer hidden but manifest to all.

The mission of the Church is to be understood, can only be rightly understood, in terms of the trinitarian model. It is the Father who holds all things in his hand, whose providence upholds all things, whose tender mercies are over all his works, where he is acknowledged and where he is denied, and who has never left himself without witness to the heart and conscience and reason of any human being. In the incarnation of the Son he has made known his nature and purpose fully and completely, for in Jesus "all the fullness of God was pleased to dwell" (Col. 1:19). But this presence was a veiled presence in order that there might be the possibility of repentance and freely given faith. In the Church the mission of Jesus is continued in the same veiled form. It is continued through the presence and active working of the Holy Spirit, who is the presence of the reign of God in foretaste. The mission of the Church to all the nations, to all human communities in all their diversity and in all their particularity, is itself the mighty work of God, the sign of the inbreaking of the kingdom. The Church is not so much the agent of the mission as the locus of the mission. It is God who acts in the power of his Spirit, doing mighty works, creating signs of a new age, working secretly in the hearts of men and women to draw them to Christ. When they are so drawn, they become part of a community that claims no masterful control of history, but continues to bear witness to the real meaning and goal of history by a life which—in Paul's words—by always bearing in its body the dying of Jesus becomes the place where the risen life of Jesus is made available for others (2 Cor. 4:10).

It is impossible to stress too strongly that the beginning of mission is not an action of ours, but the presence of a new reality, the presence of the Spirit of God in power. The whole New Testament bears witness to this, and so does the missionary experience of the Church through the ages. Perhaps this has been made especially clear to us in the present century through the experience of the Church in the Soviet Union and in China. In both these vast countries we have seen the Church crushed to a point where no kind of explicit public witness, in spoken or written word, or in service to the public, was permitted. And in exactly these situations, we have seen the marvelous growth of the Church through the active power of the Spirit drawing men and women to recognize in this human weakness the presence and power of God. This corresponds to what we have seen in the New Testament, not only in the explicit linking of the mission with the presence of the Spirit, but also in the fact that the great missionary proclamations in Acts are not given on the unilateral initiative of the apostles but in response to questions asked by others, questions prompted by the presence of something that calls for explanation. In discussions about the contemporary mission of the Church it is often said that the Church ought to address itself to the real questions people are asking. That is to misunderstand the mission of Jesus and the mission of the Church. The world's questions are not the questions that lead to life. What really needs to be said is that where the Church is faithful to its Lord, there the powers of the kingdom are present and people begin to ask the question to which the gospel is the answer. And that, I suppose, is why the letters of St. Paul contain so many exhortations to faithfulness but no exhortations to be active in mission.

The presence of the kingdom in the Church is the presence of its foretaste, its firstfruit, its pledge (*arrabon*) in the Spirit. It is the presence of power veiled in weakness. It is a presence that leads us to speak, with the New Testament, both of having and of hoping. "We ourselves," says St. Paul, "who have received the firstfruit, namely the Spirit, groan inwardly as we wait for adoption as sons, the redemption of our bodies. For in this hope we were saved" (Rom. 8:23–24). It is this indissoluble unity of having and hoping, this presence now of something that is a pledge of the future, this *arrabon* which is both a reality now and at the same time a pledge of something far greater to come, it is this which constitutes the Church as witness. But the Church is not the source of the witness; rather, it is the locus of witness. The light cast by the first rays of the morning sun shining on the face of a company of travelers will be evidence that a new day is coming. The travelers are not the source of that witness but only the locus of it. To see for oneself that it is true, that a new day is really coming, one must turn around, face the opposite way, be converted. And then one's own face will share the same brightness and become part of the evidence.

This presence of a new reality, the presence in the shared life of the Church of the Spirit who is the *arrabon* of the kingdom, has become possible because of what Jesus has done, because of his incarnation, his ministry as the obedient child of his Father, his suffering and death, his resurrection, his ascension into heaven, and his session at the right hand of God. When the apostles are asked to explain the new reality, the new power to find joy in tribulation, healing in sickness, freedom in bondage, life in death, this is the explanation they give. It follows that the visible embodiment of this new reality is not a movement that will take control of history and shape the future according to its own vision, not a new imperialism, not a victorious crusade. Its visible embodiment will be a community that lives by this story, a community whose existence is visibly defined in the regular rehearsing and reenactment of the story that has given it birth, the story of the self-emptying of God in the ministry, life, death, and resurrection of Jesus. Its visible center as a continuing social entity is that weekly repeated event in which believers share bread and wine as Jesus commanded, as his pledge to them and their pledge to him that they are one with him in his passion and one with him in his victory. Instead of the celebration of the Sabbath as the end of God's old creation, they celebrate the first day of the week, the Lord's Day, as the beginning of the new creation. In this they find enacted and affirmed the meaning and goal of their lives as part of the life of the cosmos, their stories as part of the universal story. This story does indeed lead to a glorious end and is therefore filled with meaning, but the end is not at some far distant date in terrestrial history. The end is the day when Jesus shall come again, when his hidden rule will become manifest and all things will be seen as they truly are. That is why we repeat at each celebration of the Supper the words that encapsulate the whole mystery of faith: "Christ has died. Christ is risen: Christ shall come again."

It is in this light that we must understand the purpose and goal of missions. I am here using the word "missions" in distinction from the more all-embracing word "mission." This latter word I take to mean the entire task for which the Church is sent into the world. By "missions" I mean those specific activities undertaken by human decision to bring the gospel to places or situations where it is not heard, to create a Christian presence in a place or situation where there is no such presence or no effective presence. The goal of such a missionary action has been defined in different ways. Sometimes the emphasis is on the conversion of the greatest possible number of individuals and their incorporation into the Church. The success of the mission is to be evaluated in terms of church growth. Sometimes the emphasis is on the humanization of society, the eradication of social ills, the provision of education, healing, and economic development. Success in either of these aims is hailed as success for the mission. By contrast, St. Paul's criterion seems to be different. He can tell the Christians in Rome that he has completed his work in the whole vast region from Jerusalem to the Adriatic and has "no longer any room for work in these regions" (Rom. 15:23). What, exactly, has he done? Certainly not converted all the populations of these regions. Certainly not solved their social and economic problems. He has, in his own words, "fully preached the gospel" and left behind communities of men and women who believe the gospel and live by it. So his work as a missionary is done. It is striking, for a modern reader, that he does not agonize about all the multitudes in those regions who have not yet heard the gospel or who have not accepted it. He does indeed, in the same letter, agonize over the fact that the Jews, to whom the gospel primarily belongs, have rejected it. But he is certain that in the end "the fullness of the Gentiles will be gathered in" and "all Israel will be saved" (Rom. 11:25–26). We shall have to consider in a later chapter what to make of this confidence of the apostle. The point here is that he has completed his missionary task in the creation of believing communities in all the regions through which he has passed. These communities are, as he says to the Corinthians, composed mostly of people whom the world despises. They do not look like the wave of the future. They are ignored by contemporary historians. They do not pretend to take control of the destiny of the Roman Empire, let alone of the whole world. What, then, is their significance?

One could answer most simply by saying that their significance is that they continue the mission of Jesus in accordance with his words: "As the Father sent me, so I send you." They share his weakness, and as they do so, they share in the powers of the new age which he brings. They thus perform, as he did, a critical function. They confront men and women with the ultimate issues of human existence. They therefore share, in their measure, his passion. "A servant is not greater than his master, nor a messenger [apostle] greater than the one who sends him" (John 13:16). All this is spelled out in the apocalyptic passages of the first three Gospels and the corresponding sayings in the fourth. As the coming of Jesus precipitated crisis for Israel, so the coming of the Church will precipitate a crisis for the world. The coming of light into the darkness must necessarily have this effect. In the darkness things can be hidden; when the light comes people have to choose. If Jesus was rejected, so will be his messengers. Not only so, there will be false Christs. The coming into the world of the promise of total salvation, of a radically new age, precipitates at the same time the appearing of those who offer salvation on other terms. Therefore, it will be not only the old paganisms that fight against the Church, but also the new messianisms.

Wherever the gospel is preached, new ideologies appear—secular humanism, nationalism, Marxism—movements that offer the vision of a new age, an age freed from all the ills that beset human life, freed from hunger and disease and war—on other terms. It is no accident that the only areas of India where Marxism has become a real power are areas of vigorous Christian missionary activity, or that those who led the Marxist revolution in China were the products of Christian schools and colleges. Once the gospel is preached and there is a community that lives by the gospel, then the question of the ultimate meaning of history is posed and other messiahs appear. So the crisis of history is deepened. Even more significant as an example of this development than the rise of Marxism is the rise of Islam. Islam, which means simply submission, is the mightiest of all the post-Christian movements that claim to offer the kingdom of God without the cross. The denial of the crucifixion is and must always be central to Islamic teaching. But Islam and Marxism are only the most powerful illustrations of something that must necessarily mark the progress of the Christian mission to the nations. Once the real end of history has been disclosed, and once the invitation is given to live by it in the fellowship of a crucified and risen messiah, then the old static and cyclical patterns are broken and can never be restored. If Jesus is not acknowledged as the Christ, then other christs, other saviors will appear. But the gospel must first be preached to all the nations. Every human community must have the opportunity to hear, believe, and freely accept the true goal. That goal lies beyond history. Kingdoms will pass away. The earth itself and the visible cosmos will pass away. In the end Jesus Christ will be seen as the one to whom authority is given. And so the call is for patient endurance.

What I have been saying seeks to reflect the material of the synoptic apocalypse. The corresponding Johannine teaching is to be found in Chapters 14-16 of the

Fourth Gospel. Here, too, the disciples are warned that they will be rejected and cast out (John 15:18ff.). They are promised the presence of the Spirit, who will himself be the witness and by whose presence they also will be witnesses (John 15:26–27). This same Spirit will bring the world under judgment, exercising the same power that had been present in Jesus to overturn accepted ideas of sin and righteousness and judgment (John 16:8–9). The Spirit will call for the same radical conversion to which Jesus called men and women. The Spirit is the Spirit of truth, in contrast to the many spirits of this age that lead men and women into falsehood. The Holy Spirit will lead the Church into ever fuller understanding of the truth— beyond what it was possible for the incarnate Lord to communicate to that group of disciples limited to one time and place and culture (John 16:12–15). The work of the Spirit will be to manifest the glory of Jesus by taking what belongs to him (which is in fact everything, because "all that the Father has is mine") and showing it to the Church. By the work of the Spirit the Church will be able to understand "the things that are to come" and to learn that all that exists belongs to Christ. As it lives in the power of the Spirit, and as it shares in the suffering and rejection of Jesus, the Church will learn more and more fully what it means that Jesus is the clue to history, its source and its goal. But clearly this learning process is part of and cannot be detached from the Church's missionary journey to all the nations. There is already in the life of the Church a foretaste of what is promised for the end, namely that the nations shall walk in the light of the Lamb and their kings shall bring their glory into the Holy City (Rev. 21:24). In this sense, as the mission goes its way to the ends of the earth, new treasures are brought into the life of the Church, and Christianity itself grows and changes until it becomes more credible as a foretaste of the unity of all humankind. The first steps of this journey are chronicled in the New Testament, where we see the struggles that were required before the Church could accept that the Gentiles, as Gentiles and not as Jewish proselytes, were to be part of the new community.

The fulfillment of the mission of the Church thus requires that the Church itself be changed and learn new things. Very clearly the Church had to learn something new as a result of the conversion of Cornelius and his household. And, once again, the point must be made: this is not an achievement of the Church but a work of the Spirit. In that story we see Peter's extreme reluctance to mix with the household of a pagan Roman officer. He tells the story of Jesus in that Roman house because he is directly questioned. The fruit of the telling is an action of the Spirit which takes matters out of Peter's hands. He can only confess with astonishment that these uncircumcised pagans have been made part of God's household. So the Church is moved one step on the road toward becoming a home for people of all nations and a sign of the unity of all.

The last two centuries have seen giant steps along that road. The Church is now recognizable as a universal community in which all human cultures can be welcomed. But still we are only on the way, and the Church has to continue to learn new things as new peoples are brought to Christ.

Only at the end shall we know what it means that Jesus is Lord of all. Till then our confession can only be partial, culture-bound, and thus incomplete. The whole world needs to know what Jesus' lordship means.

The writer to the Hebrews, speaking of the saints of the previous generations, says that apart from us they could not be made perfect, because God had prepared some better thing for us (Heb. 11:39–40). The same logic leads us to look into the future and say that we cannot be made perfect without those who are to.come after. God's perfect reign cannot be made manifest to all until the mission of the Church to all nations is complete.

In this sketch of the logic of mission, it is obvious that the center of the picture is not occupied by the question of the saving of, or the failure to save, individual souls from perdition. That question has dominated Protestant missionary thinking at many times and places. Clearly it cannot be left out of the picture, but I do not find that in the New Testament it occupies the center. If this were the central question, St. Paul could not have said that his work in the Eastern Roman world was finished. However many local churches had come into being through his ministry, only a tiny minority of those who had died during the years of his ministry had died as Christian believers. If this is the criterion by which missions are to be judged, then plainly they have been and still are a colossal failure. Not only today, but through all the centuries, the great majority of human beings who have died have died without faith in Christ. The missionary calling has sometimes been interpreted as a calling to stem this fearful cataract of souls going to eternal perdition. But I do not find this in the center of the New Testament representation of the missionary calling. Certainly Jesus tells us that God seeks the last lost sheep, and Paul is ready to be all things to all people in order that he may by all means save some (1 Cor. 9:22). And he goes on to say, "I do it all for the sake of the gospel that I may share in its blessings." I shall return to this verse. But meanwhile we must also consider the important passage in Romans 9-11 where Paul gives his most fully developed theology of mission, and here the center of the picture is the eschatological event in which the fullness of the Gentiles will have been gathered in and all Israel will be saved. This is in spite of the fact that the vast majority of Jews have rejected the gospel, and that the event to which Paul looks forward will certainly occur long after the death of the unbelieving Jews. Plainly Paul is not thinking in terms of the individual but in terms of the interpretation of universal history. The center of the picture is the eschatological event in which the fathomless depths of God's wisdom and grace will be revealed. His ways are inscrutable and his judgments unsearchable. He has consigned all men to disobedience in order that he may have mercy on all (Rom. 11:32–36). Until that day none can share in God's perfection. Until that day, we are all on the way. There is no room either for anxiety about our failure or for boasting about our success. There is room only for faithful witness to the one in whom the whole purpose of God for cosmic history has been revealed and effected, the crucified, risen, and regnant Christ.

So the logic of mission is this: the true meaning of the human story has been disclosed. Because it is the truth, it must be shared universally. It cannot be private opinion. When we share it with all peoples, we give them the opportunity to know the truth about themselves, to know who they are because they can know the true story of which their lives are a part. Wherever the gospel is preached the question of the meaning of the human story—the universal story and the personal story of each human being—is posed. Thereafter the situation can never be the same. It can never revert to the old harmonies, the old securities, the old static or cyclical patterns of the past. Now decisions have to be made for or against Christ, for Christ as the clue to history or for some other clue. There will always be the temptation, even for those within the Christian community, to find the clue in the success of some project of our own, to see our program (whether of church growth or of human development) as the success story that is going to give meaning to our lives. The gospel calls us back again and again to the real clue, the crucified and risen Jesus, so that we learn that the meaning of history is not immanent in history itself, that history cannot find its meaning at the end of a process of development, but that history is given its meaning by what God has done in Jesus Christ and by what he has promised to do; and that the true horizon is not at the successful end of our projects but in his coming to reign.

One may say, therefore, that missions are the test of our faith. In earlier chapters I have emphasized the fact that the Christian gospel cannot be validated by reference to some more ultimate commitment. The Christian faith is itself an ultimate faith-commitment which can be validated only in its exercise. As such it is open to the charge of subjectivity. In drawing on the epistemological work of Polanyi I referred to his insistence on the importance of the subjective pole in all our knowing. All knowing is an exercise of a knowing subject which involves personal commitment. How, then, is it saved from pure subjectivity? This is a vital question in our present cultural situation, where Christian faith is widely regarded as belonging to the world of subjective values rather than to the world of objective facts, and as being therefore merely a matter of personal choice about which the words "true" and "false" cannot be used. How is this charge to be refuted? Not by seeking some more ultimate ground on which faith could rest. There is nothing more ultimate than Jesus Christ, through whom all things came to be and in whom all things will find their consummation. Polanyi's answer to the charge of subjectivism is that while we hold our beliefs as personally committed subjects, we hold them with universal intent, and we express that intent by publishing them and inviting all people to consider and accept them. To be willing so to publish them is the test of our real belief. In this sense, missions are the test of our faith. We believe that the truth about the human story has been disclosed in the events that form the substance of the gospel. We believe, therefore, that these events are the real clue to the story of every person, for every human life is part of the whole human story and cannot be understood apart from that story. It follows that the test of our real belief is our readiness to share it with all peoples.

I do not say that that is the only way to speak of missions. Missions are also an expression of our hope: they express our belief that there is a real future for us and for the world and that there are therefore solid grounds for hope. Missions are also an expression of love. As Paul says, the love of Christ constrains us. We have been reconciled to God through the atoning love of Christ, and therefore we have an obligation to share that love with all for whom he died. We have a ministry of reconciliation entrusted to us because God has reconciled us to himself. But clearly both of these motives depend on the truth of what we believe. If it is not true, then there are no grounds for hope. And if it is not true, then to persuade men and women to follow Jesus is not an act of love. Missions are the test of our faith that the gospel is true.

It will be clear from what I have said about Paul's eschatological vision of salvation that I am not placing at the center of the argument the question of the salvation or perdition of the individual. Clearly that is part of what is involved, but my contention is that the biblical picture is distorted if this is put in the center. But it may be asked: if it is true that those who die without faith in Christ are not necessarily lost, and if it is also true that those who are baptized Christians are not necessarily saved, what is the point of missions? Why not leave events to take their course? In answer to that question, I would refer again to the word of Paul which I quoted earlier, "I do it all for the sake of the gospel, that I may share in its blessings" (1 Cor. 9:23). Jesus said as he was on his way to the cross, "Where I am, there shall my servant be" (John 12:26). The one who has been called and loved by the Lord, the one who wishes to love and serve the Lord, will want to be where he is. And where he is is on that frontier which runs between the kingdom of God and the usurped power of the evil one. When Jesus sent out his disciples on his mission, he showed them his hands and his side. They will share in his mission as they share in his passion, as they follow him in challenging and unmasking the powers of evil. There is no other way to be with him. At the heart of mission is simply the desire to be with him and to give him the service of our lives. At the heart of mission is thanksgiving and praise. We distort matters when we make mission an enterprise of our own in which we can justify ourselves by our works. I said at the beginning of this chapter that the Church's mission began as the radioactive fallout from an explosion of joy. When it is true to its nature, it is so to the end. Mission is an acted-out doxology. That is its deepest secret. Its purpose is that God may be glorified.

3

Thy Will Be Done

Mission in Christ's Way

Anastasios of Androussa *

The Plenary address by Bishop Anastasios Yannoulatos of Androussa at the conference sponsored by the Commission on World Mission and Evangelism in 1989 in San Antonio illustrates the emergence of Eastern Orthodox theology as a major contribution to ecumenical missiology in recent decades. Drawing on Scripture and the traditions of the Eastern Fathers to illuminate the conference theme, "Thy Will Be Done: Mission in Christ's Way," Anastasios sets forth an understanding of mission which is at once trinitarian, incarnational, kenotic, Spirit-guided, and future-oriented. "Just as there is no church without a worshipping life," he says, "so there cannot be a living church without missionary life." The address presents perspectives that are both timeless and relevant to the life of the churches.

Human pride, in its individual, social, or racial expression, poisons and destroys life in the world at large or in the small community in which we live. The human will obstinately exalts its autonomy. Loneliness is on the increase, nightmares multiply, fears mount up. Old and new idols are being erected in human consciousness. People dance around them. They offer them adulation and worship them ecstatically. But at the same time, every so often, new, sensitive voices speak out for a just and peaceful age. New initiatives are being taken; a new awareness of worldwide community is growing.

In our ecumenical gatherings all of these facts come to light, sometimes alarming, sometimes hopeful. Our problems overwhelm us. We describe them and try to solve them. But when we think we have solved one, three new ones spring up. Our mood keeps swinging, like a pendulum, between hope and despair.

---

* Reprinted from *The San Antonio Report*, ed. Frederick R. Wilson, with the permission of the publisher (Geneva: WCC Publications, 1990), pp. 100–14. In addition to being the former moderator of the WCC's Commission on World Mission and Evangelism, Bishop Anastasios Yannoulatos has been the acting Archbishop of the Orthodox Church in East Africa and has served as Professor of the History of Religions at the University of Athens. He has played a prominent role in the re-emergence of Eastern Orthodox missiology, having initiated several Orthodox societies for mission and inaugurated an Orthodox journal of mission studies.

In this world the faithful continue to pray: "Thy will be done, on earth as it is in heaven," proclaiming, quietly but resolutely, that above all human wills there is one will that is redemptive, life-giving, full of wisdom and power, that in the end will prevail. The choice of subject for our meeting is essentially, I think, a protest and a refusal to accept that which militates against God's loving design, and at the same time an expression of hope and optimism for the future of the world.

REALITY AND EXPECTATION

In the prayer "thy will be done, on earth as it is in heaven," the firm certainty prevails that the Father's will is *already a reality*. Countless other beings—the angels and saints—are already in tune with it. The realization of God's will is not simply a desire; it is a fact that throws light on all the rest. The center of reality is God and God's kingdom. On this the realism of faith is grounded. On this ontology is based every Christian effort on earth. To some, to mention "heaven" might seem anachronistic. We usually look for immediate answers, down-to-earth and realistic, according to our own fixed ideas. We forget, however, that contemporary science and technology have made important leaps forward with regard to a material heaven. A few decades ago we sought to solve humankind's communication problems by using wires stretched out over the earth's surface. Later on we used wireless waves, still following the surface of our planet. With the new technology, however, we have discovered that we can communicate better above the earth, by sending wireless waves heavenwards. So in our theological, ecclesial, and missionary thinking, if we turn our sight once more to the reality of "heaven," about which scripture speaks constantly, we shall certainly find new answers to the world's problems and difficulties.

Our church has not ceased to look in that direction, with prayer and festival affirming the supremacy of God's will. For this faith to clarify the mass of problems that oppress us, the two ideas that form our theme need to be looked at in combination. I shall first attempt a synoptic approach, drawing on the Orthodox tradition of twenty centuries.

"THY WILL BE DONE"

In the prayer our Lord taught us, this petition follows two others, with which it forms a group: "Hallowed be thy name, thy kingdom come, thy will be done." The chief characteristic of the three is the eschatological perspective. They all begin to be realized here below, in order to be perfected in the glory of the kingdom that is to come.

The verb of the petition is in the passive voice. Who exactly is the subject of the action? A preliminary answer says, God. In this petition God's intervention is sought for the implementation of his will, for the establishment of his kingdom. He has the initiative, he carried out his own will. The chief and decisive role in what happens to humankind and the whole universe belongs to God.

A second interpretation sees God's will being done on earth through humankind's conformity with God's commandments (cf. Matt. 7:21, 12:50; John 9:31).

We are called to "do the Father's will." It is a question of the point of view that is expressed in the insight that permeates the Old Testament and in the continuity that is a dominant feature of Jewish literature. In it our participation in the fulfillment of God's will and the necessity of obedience are emphasized.

There is, however, yet a third interpretation, a composite one, that sees as subject of the action both God and human being, that considers that the divine will is realized by divine-human cooperation. Thus the two preceding views are intertwined. Certainly, so that his will may be done, God's intervention is essential. But we, by conforming to his precepts that express God's will in the here and now, contribute to the foretaste and coming of the kingdom in historical time, until its final consummation at the last day.

"On earth as it is in heaven." In this appendage we can perhaps distinguish various closely connected aspects: ethical, social, missionary, ecumenical, and a further one, which we will call realistic. They sum up graphically most of what Chrysostom was saying: "For he did not say, 'thy will be done in me or in us'; but 'everywhere on earth,' so that error might be done away with and truth established, all evil be cast out, virtue return and so nothing henceforth separate heaven from earth."[1] The prayer that our Lord put on our lips and in our hearts aims at a more radical change: the "celestification" of the earth, so that all persons and all things may become heaven.[2]

By the phrase, "thy will be done," of the Lord's prayer, we beseech the Father that he will bring to completion his plan for the salvation of the whole world, and at the same time we ask for his grace that we may be freed from our own will and accept his joyfully. And not only we as individuals, but that all humankind may have fellowship in his will and share in its fulfillment.

After Pentecost, this prayer on the church's lips is highlighted by the facts of the cross and the resurrection. It becomes clear that the divine will has been revealed in its fullness by the word, life, and sacrifice of Jesus Christ. Each member of the church is called thenceforth to advance in its realization, "so to promote 'the' Father's 'will,' as Christ promoted it, who came to do 'the will' of his Father and finished it all; for it is possible by being united with him to become 'one spirit' with him."[3] Christ is made the leader of the faithful in realizing the divine will.

The prayer "Thy will be done" is at the same time our guide in Gethsemane, at the decisive point in the history of the new Adam, our first-born brother. "My Father, if this cannot pass unless I drink it, thy will be done" (Matt. 26:42). This prayer, in which the conformity of the human to the divine will reaches its culmination, illustrates on a personal level the meaning of the phrase "thy will be done" of the Lord's prayer. For all those who determine to be conformed to God's will, who struggle for its realization on earth, the time will come to experience God's will.

Christ's repetition of "thy will be done" in the context of the passion also illustrates the second opinion of our theme, "Mission in Christ's Way."

MISSION IN CHRIST'S WAY

By this expression we often tend to concentrate our attention on some particular stage in Christ's life, e.g., the passion, the cross, his compassion for the poor, etc.

It is certainly not strange to put particular emphasis at times on one aspect, especially when it is continually being overlooked in practice. But the theological thinking and experience of the catholic church insist on what is universal (*to kath'holou*). The same is true of the person of Christ. This distinguishes the outlook and feeling of the one, holy, catholic, and apostolic church from the schismatic, sectarian thinking that holds to that which is only a part. In this theological connection I would like to indicate five central points.

TRINITARIAN CONNECTION AND RELATIONSHIP

Jesus Christ is seen in a continuous relationship to the Father and the Holy Spirit. He is the *apestalmenos* of (who was sent by) the Father. The Holy Spirit clears the way for him, works with him, accompanies him, sets the seal on his work and continues it forever. Through Christ's preaching we come to know the Father and the Holy Spirit. But even the preaching of Christ would remain incomprehensible without the enlightenment of the Holy Spirit, impossible to put into effect without the presence of the Paraclete.

In every expression of Christian life, but especially in mission, the work of Christ is done with the presence of the Holy Spirit; it is brought to completion within historical time by the uninterrupted action of the Holy Spirit. The Holy Spirit "recapitulates" all of us in Christ. He forms the church. The source and bearing of our own apostolic activity resides in the promise and precept of the risen Lord in its Trinitarian perspective: " 'As the Father has sent me, even so I send you.' And when he had said this, he breathed on them, and said to them, 'Receive the Holy Spirit' " (John 20:21–22).

The Christ-centeredness of the one church is understandable only within the wider context of Trinitarian dogma. The one-sidedness of the Western type of Christocentrism was often caused by the restriction of the image of Christ to the so-called "historical Jesus." But the Christ of the church is the eternal word, "the only Son, who is in the bosom of the Father" (John 1:18), who is ever-present in the church through the Holy Spirit, risen and ascended, the universal Judge, "the Alpha and the Omega, the first and the last, the beginning and the end" (Rev. 22:13). The faith and experience of the church are summed up in the phrase: the Father, through the Son, in the Holy Spirit, creates, provides, saves. Essentially, mission in Christ's way is mission in the light of the Holy Trinity, in the mystical presence and working together of Father, Son and Holy Spirit.

ASSUMPTION OF THE WHOLE HUMANITY

One of the favorite terms that Jesus Christ used to describe himself was "son of man." Jesus is the new Adam. The incarnation of the word is the definitive event in the history of humankind, and the church has persisted in opposing any Docetist deviation. "Incarnate by the Holy Spirit and the Virgin Mary" remains the credo of faith. In his conception lies the human contribution, by the wholehearted acceptance of the divine will, in obedience, humility, and joy, by his mother, the most pure representative of the human race. "Behold, I am the handmaid of the Lord; let it be to me according to your word" (Luke 1:38) was her decisive statement.

The absolute distinction of matter and spirit—as imagined by representatives of ancient Greek or Indian thought—is rejected, and humanity is raised up as a whole. Jesus Christ is not only the savior of souls but of the entire human being and the whole material-spiritual creation. This is as hard for classical thought to understand as the Trinitarian dogma. Often indeed an attempt is made to simplify or pass it over. But then mission loses all its power and perspective. Christian mission does not mean taking refuge from our materiality, in one way or another, for the salvation of mere souls, but the transforming of present time, of society and all matter in another way and by another dynamic. This perspective demands creative dialogue with contemporary culture, with secular persons stuck in the materialism of this world, with the new options of physics about matter and energy and with every variety of human creation.

THE RADICALLY AND ETERNALLY NEW ELEMENT: LOVE

Christ overthrows the established forms of authority, wisdom, glory, piety, success, and traditional principles and values, and reveals that the living center of all is *love*. The Father is love. The Son is love incarnate. The Spirit is the inexhaustible power of love. This love is not a vague "principle." It is a "communion" of persons. It is the supreme Being, the Holy Trinity. God is love because he is an eternal trinity, a communication of living, equal, distinct persons. The Son reveals this communion of love (*koinonia agapes*) in the world. In it he is not only the one who invites, but also the way.

Closely bound up with love are freedom, justice, liberation and fellowship of all humankind, truth, harmony, joy, and fullness of life. Every sincere utterance and endeavor for these things, anywhere in the world, in whatever age and culture, but above all every loving, true expression of life, is a ray of God's grace and love. Jesus did not speak in vague and philosophical language about these great and holy things but revealed them in power by clear signs and speech, and above all by his life.

Among the many surprises that Christ held in store was the fact that he *identified himself with the humble*, the simplest of the people. From among those he chose his companions and apostles. And in the well-known saying about the universal last judgment he directly identified himself with the despised, the infirm, the poor, the strangers, and those in distress in the whole world. "As you did it to one of the least of these my brethren, you did it to me," he says, having "all the nations" assembled before him (Matt. 25:31–46).

This course remains determinative for his church, his mystical body, for all ages. For this, it constitutes, in its authentic form, the most benevolent power that fights for human dignity, worth, relief, the raising up of every human being throughout the length and breadth of the earth. Concern for all the poor and those unjustly treated, without exception—independent of race or creed—is not a fashion of the ecumenical movement, but a fundamental tradition of the one church, an obligation that its genuine representatives always saw as of first importance. "To the extent that you abound in wealth, you are lacking in love," declares Basil the Great, criticizing the predilection of many for a "piety that costs nothing." [4] He did not hesitate to call a "robber" not only the person who robs someone, but also the one who, though able to provide clothing and help, neglects to do so. Tersely he concludes: "You do injustice to so many, as many are those you could help."[5] The modern fact of the world's integration extends these judgments from the individual to the collective plane, from individuals to wider conglomerations, to peoples, the rich nations. The saints of the church did not simply speak for the poor, but, above all, shared their life. They voluntarily became poor out of love for Christ, who made himself poor, in order to identify with him.

THE PARADOX OF HUMILITY AND
THE SACRIFICE OF THE CROSS

From the first moment of his presence in humanity Christ makes *kenosis* (self-emptying) the revelation of the power of the love of the Triune God. He spends the greater part of his human life in the simplicity of everyday labor. Later, in his short public life, he faces various disputes and serious accusations. The power of love is totally bound up with *humility*. The opposite of love we usually call hatred. But its real name is egoism. This is the denial of the Triune God who is a *koinonia* (communion) of love. Therein also lies the drama of Lucifer, that he can do everything except be humble. And that is precisely why he cannot love. Christ destroys the works of the devil (1 John 3:8), and ransoms us chained in our egoism, by accepting the ultimate humiliation, the cross. By this humility he abolishes on the cross demonic pride and self-centeredness. In that hour the glory of his love shines forth. We are redeemed.

Christian life means continual assimilation of the mystery of the cross in the fight against individual and social selfishness. This holy humility, which is ready to accept the ultimate sacrifice, is the mystical power behind Christian mission. Mission will always be a service that entails acceptance of dangers, sufferings and humiliations, the experience of human powerlessness, and at the same time of the power of God. Only those who are prepared to accept, with courage and trust in Christ, sacrifice, tribulation, contradiction, and rejection for his sake, can withstand. One of the greatest dangers for Christian mission is that we become forgetful in the practice of the cross and create a comfortable type of a Christian who wants the cross as an ornament but who often prefers to crucify others than to be crucified oneself.

EVERYTHING IN THE LIGHT OF THE RESURRECTION
AND ESCHATOLOGICAL HOPE

The first precept of the universal mission is given in light of the resurrection. Before the fact of the cross and resurrection Jesus had not allowed his disciples to go out into the world. Unless one experiences the resurrection, one cannot share in Christ's universal apostolate. If one experiences the resurrection, one cannot help bearing witness to the risen Lord, setting one's sights on the whole world. "All authority in heaven and on earth has been given to me. Go, therefore, and make disciples of all the nations" (Matt 28:19). The first sentence takes our thought back to "on earth as it is in heaven" in the Lord's prayer. Authority over the whole world has been given to the Son of man, who fully carried out the Father's will.

He is the Lord, "who is and who was and who is to come, the Almighty" (Rev. 1:8). The faith and power of the church are founded precisely on this certainty. Cross and resurrection go together. To conform one's life to the crucified life of Christ involves the mystical power of the resurrection. On the other side, the resurrection is the glorious revelation of the mystery and power of the cross, victory over selfishness and death. A mission that does not put at its center the cross and resurrection ends up as a shadow and a fantasy. As do simple people, so also the more cultivated—who wallow in wealth, comfort and honors—come at some moment of crisis face to face with the implacable, final question: what happens at death? In this problem that torments every thinking person in every corner of the world, the church has the task of revealing the mystery of Christ's word: "For this is the will of my Father, that every one who sees the Son and believes in him should have eternal life; and I will raise him up at the last day" (John 6:40).

I recall a personal experience, in an out-of-the-way region of western Kenya. We arrived at night at a house that was in mourning. The little girl, stricken mortally by malaria, was lying on a big bed, as if sleeping peacefully. "She was such a good child. She was always the first to greet me," whispered the afflicted father in perplexity. We read a short funeral prayer, and I said a few words of consolation. Alone in the room of the schoolhouse where we were staying, by the light of the oil lamp, with the sound of rain on the banana leaves and zinc roof, I remembered the events of the day. Away in the darkness a drum was beating. It was in the house of mourning. In my tiredness I wondered: why are you here? There came confusedly to my mind the various things that are spoken about in connection with mission: preaching, love, education, civilization, peace, development. Suddenly a light flashed and lit up in the mist of my tired brain the essence of the matter: You bring the message, the hope of resurrection. Every human person has a unique worth. They will rise again. Herein lies human dignity, value, and hope. Christ is risen! You teach them to celebrate the resurrection in the mystery of the church; to have a foretaste of it. As if in a fleeting vision I saw the little African girl hurrying up to greet me the first, as was her habit, helping me to determine more precisely the kernel of the Christian mission—that is, to infuse all with the truth and hope of the resurrection; to teach them to celebrate it.

What our brothers and sisters in the isolated corners of Africa and Asia or in the outskirts of our large and rich cities long for, in their depression and loneliness, is not vague words of consolation, a few material goods or crumbs of civilization. They yearn, secretly or consciously, for human dignity, hope, to transcend death. In the end they are searching for the living Christ, the perfect God-man, the way, the truth, and the life. All, of whatever age and class, rich or poor, obscure or famous, illiterate or learned, in their heart of hearts long to celebrate the resurrection and the "celestification" of life. In this the prospect of a mission "in Christ's way" reaches its culmination.

FULLNESS AND CATHOLICITY

The consequences of such a theological understanding are many-sided. The important units, among which will be groups of problems critical for our time in the days that follow, have already been fixed: (1) turning to the living God; (2) participating in suffering and struggle; (3) the earth is the Lord's; and (4) towards renewed communities in mission. Already, much study, leavened with prayer, has taken place in small and larger groups, in conferences and congresses. The third part of this summary report will turn on only two axes.

1. "Thy will be done," as it is repeated by Christ himself in Gethsemane, helps us to overcome a great temptation: *the tendency for us to minimize the demands and cost of doing God's will in our personal life.* It is usually easier for us to rest in the general, in what concerns mostly others.

a) But the will of God, as it is revealed in Christ, is a single and indissoluble *whole* (" . . . teaching them to observe *all* that I have commanded you"). "Thy will be done"—entirely, not by halves. The various so-called corrections that have at times been made to make the gospel easier and the church more acceptable or, so to speak, more effective, do not strengthen but rob the gospel of its power. While waiting at a European airport a couple of years ago there came into my hands a leaflet in which, framed between other things, was written: "Blessed are those who are rich. Blessed are those who are handsome. Blessed are those who have power. Blessed are the smart. Blessed are the successful. For they will possess the earth." I thought to myself: How many times, even in our own communities, do we prefer, openly or secretly, these idols, this worldly topsy-turvy representation of the beatitudes, making them criteria of our way of life?

The name of the city in which this meeting of ours is taking place reminds us not only of San Antonio of Padua to which the toponymy refers but also of St. Anthony the Great, one of the universal church's great personalities, who traced a model of perfect acceptance of God's will. This great hermit, in perfect obedience to "if you would be perfect, go, sell what you possess and give it to the poor, and you will have treasure in heaven; and come, follow me" (Matt. 19:21) went out in an adventure of freedom and love, which led to the outpouring of a new breath of the Spirit in the church at a time when it was in danger of compromising with secular power and the spirit of the world.

In the midst of our many sociopolitical concerns we have to bear in mind and act on the understanding that "this is the will of God, your sanctification" (1 Thess. 4:3). Our *sanctification*, by following the divine will in all things, in our daily obligations, in our personal endeavors, and in the midst of many and various difficulties and dilemmas. The simplistic anthropology that encourages a naive morality by passing our existential tragedy by does not help at all. Human existence is an abyss. "I do not do what I want, but I do the very thing I hate. . . . I see in my members another law at war with the law of my mind and making me captive to the law of sin which dwells in my members" (Rom. 7:15–23). Many of us, in critical situations, while we easily say "thy will be done," in practice add: "not as thou wilt, but as I will." This overt or secret reversal of the divine will in our decisions is the main reason and cause of the failure of many Christian missions and initiatives. The hard inner struggle for purification and sanctification is the premise and mystical power of the apostolate.

The carrying out of God's will in the world will always be assisted by *continuous repentance*, so that we may be conformed to the model of Christ and be made one

with him. That is why in the Orthodox tradition monasteries have special importance, above all as centers of penitence. Everything that accompanies this struggle—worship, work, comforting the people, education, artistic creativity—follows,
as a reflection of the spiritual purification, the transforming personal experience of
repentance. The quest for new types of communities that will serve the contemporary apostolate must be closely bound up with the spiritual quest in the contemporary social reality for concrete forms of communities that will live out thoroughly,
on the personal level, repentance and longing for the coming of the kingdom. The
critical question for a mission in Christ's way is to what extent others can discern
in our presence a ray of his presence.

b) Conformity to God's will does not mean servile submission or fatalistic
expectation. Nor is it achieved by a simple, moral, outward obedience. Joyful
acceptance of God's will is an expression of love for a new relationship in the
Beloved; it is a restoration of humanity's lost freedom. It means our communion
in the mystery of the love of the Holy Trinity, communion in freedom of love. Thus,
we become "partakers of the divine nature" (2 Pet. 1:4). Conformity to God's will
is in the end a sharing in what the Orthodox tradition calls "uncreated energies,"
by which we reach theosis, we become "good by grace."[6] The most blessed pages
of Christian mission were written out of an excess of love for Christ, an identifica-
tion with him.

c) The church continually seeks to renew this holy intoxication of love, especially by the sacrament of the holy eucharist—which remains the pre-eminently
missionary event—everywhere on earth. In the divine liturgy the celebrant, as
representative of the whole community, prays: "Send thy Holy Spirit upon us and
upon these gifts here present." Not on the gifts only, but we beg that the Holy Spirit
may be sent "upon us" also, so that we may be "moved by the Spirit." The whole
prayer moves very clearly in a *Trinitarian* perspective. We beseech the Father to
send the Spirit to change the precious gifts into Christ's body and blood, and in
receiving holy communion we are united with him; we become "of one body" and
"of one blood" with Christ, that we may bear the "fruit" of the Spirit, become
"God's temple," receivers and transmitters of his blessed radiance.

The enthusiasm for the *acquisition of the Holy Spirit*, which is of late much
sought after in the West, has always been strong in the East, but in a sober
Christological context and in a Trinitarian perspective. The church's experience is
summed up in the well-known saying of St. Seraphim: "The purpose of Christian
life is the acquisition of the Holy Spirit." And the saint continues: "Prayer, fasting
and almsgiving, and the other good works and virtues that are done for Christ, are
simply, and only, means of acquiring God's Holy Spirit."[7] This presence of the
Holy Spirit has nothing at all to do with spiritual pride and self-satisfaction. It is at
bottom connected with the continual exercise of penitence, with holy humility. "I
tell you the truth," wrote a holy monk of Mount Athos, Starets Silouan. "I find
nothing good in myself and I have committed many sins. But the grace of the Holy
Spirit has blotted them out. And I know that to those who fight sin is afforded not
only pardon but also the grace of the Holy Spirit, which gladdens the soul and
bestows a sweet and profound peace."[8]

2. The fact that the will of God refers to the whole world, the whole universe,

excludes any isolating of ourselves in an individual piety, in a sort of *private Christianity.*

a) The will of God covers the whole human reality; it is accomplished in the whole of history. It is not possible for the Christian to remain indifferent to historical happenings in the world, when faith is grounded on two historical facts: the incarnation of the word and the second coming of Christ. The social, human event is the place in which the church unfolds. Every expression of human creativity, science, technology, and the relationships of persons as individuals, peoples, and various groupings are to be found among its concerns. We are living at a critical, historic juncture in which a new universal culture, the electronic culture, is taking shape. The natural sciences, especially biomedicine, genetics, and astronautics, are creating and posing new problems. Half of the earth's population is crushed into huge urban centers; contemporary agnosticism is eating away at the thought and behavior of the city-dwellers. The passage from the "written" to the "electronic" word is opening up undreamed-of possibilities for the amassing of a whole universe of increased knowledge and creating a new human thinking. A new world is emerging. A new sort of human being is being formed. The church, the mystical body of "the one who is and was and is to come" has a pledge and a duty to the march of humanity in the future, the whole society in which it exists as "leaven," "sign," and "sacrament" of the kingdom that has come and is coming. What the church has, it has to radiate and offer for the sake of all the world.

But if one temptation is for us not to see the universal duty when we pray "thy will be done," the reverse is for us to be occupied only with universal themes, indifferent to concrete reality; to be too sensitive to certain situations and indifferent to others. (To speak, for example, constantly about injustice in such-and-such a publicized region and be indifferent to injustice in Europe, as, for example, in Albania, where four hundred thousand Christians are oppressed, deprived constitutionally of every expression of faith, even of the elementary right to have a church.)

In various corners of our planet, want, disease, oppression, injustice, and the raw violence of arms oppress millions of our fellow human beings. All of these are cells of the same body—the great body of humanity to which we belong. Their suffering is the suffering of Christ, who assumed the whole of humanity, and the suffering of the church, his mystical body. It is—must be—the suffering of us all.

The prophetic voice, both for the immediate and actual and worldwide, remains always the church's obligation, even if it annoys certain people who do not wish to touch any unjust establishment. In many situations, within and outside, the church is obliged today to speak in the way of the biblical protest: Woe to those who talk about justice but who in practice seek only their own right and their own privileges. Woe to those who rejoice, crying "peace, peace," but forge the fetters of the defenseless. Woe to the rich nations that continually celebrate freedom and love, but by their policies make the developing peoples poorer and less free. Woe to those who appear as God's lawyers and representatives, making a mockery— deliberately or unintentionally— of what is finest in humanity, the witness of Jesus Christ.

b) But still the gospel cannot remain the possession of only certain peoples who had the privilege of hearing it first. By putting on our lips the prayer "thy will be done," the Lord "bade each one of us who prays to take thought for the ecumene" (John Chrysostom).[9] God's will, as it was fulfilled and revealed in Christ, has to be made known in every corner of the earth, in every cranny of the world, in every expression of our contemporary many-centered civilization. A world missionary conference like our own cannot relegate to a footnote the fact that millions of our fellow men and women have not heard, even once in their lives, the Christian message; that hundreds of races still, after twenty centuries of Christian history, do not have the gospel in their mother tongue.

Distinctions between Christian and non-Christian nations are no longer absolutely valid in our days. In all nations there is a need for re-evangelization in every generation. Every local church finds itself in mission in its actual geographical and cultural territory and context. But its horizons, outside the place in which it is active, must extend in the catholic church "from one end of the earth to the other." Despite cultural differences, all of us face more or less the same basic human problems. All the local churches, expressing the life of the "one, holy, catholic and apostolic church," are in a state of mutual interdependence and interchange, on both receiving and sending. The distinction between sending and receiving churches belongs to the past. All should, and can, both receive and send. In proportion to the gifts (*charismata*) that every local church possesses (personnel, knowledge, expertise, financial resources) it can contribute to the development of the worldwide mission "to the end of the earth" (Acts 1:8). It is time for every Christian to realize that mission is our own obligation and to take part in it looking to the whole of humankind. Just as there is no church without a worshipping life, so there cannot be a living church without missionary life.

c) Those outside the Christian faith, who still have no knowledge of the will of God in its fullness, do not cease to move in the mystical radiance of his glory. God's will is diffused throughout the whole of history and throughout the whole world. Consequently it influences their own life, concerns them and embraces them. It is expressed in many ways—as divine providence, inspiration, guidance, etc. In recent times in the ecumenical movement we have been striving hard for the theological understanding of people of other faiths; and this difficult, but hopeful, dialogue very much deserves to be continued at this present conference.

Certainly for the church, God's will, as it was lived out in its fullness by Christ, remains its essential heritage and contribution in the world. But respect for others will not be a so-called agreement on a common denominator that minimizes our convictions about Christ, but an injustice, if we are silent about the truth that constitutes the givenness of the church's experience; it is another thing, the imposition by force, that is unacceptable and has always been anti-Christian. A withholding of the truth leads to a double betrayal, both of our own faith and of others' right to know the whole truth.

Jesus Christ went about doing good among people of other faiths (let us recall the stories of the Canaanite woman and the centurion), admiring and praising their spontaneous faith and goodness. ("I say to you, not even in Israel have I found such faith," Matt. 8:10.) He even used as a symbol of himself a representative of another religious community, the good "Samaritan." His example remains determinative: beneficent service and sincere respect for whatever has been preserved from that which was made "in the image of God." Certainly in today's circumstances our duty is becoming more clear and extensive: a journey together in whatever does not militate against God's will, an understanding of the deepest religious insights that have developed in other civilizations by the assistance of the Spirit, a cooperation in the concrete applications of God's will, such as justice, peace, freedom, and love, both in the universal community and on the local level.

d) Not only the so-called spiritual but also the whole physical universe moves in the sphere of God's will. Reverence for the animal and the vegetable kingdoms, the correct use of nature, concern for the conservation of the ecological balance, and the fight to prevent nuclear catastrophe and to preserve the integrity of creation, have become more important in the list of immediate concerns for the churches. This is not a deviation, as asserted by some who see Christ as saving souls by choice and his church as a traditional religious private concern of certain people. The whole world, not only humankind but the entire universe, has been called to share in the restoration that was accomplished by the redeeming work of Christ. "We wait for new heavens and a new earth in which righteousness dwells" (2 Pet. 3:13). Christ, the Almighty and Logos of the Universe, remains the key to understanding the evolution of the world. All things will come to pass in him who is their head. The surprising design, "the mystery of his will," which has been made known to us "according to his purpose," is "a plan for the fullness of time, to unite all things in him (*anakephalaiosasthai ta panta en tō Christo*—according to another translation: 'bring everything together under Christ, as a head'), things in heaven and things on earth" (Eph. 1:9–10). The correspondence with the phrase of the Lord's prayer is obvious. The transforming of creation, as victory over the disfigurement that sin brought to the world, is to be found in the wider perspective and immediate concerns of Christian mission.

Through all the length and breadth of the earth millions of Christians of every race, class, culture, and language repeat "thy will be done, on earth as it is in heaven"—sometimes painfully, faithfully, and hopefully; sometimes mechanically and indifferently. But we seldom connect it intimately with the missionary obligation. The conjunction of the two phrases "thy will be done" and "mission in Christ's way" gives a special dynamic to our conference. Understanding the missionary dimensions of this prayer will strengthen in the Christian world the conviction that mission is sharing in carrying out God's will on earth—and, put the other way round, that God's will demands our own active participation, working with the Holy Trinity.

By sharing the life of the risen Christ, living the Father's will moved by the Holy Spirit, we have a decisive word and role in shaping the course of humankind. The Lord is at hand. The history of the world does not proceed in a vacuum. It is unfolding towards an end. There is a plan. God's will shall prevail on earth. The prayers of the saints will not remain unanswered! There will be a universal judgment by the Lord of love. At that last hour everything will have lost its importance and value, except for disinterested love. The last word belongs to Christ. The mystery of God's will reaches its culmination in the recapitulation of all things in him. We continue to struggle with fortitude. We celebrate the event that is coming. We enjoy a foretaste of that hour of the last things. Rejoicing in worship. With this vision. With this hope.

Lord, free us from our own will and incorporate us in your own. "Thy will be done."

NOTES

1. John Chrysostom, "Commentary to Saint Matthew the Evangelist," Homily 19, 5. P.G., (= J.P. Migne, *Patrologiae Cursus Completus, Series Graeca*, Paris), Vol. 57, col. 280.

2. Origen, "On Prayer," XXVI, 6 *BEPES* (Library of Greek Fathers and Church Writers, Athens), Vol. 10, p. 279.

3. *Ibid.*, XXVI, 3. p. 277.

4. Basil the Great, "To those who become wealthy," *BEPES*, Vol. 54, p. 67.

5. Homily on "I will pull down my barns," 7 *BEPES*, Vol. 54, pp. 64–65.

6. Maximos the Confessor, "On various questions. . . ?," *P.G.*, Vol. 91, col. 1084AC, 1092C.

7. P. A. Botsis, *Philokalia ton Roson Neptikon* (Philocalia of the Russian Vigilents), Athens, 1983, p. 105.

8. Archimandrite Sophrony, *Starets Silouan, moine du Mont-Athos* (translated from Russian into French by the Hieromoine Symeon), Sisteron, 1973, p. 318.

9. Chrysostom, *ibid.*, col. 280.

4

The Exclusiveness of Jesus Christ

*George Brunk, III**

George Brunk's essay probes the requirements of a Christ-centered faith that avoids both historical relativism and confessional fanaticism. The essay seeks to answer not only the question of Christ's identity but also the issue that is intimately connected to it, Christian identity. The author examines not only scriptural and historical claims for the exclusiveness of Christ, but goes on to set missiological and ethical requirements of faithful Christian practice. The missionary style flowing from loyalty to the claim to Christian exclusiveness is described by this Mennonite author as "mediatorial" and "irenic." The follower of Christ is called to share the truth about Christ and the way of salvation with others without passing judgment on the value of other faiths or the question of their followers' eternal destiny.

Many sectors of contemporary Christendom are experiencing a "Christological failure of nerve."[1] Convictions regarding the significance of Jesus Christ for the human experience are wavering; actions aimed at mediating Jesus Christ to the human race are weakening. This is the loss of nerve.

On the other hand, in our time as in the past, there are those of a fanatical mindset who confuse their limited human cause with the final cause of God and his Christ.[2] Interestingly, those who choose either one of these extremes often appear to do so as an escape from the evils of the opposite extreme. This vacillation between a loss of nerve and a spirit of presumption illustrates the central problem in the question of the exclusiveness of Jesus Christ, especially as that question bears upon the mission of the church. Is there an alternative to these opposites that both answers to the claims of the Christian message and provides a viable style of mission activity?

* Taken from *Jesus Christ and the Mission of the Church: Contemporary Anabaptist Perspectives*, ed. Erland Walter, and reprinted with permission of the publisher (Newton, KS: Faith and Life Press, 1990), pp. 1–23. George R. Brunk, III, is Vice-President and Academic Dean of Eastern Mennonite Seminary, Harrisonburg, Virginia, where he also serves as professor of New Testament. He received his doctorate from Union Theological Seminary in Richmond, Virginia. This paper was commissioned for a 1989 study conference on christology sponsored by Mennonite and Brethren churches "to clarify their respective faith positions, identify areas of commonality and differences, and to promote better mutual understanding and greater unity among our groups as we together witness that Jesus Christ is Lord." Brunk is author of *The Christian's Future* (1987).

What exactly do we mean by the exclusiveness of Jesus Christ? We mean that which marks the person of Jesus Christ as singular and unique so as to make of him an unparalleled and unsurpassable means of salvation. Parallel expressions are the finality of the supremacy of Jesus Christ. Yet another phrase with a similar concern is "the absoluteness of Christianity."[3] However, posing the question in relation to Christianity is, as we will see, not the same as posing it in relation to Jesus Christ. Christianity, in the sense of the historical manifestation of Christian belief, is not the same as the historical manifestation of truth in the person of Jesus Christ. The various modes of expression have their strengths and shortcomings. It is not the present purpose to decide on the relative merits of the language. We will use a variety of terms.

While the term *exclusiveness* has a long history, it has a negative ring in our inclusive age. Perhaps this is helpful in the end for it helps sharpen the issues for us. In all events, when used in relation to Jesus Christ, the term does not carry the common connotation of shutting out another or dissociation from others. However the uniqueness of Jesus Christ is to be construed, no one will contest the fact that this uniqueness coexists with and, indeed, supplies the ground for a universal significance of this person. Here exclusiveness and inclusiveness commingle.

To develop our theme further, we will first consider the current cultural context that conditions our question. Then attention will be given to the scriptural evidence as it bears on the subject. Finally, the focus will be on the implications of a right understanding of Christ's claim for the missionary practice of the church.

THE PRESENT STATE OF THE QUESTION

It has practically become a truism to describe our times as relativistic. Allen Bloom in his best-selling book, *The Closing of the American Mind*, aptly expresses our situation by what he sees among university students:

> They are unified only in their relativism and in their allegiance to equality. . . . The relativity of truth is not a theoretical insight but a moral postulate, the condition of a free society, or so they see it. . . . The danger they have been taught to fear from absolutism is not error but intolerance. Relativism is necessary to openness; and this is the virtue, the only virtue, which all primary education for more than fifty years has dedicated itself to inculcating. Openness—and the relativism that makes it the only plausible stance in the face of various claims to truth and various ways of life and kinds of human beings—is the great insight of our times. The true believer is the real danger (pp.25–26).

What is here attributed to the mindset of the student generation is equally true of Western society as a whole. Tolerance is the great virtue and a relative understanding of truth is its corollary. Pluralism is both a cause and effect of this outlook. Perhaps its deeper root is the autonomous reason of the Enlightenment which, once set free from any authority, fragments into a multiplicity of viewpoints and finally loses all confidence in itself. Pluralism and relativism are the products.

The point for the present discussion is simply this: if tolerance is the sole virtue, then exclusiveness becomes the vice. Whether tolerance and exclusive claims to truth are necessarily incompatible is not the point here. Our society, given its understanding of tolerance based in relativism, finds the question of exclusiveness to be a stumbling block and a scandal. We can harbor no illusion about the status of our interest in the exclusiveness of Jesus Christ. The matter will be coolly rejected or hotly resisted.

It was noted that relativism and pluralism are mutually related. The relativism from the Western enlightenment has contributed to the breakdown of uniform beliefs in society. On the other hand, pluralism has its own long history of diverse religions and world views among peoples. Within Christianity, Anabaptism itself has been a major contributor to the rise of pluralism in the West, with its commitment to voluntarism in faith and a church free from political control. Pluralism antedates relativism and has helped to create it.

Developments in the modern world bring us increasingly in contact with the pluralism of religious beliefs. Faraway places have been brought closer by new means of travel and communication; the faraway peoples have come nearer by massive migration to new cultural and religious contexts. Alternate visions of life become part of our daily experience and the questions of coexistence with them are unavoidable. One writer concludes that "The new perception of religious pluralism is pushing our cultural consciousness toward the simple but profound insight that there is no one and only way."[4] Here it is not a question of whether this perception is correct or not. We simply recognize that the pluralistic context of our times places increasing pressure on the claim of exclusiveness of all faiths, including Christianity.

While pluralism has long been present in the human experience, it was looked upon as abnormal, reflecting the limitations of human understanding or the moral failure of the human family. Today, many are inclined to search for a way to accommodate pluralism, to normalize it by acknowledging that reality is fundamentally plural in nature. This is tersely expressed in the statement: "Today, the universe of meaning has no center."[5]

Those with this outlook are not arguing for a pure relativism of truth nor for a fixing of the diversity of religious faiths. Rather they are attracted to the general outlook of process philosophy for making sense of pluralism. According to this outlook, the world is in the process of becoming. What we experience now is pluralism, but the process is leading toward unity. In this vision, all aspects of present reality are seen as significant, for each aspect contributes to the movement toward convergence. The shape of that convergence is by definition unknown, although Christian thinkers with this perspective may characterize that future in the light of past revelation.[6] Along with the key concept of becoming is an emphasis on interrelating. The process of becoming takes place in the interrelating of all aspects of reality. Relationship defines being, not the other way around. This principle holds true for the realm of human experience as in other realms. The emphasis on interrelating carries into the religious arena since the search for truth occurs in the interaction between religions.

When one takes this approach to understanding reality, many of the Christian beliefs must be either rejected or reinterpreted. For example, the doctrines of Creation and the Fall have said that the universe began with a unity in the act of creation but lost that unity by reason of sin and its fragmenting consequences. This requires that the plurality of truth claims in history be weighed in the light of both a principle of coherence with the beginning norm and a principle of morality. In other words, the question of right or wrong has to be addressed to the diverse claimants of truth. The radical affirmation of pluralism, however, appears to renounce any ground or right to pass such judgment, since truth is in the becoming process.

In the preceding paragraphs, we have explored two important tendencies of our social context—relativism and pluralism. The purpose has been evocative rather than exhaustive. The intention is to illustrate why and how the exclusiveness of Jesus Christ is a problem in our time. A critique of this contemporary viewpoint is not our primary interest. What is of significance is the recognition that we are not immune to the formative impact of these issues.

The spirit of the age has taken root and bears its fruit in our souls, perhaps more than we realize. We, as followers of Christ, are conditioned to stumble at his claim. All of this does not yet answer the question of how we are to understand the question of the exclusiveness of Jesus Christ. It does, however, alert us that the temptation we face is not only to be driven by self-interest and will-to-power under the guise of exclusive claims for our religion, but also to sell out the exclusive claim of another under the pretense of acknowledging the relativity of our own knowledge and achievements.

THE CLAIMS OF SCRIPTURE FOR
THE EXCLUSIVENESS OF JESUS CHRIST

The evidence of Scripture suggests that the question before us does not yield to a simple, unilateral answer. It is not a matter of the New Testament sounding an uncertain note about Christ's absolute significance for all people. Friend and foe alike tend to agree that, when taken on its own terms, the New Testament does make exclusive claims for Jesus the Christ. However, in the biblical writing, there is no systematic and full defense of these claims as a theoretical problem set against other religions. In fact, the biblical writers are reserved about speculation concerning the present status or the future destiny of individual nonbelievers. They are profoundly interested, however, in the moral condition of humanity and its relation to the future destiny of humankind. They are deeply committed to sharing the gospel with all persons in the belief that Christ offers something to everyone. But is there a disinterest or reticence to draw a precise line between truth and nontruth, between salvation and damnation, in their *historical expression*?[7]

A clue to this status of the question is found already on the lips of Jesus himself. On one occasion, the disciple John informed Jesus that a certain man was casting out demons in Jesus' name but was not ready to follow him. To this Jesus responded, "He who is not against us is for us" (Mark 9:38–40, RSV). On another occasion, however, when Jesus defended his deliverance ministry as a conflict of God's kingdom with the kingdom of Satan, he made a parallel but reverse assertion:

"He who is not with me is against me; and he who does not gather with me scatters" (Luke 11:23).

It seems apparent that for Jesus the question of his own exclusive claim cannot be answered in the same way in relation to every other claimant of truth. In the second instance, Jesus sets himself clearly in exclusive contrast to the kingdom of evil. This is not surprising. The world is the arena for the clash of good and evil. All must, and, in fact, inevitably do, take sides on the issue. In the other account, there is a religious leader who, while using Jesus' name, does not identify with the same program and community of Jesus and his immediate disciples. Jesus includes him without demanding that he participate in his own social circle. The movement of Jesus is bigger than the historical structures organically related to him.

But the story does not answer our question definitively. Since the independent exorcist uses the name of Jesus, there is a link to the messianic claim of Jesus. This is not just any religionist. We do not have here, for instance, the grounds for affirming that the movement of God is larger than the messianic movement of Jesus. The case falls within the classical formulation of Acts 4:12: "no other name . . . by which we must be saved." We are, however, put on notice that error lurks on more than one side of the question of Jesus' exclusive claim and its bearing on the practice of mission by the church. In the expression, "he who is not against us is for us," there is disclosed both a clear sense of a cause promoted by an identifiable movement (us) and a recognition that this cause, the cause of God, is not dependent exclusively upon that one movement. The necessary implication is that the nature of this cause is one that can be related to and supported in unexpected ways, perhaps even unwittingly.

THE CLAIM OF JESUS

The search turns then toward the wider evidence of the New Testament to confirm and to clarify the kind of perspective seen in the above sayings of Jesus. There are, of course, the well-known standard passages to which appeal is rightly made. "I am the way, and the truth, and the life; no one comes to the Father, but by me" (John 14:6). "There is salvation in no one else, for there is no name" by which persons must be saved (Acts 4:12), "For there is one God, and there is one mediator between God and men, the man Christ Jesus" (1 Tim. 2:5). The book of Hebrews sounds a strong exclusivist note with the definition of Christ's work as "once for all" (9:12).

While no one is prepared to argue that the early Christians intended anything other than what is implied by this exclusive language, there are some who wish to reinterpret its meaning for today. They may argue that the world view of the first Christians—with its static view of truth and God-determined, end-oriented view of history, and upon which the language of Christ's finality is based—is no longer tenable. Moreover, this language is said to express the believers' confidence in their faith experience, rather than to formulate with precision the relationship of Jesus Christ to all other claims of salvation.[8]

In order to attempt some weighing of these matters for ourselves, we should look again at the fundamental reality of New Testament beliefs as rooted in the life and teaching of Jesus. As careful biblical students know, it was not the practice of Jesus to center his message in himself directly nor to make explicit claims about his person.[9] Nothing illustrates this more strikingly than Jesus' use of the self-designation of "son of man." This enigmatic expression, with its potential meanings of either the most human or most transcendent, divine dimensions, was as puzzling then as it is now. It is as if Jesus' self descriptions are to his person what his use of parables was to his teaching—they helped those inclined to perceive, but caused those inclined to unbelief to misunderstand (see Mark 4:11,12). This may well explain also why Jesus avoided the messianic titles, since they carried connotations of Jewish political and material aspirations that Jesus renounced. The reticence of Jesus to spell out his personal claims means that we face considerable difficulty in answering the question of his exclusiveness on the basis of his own direct claims for his person, i.e., who he was. We must look for more indirect evidence from his teaching and actions.

Certainly one of the amazing features of Jesus' teaching is the way in which he makes a person's ultimate destiny with God dependent upon that person's response to himself. "For whoever is ashamed of me and of my words in this adulterous and sinful generation, of him will the Son of man also be ashamed, when he comes in the glory of his Father" (Mark 8:38).[10] There is ultimate, that is, final significance in Jesus and his teaching because the ultimate consequences of life are linked to him. A correlation exists between the response to Jesus now and the response of God's eschatological agent to the individual in the culmination of history.

In other ways also, the teaching of Jesus discloses an implicit claim of uniqueness and finality. This is especially conspicuous in Jesus' manner of placing himself above the law by claiming to speak for the will of God so as to interpret the law rightly and even to set aside parts of it (see especially the Sermon on the Mount). Interpreters have noted that even the parables have an implicit Christological claim. In this light, the disputed statement of Jesus in Matthew 11:27 rings true: "All things have been delivered to me by my Father; and no one knows the Son except the Father, and no one knows the Father except the Son and any one to whom the Son chooses to reveal him."

These elements from Jesus' teaching point to a close linkage between the content of the message and the person of the messenger. Jesus has been given a message from God of such final significance that one asks who this person is with such authority. On the other hand, statements like Matthew 11:27 just quoted speak expressly of the unique relationship of this person to God that grounds the teaching authority. On the occasion of his teaching about servanthood, Jesus used the example of the child but drops another astonishing statement of his mediatorial role for God himself: "Whoever receives one such child in my name receives me; and whoever receives me, receives not me but him who sent me" (Mark 9:37).

All of these features have their place within the larger theme of Jesus' message of the kingdom of God which has drawn near in his ministry. "The time is fulfilled, and the kingdom of God is at hand; repent, and believe in the gospel" (Mark 1:15). The presence of the kingdom is mediated in Jesus' teaching. It is also actualized in his ministry of healing and exorcism (Luke 11:20). Once again it is evident that the person and the ministry are inseparable. In the presence of this person, the kingdom of God is present. This appears to be the plain sense of Jesus' retort to the Pharisees in Luke 17:21 when they ask about the time of the kingdom's coming: " . . . the kingdom of God is in the midst of you." Jesus is the kingdom present.

With the concept of the kingdom there is an additional dimension. The time is fulfilled; the kingdom has drawn near. There is a note of finality here. This is not the finality of a message, or even of a person, although they are related. This is a finality of context: history has reached a point of completeness, a stage of maturity. The character of the time is different; it is unique. What is claimed in all this is not that some change in the external structures of history explains the special role of Jesus (in a manner rather like Jewish apocalyptic). Rather, it is the other way around. The historical presence of the person of Jesus modifies the character of the historical situation.[11] Where Jesus is, the situation changes for every person.

This is then the basis for the call to repentance that Jesus announces. Jesus asks all to repent. The implication of this must not escape us. Jesus does not see repentance as something just for the ungodly and the immoral. The righteous are eligible for repentance even though they tend to miss the point of Jesus' call. (Hence his statement that he came not to call the righteous but sinners to repentance.) A new offer of God is now present and all are called to reorient their lives (repent) to the new possibilities of righteousness in Jesus. It is not a question of what level of godliness one had reached or whether one had already experienced salvation. In Jesus, all—with no exceptions—are summoned to step into a new kingdom reality not possible before. (See the story in Luke 13:1–5.)

It would be preposterous to conclude that Jesus thought no salvation had preceded him in Israel (or the nations?) or that no saints existed during his lifetime before his ministry to them. However one understands the exclusiveness of Jesus, it is not a simple matter of salvation here, non-salvation elsewhere. One must speak of salvation in Jesus as final in the sense that it supersedes all previous modes of salvation. It fulfills the older in a manner analogous to Jesus' fulfillment of the law—the former is not negated, but is taken up into something greater. And, in this sense, it claims acceptance from all. This then is the basic paradigm with which we are to understand the exclusiveness of Jesus Christ.

A crucial question emerges at this point. Does this paradigm apply to all peoples and religions? What has just been described answers to the relation of Jesus to the older covenant with Israel. The idea of fulfillment itself is a salvation history concept and this concept is rooted in the special history of Israel's God saving this chosen people. We will return to this question at a later point. Here it will suffice to note that the early church understood the meaning of Jesus' life to be relevant for universal history, i.e., all nations.

In the light of the discussion above concerning repentance, the report in Acts 17 of Paul's sermon in Athens is particularly interesting and illuminating. At the conclusion of the sermon, Paul remarks, "The times of ignorance God overlooked, but now he commands all men everywhere to repent . . ." (Acts 17:30). Here is the call to repentance in the light of a changed situation brought about by God's action in Jesus. In this it parallels the preaching of Jesus himself. But now, the proclamation is directed to the Gentiles. According to the book of Acts then, the paradigm of final salvation in Jesus applies to all nations as well as Israel. But, with this

example, we have passed over into the claims of the early church for Jesus'
uniqueness.

THE CLAIMS OF THE EARLY CHURCH

What was a matter of reticence for Jesus became a matter of bold statement and
proclamation for the early church. In direct language and standard titles, the first
believers speak of one whom God has exalted to his own right hand. The status of
Jesus as Son of God is now plainly set forth in its rightful meaning and in effective
demonstration by his resurrection from the dead (Rom. 1:4). The implied sonship
of the Abba-relation of Jesus to God is now understood as sonship of the highest
divine status (Phil. 2:9,10). The church not only is more explicit in its confession
of Jesus the Christ; it now makes the person of Jesus Christ the starting point of the
gospel, not the subtle presupposition of the message as in Jesus' own teaching.
Therefore, we recognize that heightening of the Christological confession takes
place and, by consequence, also a heightening of the exclusive claims for the person
of Christ.[12]

In order to trace this confession of the uniqueness and finality of Jesus Christ,
we will limit ourselves to two crucial contexts: the book of Acts and the prologue
of John. Reference was made to the sermon of Paul at Athens, as recorded in Acts
17. We noted how the call to repentance has become a universal call to every
person. In the sermon, this is anchored on one side in the resurrection (17:31) and
on the other side in the monotheism of the Old Testament by which there is one
creator God who unites all peoples in a common spiritual quest. The relevance of
both of these presuppositions for the universal relevance of Jesus Christ can hardly
be overemphasized. The resurrection is the sign beyond all signs that the highest
of all salvation acts—the defeat of death—has been made a realistic expectation
because of its accomplishment in human experience in history. A truly universal
hope has been opened up. The early missionaries seem to reflect the conviction that
such a message would find no rival claim and should be withheld from no one. On
the other hand, the belief in the one God leads to a view of oneness in human
experience. All peoples come from the one source and have a common destiny in
this God. In this way, the early church builds a bridge of solidarity with all persons
and nations by means of which they share the novelty of God's final saving acts in
Jesus of Nazareth.

This sharing, however, is not done in Paul's sermon (or elsewhere in Acts) by
an absolute polarity of negative and positive, in which the other religion is
completely negated. The religiosity of the Athenians is an expression of the search
for the one God. Moreover, is there not even a sign of grace in the comment, as
fascinating as it is enigmatic, that God has overlooked the former times of
ignorance, but now commands repentance? Behind the description of ignorance,
which does not have the connotation of stupidity but of unawareness, is a God who
shows patience and mercy towards those without knowledge.[13] Parallel ideas to
these are found in Acts 14:16–17: "In past generations he [God] allowed all the
nations to walk in their own ways; yet he did not leave himself without witness,
for he did good. . . ." The theme of God's patient indulgence is repeated here. The

assertion of God's positive blessing is stated more strongly by reference to acts of goodness leading to a fulfilled life. This is quite a generous view of God's dealing with those outside both the Christian and the Jewish streams of salvation.

It is not the practice of the Bible to use the language of salvation for this general blessing of God to the nations. Presumably that language is intended to carry the special meaning of the deliverance acts accomplished on behalf of the elect people. When today the question is posed whether salvation is found outside of Christ, the term *salvation* is being used more widely. The Acts passages give us ground for saying that God does accept and bless (and, in this sense, saves) in other traditions. For many, including conservative Christians, the term *salvation* refers to the final destiny of the individual. While this is a partial understanding from the biblical point of view, the question is important. What is striking in this regard is that biblical writers do not press this question, one way or the other. It is as if they respect the freedom and sovereignty of God and refrain from judgment. This observation needs to be qualified carefully. The biblical writers believe in the separation of the righteous and wicked in eternity; but they show no inclination to make these lines of separation synonymous with the lines of the covenant people. The wicked will perish; but never is there the simple equation of the nations with the wicked.[14]

There is evidence in Acts, as in the life of Jesus, that no need is felt to limit God's saving interest and intervention in other peoples. What is felt is a compelling drive to share the *final* salvation of Jesus that supersedes all other knowledge and experience with God. In Acts, the God-fearing Cornelius is just such an example (Acts 10:1,2). He is a devout man who fears God. Peter makes the astounding comment at the moment of his meeting Cornelius: "Truly I perceive that God shows no partiality, but in every nation any one who fears him and does what is right is acceptable to him" (10:34,35). With the language of acceptance used here, one could hardly affirm that Cornelius was a subject of God's eternal rejection outside of Christ. But just as important is the fact that God does not hold back from Cornelius a greater salvation. The forgiveness of sin in Jesus and the blessing of the Spirit—both signs of God's final salvation—are appropriate to Cornelius without negating the acceptance of any earlier time.

But what about that classical passage on our subject in Acts 4:12 to the effect that there is salvation in no other for there is no other name known to the human race by which we must be saved? Does that not have the obvious meaning that no one can be saved unless they know the name of Jesus? How does this relate to Acts 10, 14, and 17? Some light is thrown on the matter when we consider the meaning of the word *must* in Luke/Acts. This is a common word to the author, having a special theological meaning. It points to the purposes of God which are being realized in the movement of events in Israel, Jesus, the church, and the world. The *must* in our verse does not refer to an intrinsic logic of reality as if there is no material possibility of salvation elsewhere. Rather, it is God's intention that, at this stage in the fulfillment of his purposes, all persons might be summoned to faith in Jesus. This kind of salvation exists in no other. Such an understanding of the verse would then parallel the proclamation of Jesus regarding the kingdom whose approach has called for reorientation on the part of all, even the righteous.

A further, fascinating implication of this understanding is that the *must* of this salvation bears not only upon the hearer of the gospel but lays upon the believer a sense of obligation to proclaim this message God intends for all nations. We believers are involved in the process of fulfilling the grand design of the Lord of history. A divine necessity has been laid upon us.

Beyond any doubt, the book of Acts represents the concerns of a Christian mind that wrestled with the relationship of the particularity of the means of salvation in Jesus of Nazareth and the universality of the mission of the church to all peoples. The stories show clearly a church that is responding to how the exclusive claim of the message (no other name) relates to the universal religious experience of humankind (anyone who fears God is acceptable).

Another key passage of the New Testament which reveals the same interest is the prologue to the Gospel of John. In all probability, the evangelist has chosen the concept of *logos* (word) to bridge between the wisdom tradition of the Old Testament (salvation history) and the philosophical tradition of the Greco-Roman world (universal history). Jesus is that bridge: the Word which became flesh in the particular man Jesus is also the creative agent of God from which comes all life and light in every age. This Word "enlightens every man" (John 1:9). These qualities of life and light are the very qualities that Jesus brings in the gospel. Our author is prepared to see these gospel values linked to some degree with the universal experience of humankind. Here we see a new kind of theological development in which the exclusiveness of Jesus Christ, which disclosed itself out of the life and message of one person in a particular historical setting, is projected backward in time and outward in space. Now the true and the right of Israel's saving history and of the entire human race—the total creation—are shown to be grounded in Jesus Christ. A new bold step is taken; not only is final salvation found in Jesus Christ, but all penultimate salvation is from him as well.

Nevertheless, the prologue does not leave us with a positive picture of the condition of that universal world. Light is in conflict with darkness. When the light came into the world, it was more likely rejected than received. The general picture of humanity outside of Christ, no matter what evidence of light and life there may be, is one of disobedience and failure. This outlook is shared by other scriptural writers. Paul especially, in his letter to the Romans, articulates this viewpoint. God has made himself plain to all so all are without excuse. The Gentiles may have a law on their hearts that may "perhaps excuse them on that day" of judgment (Rom. 2:15). Still "all men, both Jews and Greeks, are under the power of sin" (Rom. 3:9) and are therefore proper objects of the liberating grace of God in Jesus. In fact, it is the death of Jesus that reveals the degree of spiritual death of every person. "We are convinced that one has died for all; therefore all have died" (2 Cor. 5:14).

In summary, the range of New Testament teaching we have examined indicates that the early Christian outlook did not negate the presence of good in other cultural and religious settings. How God will judge these persons is not a matter of specific speculation. There is the recognition that moral uprightness is found among all nations and that God finds this a ground for his favor even in the final judgment. "God shows no partiality" is the ruling principle (Acts 10:34 and Rom. 2:11, both in the same contexts cited above). On the other hand, a new work of salvation has occurred in Jesus of Nazareth, the Messiah of God, that surpasses all other ways of knowing God. To withhold this news from anyone is unconscionable. To announce this saving message is both to render the hearer more responsible before God and to offer him/her a new dimension of hope not known or experienced before. Here both sinner and saint, according to other religious and moral standards, are summoned to a radical turning in adjusting their lives to a new Master. This is the exclusiveness of Jesus Christ.

THE IMPLICATIONS FOR
THE CHURCH'S PRACTICE OF MISSION

The question to which we now turn is how we as believers in our time and place shall respond to the claims of this Lord. There are two areas which will be explored. The treatment will be only introductory in nature. That there is a degree of scandal in the exclusive claim of Jesus Christ is undeniable for the person of modern sensitivities and for many persons of deep moral sensitivity in any age. If this claim were the projection on Jesus of our self-worship and cultural imperialism it would be most despicable. As it is, the claim comes from One who impresses all who encounter him as humble of spirit and sterling in moral integrity. Jesus Christ himself places before us the either-or of decision without obvious evidence on which to reject him and without unambiguous proof by which to guarantee him. We can only accept (or reject) him and live within the ensuing demonstration of the good of his claims. As a finite human, I cannot master the absolute claim of exclusiveness. It is unattainable and unverifiable for me. I can only receive and experience it for what it is in itself. The problem of the exclusiveness of Jesus Christ is, after all, a question of faith.

We do find, however, some perspective on the whole matter from two areas to which we ought to give more careful attention than before.

Universal and particular. We must sharpen our understanding of the relationship between a theology of creation and a theology of redemption. Woven throughout the presentation of the biblical evidence have been allusions to this issue. The biblical story of salvation is one of specific acts of God in history for a particular people in a concrete time and place. Salvation is particular. This perspective is the dominant one of the biblical narrative—but not the only one. There is also the story of God's concern and responsibility for all of creation. There is a universal history of salvation. One can trace the unfolding of this double perspective in the Old Testament as the conviction of absolute monotheism emerges in Israel paralleled by a heightened emphasis on God as maker of heaven and earth. The shared wisdom of all people is incorporated into Israel's faith. In the New Testament, the movement is from the Messianic salvation of Jesus for Israel to the universal mission. We have seen the evidence of the theological development in response to this movement in Acts and John. Thus the particular and the universal co-exist in biblical revelation.

There is a kind of "ugly ditch"[15] that easily opens up between these perspectives. Taken alone, the particularistic stream (cf. special revelation) becomes sectarian and exclusivistic, unable to see truth and good elsewhere and uninterested in the sharing of its truth, to say nothing of learning from others. On the other side, the universalistic stream (cf. general revelation) alone tends towards syncretism, bland inclusivism, and indifferent tolerance, unable to accept a view of God who allows truth to be conditioned by the historical process. By holding on to the value of both perspectives, the Bible gives us a clue about how to think and act rightly, even though the implications are often not worked out. Put in the broadest of terms, the mission of Christ's community takes the stance of anticipating and acknowledging the activity of the creator God in every place while at the same time openly telling its own story.[16] God, and the working of God's Spirit, will have always preceded his people in their mission; the latter mission must harmonize with the former.

Finite and infinite. We must learn to live creatively with the tension between the finality of Christ and the finitude of the church—and never ease the tension. Practically speaking, the deepest scandal in our commitment to exclusiveness is not the claim of exclusiveness of Jesus Christ but the burden for the followers of Christ to represent his exclusiveness through the actions and structures of finite history and imperfect humanity.

It is true that the idea of incarnation, in which the infinite and the finite unite, involves the same dilemma. For the non-Christian, this too is a scandal. For the person outside of faith, there is a tendency to lump these two levels of the question together—all of the Christian religion appears to claim exclusiveness and is judged accordingly. For the believer, *at the theoretical level*, a clear distinction is made between the finality of Christ and the human condition of the church in all of its aspects. At the *experiential level*, however, it is quite another matter. As for the nonbeliever so for the believer, the two dimensions easily are confused. The result of this blurred distinction is one or the other of two opposite distortions of our missionary stance. In both instances the quality of finality is attributed (erroneously) to the church as a religious phenomenon. The one distortion is a pretentious attitude of superiority that is readily accompanied by the abusive use of power to achieve one's ends since one is playing the part of God for the world. The other distortion is a falsely assumed inferiority that is ashamed of being associated with anything claiming exclusiveness.

Both of these distortions are alive and well in the church. I sense that for the Anabaptist tradition churches it is the second one that is more insidious today. What happens is that we identify ourselves too closely with the claim of Christ as if we are responsible for it. When traditional Anabaptist humanity mixes with modern relativism (of the kind described above), a powerful impulse is created to distance ourselves from any appearance of exclusiveness. But no authority has been granted us to create such a claim, and no authorization has been granted us to dismantle it. This claim belongs to Jesus of Nazareth who is now exalted Lord. He must answer for himself—or rather, every person must answer to this claim for himself/herself.

Still, this is not a simple matter. In a fundamental sense, the exclusiveness of Jesus Christ is not transmitted to his followers. It is a nontransferable trait. Yet we cannot disassociate ourselves from it. The church as a new community is to demonstrate the more-than-they level of righteousness (Matt. 5) that is made possible because of the empowerment of Christ's final salvation. Also, we are to be messengers of this claim and the listener will be hard put to appreciate a distinction between message and messenger. In a derivative sense, therefore, the church participates in Christ's finality. However, we can at best be merely a sign, not a sample of that finality. This role will never become easy. It is a burden; but woe to us if the burden is not carried.

FAITHFUL PRACTICE

What will the practice of mission look like when it reflects the preceding perspective on the claims of its Lord? We will offer only three basic theses.

The *self-understanding is apostolic*. The characteristic self-consciousness of the biblical messenger is that of the reluctant draftee. This trait ought not be passed off as a sign of weak faith. More profoundly, it is an awareness of the contradiction between a divine claim of such greatness and a human instrument of such weakness. Any other attitude would prove that the individual is out of touch. The sense of being sent—i.e., the apostolic consciousness—is the only legitimate condition under which a mission in the name of a unique Savior can be carried forward. That the self-awareness of an authentic witness is not grounded in any sense of pretentiousness is illustrated by the curious tendency to see oneself as a debtor (Rom. 1:14). The messenger is not a profiteer and the style is not exploitative when all sense of creditorship is absent. The exclusiveness of Jesus Christ is not a problem at the level of self-consciousness of the one who is motivated by a mandate outside oneself. Embarrassment at such a claim can only be a sign that our sense of call is more humanly derived than divinely impressed upon us.

Our *stance is mediatorial*. The typical biblical metaphors for those in the mission of God are *messenger* and *witness*. In both instances, the roles so described are ones in which the authorization rests outside of the communicator. The messenger is sent by a person in authority, the witness is empowered by having seen or experienced an external event or person. The truth of these persons is mediated. To communicate a claim of finality from within oneself is absurd for a finite human being. Absoluteness is something which I as a human being can neither ground nor demonstrate; I can pass on such a claim only as a witness or messenger from an absolute source.

There is a certain freedom, then, over against the question of Christ's exclusiveness. Although we have staked our lives on this truth, we are not responsible to answer for it, nor to determine the future shape of historical events in order to fulfill the claim. How God, in history or beyond it, will make good on the finality of his Son and how this will affirm or deny other religious systems is mine to observe more than to determine. "We cannot but speak of what we have seen and heard" (Acts 4:20)—if indeed we have been so moved by the hand of God.

Our *style is irenic*. It is surprising that we in the peace church tradition have not made more of our peace theme as a criterion for our evangelism and mission. Peace tends to be viewed as one part of the mission, less as a way of doing all mission. In the English language, we have the word *irenic* which comes from the Greek word for peace. When therefore we speak of an irenic style, we are not calling on general usage for its meaning. We mean to pour into the word all the biblical content of peace which implies both a goal and a way of attaining the goal. In mission, "the harvest of righteousness is sown in peace by those who make peace" (James 3:18).

Irenic witness to the claims of Christ is one that takes its strong, unapologetic stand on the stage of history to be seen and heard. It is strong in commitment and conviction without resorting to psychological manipulation or external coercion. Just as in instances of suffering evil we defer to the retribution of God, so in our mission, once we have shared the story of God's grace to us in Jesus, we defer to the visitation of God's spirit in the listener to persuade. An irenic witness can afford to exercise great patience while the Lord works. This witness can also be dialogic in style, because it realizes its human need to listen and learn with respect for fellow human seekers, being confident that the monologic address of the divine call comes authentically from God alone. The irenic witness is as wise as a serpent and as harmless as a dove (Matt: 10:16).

EXCLUSIVE TRUTH IN JESUS THE CHRIST

Out of a review of the biblical sources, we have attempted a defense of the exclusiveness of Jesus Christ. Put tersely, the biblical claim is this: God's *conclusive* revelation and action in Jesus the Christ gives to this One an *exclusive* dimension of truth which, because of its universal relevance, is *inclusive* of all humanity.

The fact that this saving action in Jesus takes place in the midst of a history in which God is universally at work means that truth is not the sole possession of the tradition of this Jesus. It does, however, signify that a truth is here revealed that bears a finality beside which all other claims are made second best.

The followers of this way are called to share this truth, this way of salvation, with all others without passing judgment on the value of their faiths or the question of their eternal destiny (apart from self-evident wickedness). The irony of a finite people bearing a final message must not be forgotten or dissolved away by absolutizing the church or relativizing the claim. The scandal of Christ's exclusiveness is to be embraced with faithfulness, humbly but joyfully.

NOTES

1. This helpful expression was used in the pluralistic context of the Association of Theological Schools in a statement on globalization presented at its 1988 biennial meeting and therefore has the force of a confession, not a condemnation.

2. It has become common practice to use the term *fundamentalist* to describe movements of this kind, both of Christian and other religious orientation. This is unfortunate. In its plain meaning, this term describes one with convictions about certain foundational truths held to be indispensable. Its usage in this pejorative sense only reinforces the perception of our age that intolerance is the inevitable result of holding convictions.

3. The former language is illustrated by the recent book by Stephen Neill, *The Supremacy of Jesus* (Downers Grove: Intervarsity, 1984). The latter terminology was given prominence by Ernest Troeltsch early in the century. His writing is available in English translation as *The Absoluteness of Christianity and the History of Religion* (Richmond: John Knox, 1971). Troeltsch embraces a relativistic position; Neill defends the uniqueness of Jesus.

4. Paul Knitter, *No Other Name?* (Maryknoll: Orbis Books, 1985) p. 5. The following

discussion on pluralism is indebted to Knitter.

5. Nicholas Lash, *Theology on Dover Beach* (New York: Paulist, 1979), p. 71.

6. The most notable of Christian attempts with this approach is that of Teilhard de Chardin.

7. These statements are open to misunderstanding. They do not mean that the Bible expresses uncertainty about its claims or indifference about the moral and spiritual consequences of human action. There is even a readiness to pass judgment on clear cases of right and wrong, truth and error. Still, we need to recognize that biblical writers do not pretend to know where the precise line of God's saving pronouncement falls for individuals and peoples.

8. So, for example, Knitter, *No Other Name?*, pp. 182-86.

9. Some readers will wonder how this relates to the Gospel of John where Jesus (and the writer) are more direct, as in John 14:6 quoted earlier. The synoptic Gospels no doubt reflect more of the feel of Jesus' lifetime. John's Gospel teaches that the disciples understood Jesus' life *after his exaltation* in a better way by the Spirit's leading (2:22, et al). The Gospel appears to be written in the light of the latter, fuller understanding. To what extent this fuller perspective is placed in Jesus' mouth or Jesus' statements are special recollections of John that the synoptic writers did not have is impossible to say. Either way should be no problem for a belief in inspiration once John's form of literary expression is recognized.

10. For purposes of our question, it makes no material difference where one stands on the meaning of "son of man" and whether Jesus identifies himself with the Son of Man or not. Compare and contrast Matthew 10:32,33 and Luke 12:8,9: "I" in Matthew is "Son of Man" in Luke, which is a similar but not parallel saying. The double attestation of the Marcan tradition and the special source (Q) of Matthew and Luke to this concept of one's status on the last day being dependent on present response to Jesus strengthens its claim to authenticity.

11. This is not to deny the typical New Testament salvation history perspective that history, under the control of God, has moved to a point of being prepared for the ministry of Jesus (for example, Gal. 4:4 and Mark 1:15).

12. We cannot probe into the currently burning question of whether the development of Christology in the early church and on into the patristic period in the great creeds is an authentic and authoritative one or not. That there is some kind of development is indisputable. In the present state of the question, this writer prefers the position of C.F.D. Moule in *The Origin of Christianity* (New York: Cambridge University Press, 1977), who defends a consistent unfolding of understanding and articulation in the New Testament (development rather than evolution). Norman Kraus in his book, *Jesus Christ Our Lord* (Scottdale: Herald Press, 1987), has placed this whole matter on the Mennonite agenda. Kraus is right that an Anabaptist hermeneutic has no reason to defend the Christology of the patristic creeds *a priori*. We answer to the canonical writings; the creeds are open to criticism. In my opinion, we have no ultimate stake in the conceptual framework or language of these creeds. However, the experience of the church (tradition) is certainly of value to us. That experience indicates that the formulas of Chalcedon have withstood the testing of philosophical changes and attempts at theological restatement. Chalcedon has a resistant quality; it should be abandoned only on overwhelming evidence and after the clear construction of something better that communicates a "high Christology" able to elicit the adoration of Jesus Christ as living Lord. I have not found other approaches convincing in this respect. This is not to condemn the search, however.

13. Compare the ideas of Paul in the second chapter of Romans.

14. It is appropriate to raise the question whether the biblical expressions that speak of the lack of righteousness in every individual do not mean that apart from the right making (justification) in Jesus all will perish. This implication drawn from the concept of justification

is strong among churches of the Reformation tradition. Jesus' statement that "unless you repent you will all likewise perish" (Luke 13:5) seems to say the same thing. This is not easy to reconcile with the kind of viewpoint we are seeing in Acts. A possible resolution lies in the perspective on repentance described above in the setting of Jesus' life. When the announcement of final salvation in Jesus comes, then a new decision for or against God must be made. To reject the kingdom offered by Jesus the Christ is to turn definitively from God. This warning would not need to imply that all who have not encountered the Jesus claim are destined to perish. In any event, even when we take seriously the biblical, and especially Pauline, analysis of the sinfulness of every human person, we still must reckon with the religious sentiment found not only in biblical religion that a person is not perfect or worthy before God and, therefore, calls upon the mercy of God.

15. The reference, of course, is to Lessing's phrase which contrasts the universal truths of reason and the particular truths of history. This is the philosophical problem that parallels our present discussion and is a backdrop to it. See, for example, the discussion in Edward Schillebeeckx, *Jesus: An Experiment in Christology*, Vintage Books (New York: Random House, 1981), p. 583ff.

16. This viewpoint is well expressed in the title and content of Lesslie Newbigin's book, *The Open Secret* (Grand Rapids: Eerdmans, 1978).

5

The Impact of Modern Ecclesiology on the Local Church

Charles Van Engen *

Charles Van Engen focuses here on the ecclesiology of churches stemming from the reformation tradition as an obstacle to the fulfillment of the church's mission in the modern world. Van Engen identifies these ecclesiologies' nonfunctionality in relation to mission as an important structural problem and pleads for a new mission-oriented ecclesiological paradigm. The missionary church, he believes, must be seen as an "emerging reality" that "becomes in fact what it is in faith." The uniqueness of his thesis lies in its recognition that the church in mission is always in a state of becoming rather than existing as established fact.

Each person relates church and mission according to an individual perception of what the Church is. For those in the Church to see themselves as the missionary people of God they need to visualize the Christian community as simultaneously a human organization and a divinely created organism. Its mission then is both gift and task, both spiritual and social. This paradigm is a rather recent development.

Until the 20th century, the theology of the Church did not receive its share of attention. Paul S. Minear and others have pointed out that during the early centuries ecclesiology amounted to the use of various images to stimulate the Church into taking on certain characteristics. Whether the Church was viewed as body, community, servant, or bride, as vineyard, flock, household, or building—each image in its own way was meant not only to describe the Church (indicative), but within that description to represent a normative (imperative) relationship between the congregation and the Church's nature.[1] Augustine's day marks a watershed period when the Church's self-understanding moved from categories of self-examination and criticism to categories of self-congratulation and static definition—culminating in the triumphalism of the Council of Trent, where there was a near-identifica-

* Taken from Charles Van Engen, *God's Missionary People: Rethinking the Local Church*, and reprinted with the permission of the publisher (Grand Rapids, MI: Baker, 1991), ch. 2, pp. 35–45. Charles Van Engen is Associate Professor of Theology of Mission at the School of World Mission, Fuller Theological Seminary, Pasadena, California. He holds a Th.D. degree from the Free University of Amsterdam and has worked with programs of theological education by extension in Mexico.

tion of the Roman Church with the Kingdom of God and a celebration of the fact that the four attributes (one, holy, catholic, and apostolic) were to be identified within the Holy Roman See alone. During the Middle Ages Christians had set their Church on a mystical instrumental pedestal; its mission was essentially shaped around the sacraments as a means of grace to the world.

The Protestant Reformation of the 16th century sought to return to a self-critical corrective with the idea of the ''marks'' of the Church. For example, the Belgic Confession defines the Church in article 27:

We believe and profess one catholic or universal Church, which is a holy congregation and assembly of true Christian believers, expecting all their salvation in Jesus Christ, being washed by his blood, sanctified and sealed by the Holy Ghost.

This is followed by article 29:

The marks by which the true Church is known are these: If the pure doctrine of the gospel is preached therein; if she maintains the pure administration of the sacraments as instituted by Christ; if church discipline is exercised in punishing of sin; in short, if all things are managed according to the pure Word of God, all things contrary thereto rejected, and Jesus Christ acknowledged as the only Head of the Church.

This view of the Church remained mostly unchallenged until Dietrich Bonhoeffer wrote *The Communion of Saints*, marking a radical change in ecclesial perspective. Until Bonhoeffer's work, most ecclesiology involved an a priori, logical, scholastic thought process. The Church was defined and explained with such logic and reason that it had no recognizable counterpart in real-world congregations. From world-dominating churches of the Constantinian and Holy Roman Empire eras to the reforming evangelicals and Anabaptists—all had derived logical ordered systematic definitions for church, either from Scripture or from other aspects of their theology. Even reformation church leaders had no way of empirically verifying what "pure preaching of the Word," "right administration of the sacraments," or "the proper exercise of church discipline" meant in practice. Witness the divisions of early Protestantism and the use of the marks of the Church to defend one's own church as "true" and all others as something less than "true." Logical, a priori ecclesiology created a very serious chasm between the idea of what should be and the reality of what is. The result was that ecclesiology ended up having two separate natures. One nature was that of the "visible" church, which was far less than what it should be, but at least its practices were verifiable. The second nature was that of the "invisible" church, which was ideal and perfect but which could not be found in the real world.

In the early 20th century the question of the nature and mission of the Church began to take on new urgency. Some questions came to the fore through Gustav and Johannes Warneck's writings,[2] and others developed through the International Missionary Council (IMC) conference of Madras, India, in 1937.[3] What Warneck and others began questioning was the Church's relation to mission and the Church's nature in terms of its mission in the world. The questions were further refined at IMC conferences at Willingen, 1952; Evanston, 1954; and Ghana, 1957. This rethinking strived to be biblical and to take theological study seriously, but the new perspective of church and mission definitely rejected the a priori, logical assumptions. The new starting point considered the real place of the real Church in the real world.

During the 19th century a large share of European and North American mission sending was carried out through such specifically focused "parachurch" missionary agencies as the China Inland Mission and the British and Foreign Bible Society. Churches were not directly involved. Warneck and others began questioning the missions' relationship to the churches and the Church's mission in the world. They began to see that the Church's nature could not be defined apart from its mission and mission could no longer be defined apart from the Church's relation in the world. The Church's nature, reason for being, and mission in the world were progressively elaborated and shaped through missionary outreach. Additional questions about the relationship of the mission churches to other religions, to developing Third World governments, to new technologies, and to Western colonial expansion called for attention. To establish self-supporting, self-governing, self-propagating churches did not seem sufficient in the light of these new questions.

BRINGING CHANGE TO MODERN ECCLESIOLOGY

The forces that stimulated a new way of thinking in modern ecclesiology were varied:

1. The historic world missionary conference at Edinburgh, Scotland, in 1910, the rise of the International Missionary Council, founded at Lake Mohonk, New York, in 1921,[4] and the global Christian missionary movement all brought a missions perspective into the European and North American churches. Those involved in this new missions ideal tended to see the church as living in order to bear the fruit of mission.

2. The capitulation to the forces of evil, particularly by the European churches during the 1930s and 1940s, led to an intensely introspective period after World War II in which many theologians demanded a rethinking about the role of the national church in society.

3. As the Church developed a more mature indigenous organization and leadership in all six continents the tremendous diversity of cultural, national, anthropological, socioeconomic, and ecclesiastical forms assumed by this increasingly global Church began to impress itself on ecclesiology.[5]

4. The rise of the World Council of Churches (WCC) and various national Christian councils demanded answers to searching questions about the relation of the one Church to diverse movements seeking membership. Because they were councils of churches, it was important to know by what criteria of beliefs and organization these groups could be called churches and accepted as members. The African independent churches, the Oceania cargo cults and prophet movements,

the Latin American "base ecclesial communities," socially active faith communities such as Sojourners in Washington, D.C., and the gay church all stretched known definitions of Christianity and ecclesiology. Admitting these groups to membership in a national or world council legitimized their claims as churches; but if they were churches what is church?[6]

5. Our radically shrunken global village, the rise of the Third World nations, the increased facility in travel, and the increase in communications called for the Church to be a global Christian community, relevant to global issues to an unprecedented degree.

6. The renaissance of "faith missions" after World War II with their "interdenominational" or "nondenominational" makeup has forced many to ask some very searching questions about the nature of the Church. While the parachurch missions movement was vitally active from the early 1800s, since 1900 David Barrett counts "15,800 distinct and separate parachurch agencies serving the churches in their mission through manifold ministries in the 223 countries of the world yet organizationally independent of the churches."[7] The relationship of these agencies to the Church, their own nature as Church, and the converts from these ministries who themselves became a national church has de facto redefined the nature of the Church in many countries. It was impossible to say that these parachurch agencies (or "sodalities" using Ralph Winter's term[8]) were not a part of the "one, holy, catholic, and apostolic Church"; yet the confessional and organizational makeup of their membership was very different from the traditional churches as known throughout previous church history.

7. The worldwide development of what at one time were called "younger" churches in the Third World from "mission" to "church" has raised new issues about how to appropriately contextualize ecclesiology in the Third World, allowing relevance yet protecting biblical Christianity.[9]

8. The post-Vatican Council II ecclesiology, articulated, for example, in "Lumen Gentium" and "Ad Gentes," stressed a conception of the Church as the "People of God" and led to a broad re-examination of Roman Catholic ecclesiology.[10]

9. The rise in the United States of faith communities whose members have a high degree of personal commitment to each other, a communal style of living, a strong social activism, and creative forms of worship and common life, has demonstrated the breadth of forms and the depth of involvement possible in the Church.[11]

A new paradigm was needed to take into account these new directions. The Church's nature in confronting new realities was squarely faced by Dietrich Bonhoeffer when he considered the relation between the community of the saints (*communio sanctorum*) as a sociological entity within world society and the spiritual community (*sanctorum communio*) when viewed as the fellowship of the followers of Jesus.[12]

Though not everyone who came after Bonhoeffer followed his approach to ecclesiology, his work marks the beginning of a new viewpoint that continually wrestled with holding together both sides of the Church's nature—the empirical and sociological on the one hand; the a priori, biblical, and theological on the other.

MISSIOLOGICAL SIGNIFICANCE OF A NEW PARADIGM

With increasing urgency, pastors, missiologists, and theologians have called for redefining the Church's nature, its mission, its reason for being, its relation to the Kingdom of God, and its calling in the world. It has become increasingly difficult to separate the "visible" from the "invisible," the hope from the reality. These modern Bonhoeffers have convincingly demonstrated that the Church must live out its missionary nature in the here and now.[13]

A new missiological paradigm in ecclesiology is needed so that we might see the missionary Church as an "emerging" reality which, as it is built up in the world, becomes in fact what it is in faith. By grasping and internalizing this new paradigm we will find our thinking about the Church and its mission becoming highly contextual, radically transformational, and powerfully hopeful, exercised with eternity in view. This viewpoint involves a process whereby the Church *is* and becomes.[14] It is a fully formed community, a living sacrament and a sign before God, its members, and those outside its walls. But simultaneously it is in the process of *becoming* through carefully contextualized goal-setting, planning, and evaluation. The gap will be bridged between the Church's human, often sinful, visible, and organizational side and its divine, holy, invisible, and organic side.

In this view the essential Church is never the same during any two days, because it is constantly becoming, developing, and "emerging." Yet in another sense the Church *is* already by nature what it is *becoming* and simply must continually change, improve, reform, and emerge. The shape this constant change develops follows well-defined and clear sociological lines but each new form is the mysterious *creatio Dei*, directed wherever the Holy Spirit pleases to blow. We know that people join a church for social, demographic, cultural, political, and economic reasons. Yet no one joins *the Church* who is not called, elected, justified, and adopted by Jesus Christ. His Spirit mysteriously creates his Body outside of which there is no salvation.

The Church thus emerges naturally but with supernatural characteristics; it is a sociological entity with a spiritual nature. Churches grow because of certain internal spiritual characteristics, because members desire to grow and prioritize and strategize for such growth, and because significant social and demographic factors affect growth. This Church will continue to become what it is in the power of the Spirit and even "the gates of Hades will not overcome it" (Matt. 16:18 NIV). This process of change reflects the desire of the Church since its inception to be in fact what it is in vision, in hope, and in potential. Paul S. Minear counts ninety-six images or word pictures used to describe the Church and notes that such images establish vision and self-concept within the body:

One function of a church image is to satisfy (a need to relate dream and vision to reality). For example we may consider the blunt, prosaic injunction: "Let the church be the church." Such a slogan implies that the church is not now fully the church. It implies that the true self-image is not at present the effectual image that it should be. But what is the church when it allows itself to become the church? Do we know? Yes. And no. We who stand within the church have allowed its true character to become obscured. Yet we know enough concerning God's design for the church to be haunted by the accusation of the church's lord: "I never knew you." So there is much about the character of the church to which the church itself is blind. . . . In every generation the use and re-use of the Biblical images has been one path by which the church has tried to learn what the church truly is, so that it could become what it is not.[15]

When Jesus left his disciples after the resurrection his commission to them was at once a dream, an image, and a view of the "emerging" church: "You shall receive power when the Holy Spirit has come upon you; and you shall be my witnesses both in Jerusalem, and in all Judea, and Samaria, and even to the remotest part of the earth" (Acts 1:8 NASB).

Jesus' statement has been overworked in missionary theory, especially in regard to the expansion of the Church in ever-widening national, cultural, and geographic circles. But few have looked at Jesus' promise as an image of the self-understanding of the Church. Could it not be that Jesus is telling his disciples that they are a certain kind of fellowship which in its essential nature is an ever-widening, mushrooming group of missionary witnesses? It seems Jesus is telling the disciples that by the very fact of being "witnesses" they are and will be endlessly emerging into what he has made them.

W. Douglas Smith has pointed out that there is a cyclical pattern to what we are calling the emerging of the missionary Church. The cycle is one of "going, teaching, equipping, and sending."[16] In fact, the historical expansion of the Church could be described as the missionary people of God striving to emerge not only numerically, culturally, and geographically, but also spiritually, structurally, organizationally, theologically, architecturally, musically, and economically. Clearly the human, fallen, and sinful aspect of the Church's nature has worked as a counterforce in this search for the Church's emerging to become what it is.

Hendrikus Berkhof has pointed to the emerging dynamism of the Church's nature in terms of the Church's "mediating" function:

The interposition of the community between Christ and the individual gives us a clear focus on the mediating function of the church, and that is part of its twofold character. Mediation means that the church comes from somewhere and goes somewhere, in order to link the beginning and the end. She must bridge the gap between Christ and man. . . . The final goal of the church cannot possibly be the individual believer. God wants a whole humanity for himself. In the movement of the spirit to the world, the church as the provisional terminal is at the same time a new starting-point. . . . The church thus stands between Christ and the world, being as it were equally related to both.[17]

SEVEN STAGES OF EMERGING
WITHIN MISSIONARY CONGREGATIONS

This emerging characteristic of mission drives the Church toward becoming a dynamic, growing, developing reality. The same commands, experiences, images, and hope that empowered the disciples on the Day of Pentecost still goad the Church to emerge to become what Christ has been creating. Since its birth, the Church has been called to grow up to the "mature man, to the measure of the stature of the fullness of Christ" (Eph. 4:13). Since this fullness is infinite, eternal, and unchanging, the vision of the Church is never limited to seeing only what is there; it always sees what, by God's grace, could and will be there.

We can illustrate this fantastically dynamic characteristic of the Church by looking at mission history. There we see at least seven stages in the emerging of a local and national missionary church—stages that have been repeated time and again in church-planting situations. We might summarize the development of the church in a given context in this way:

1. Pioneer evangelism leads to the conversion of a number of people.

2. Initial church gatherings are led by elders and deacons, along with preachers from outside the infant body.

3. Leadership training programs choose, train, and commission indigenous pastors, supervisors, and other ministry leaders.

4. Regional organizations of Christian groups develop structures, committees, youth programs, women's societies, and regional assemblies.

5. National organization, supervision of regions, and relationships with other national churches begin to form.

6. Specialized ministries grow inside and outside the church, with boards, budgets, plans, finances, buildings, and programs.

7. Indigenous missionaries are sent by the daughter church for local, national, and international mission in the world, beginning the pattern all over again.[18]

The concept of emerging that lies behind those seven stages provides a clue to the interaction of missiology and ecclesiology as we apply our understanding of the dialectical tension between present reality and future hope:

The missionary Church is *becoming* what it is.

The missionary Church *is* what it is becoming.

The missionary Church cannot *become* more than what it is.

The missionary Church cannot *be* more than what it is becoming.

Thus it is important for missionaries, mission executives, pastors, and church-planters to build up the Church's missionary nature. By so doing they more completely edify the building which, though constituted by humans, is not made with human hands. This is at once the sociological theology and the theological sociology of the Church. The Church is uniquely the body of Jesus Christ who is uniquely the God-man, at once divine and human, other-worldly and this-worldly. It is not by accident but by design that the Church which is his body should be "in the world but not of the world," should be at once a fallen, human institution and a perfect, divine organism. Only as we join the human and divine aspects of the Church's nature in a unified perspective can we possibly arrive at a true understanding of the Church's mission. Only as congregations intentionally live out their nature as the missionary people of God will the Church begin to emerge to become in fact what it is by faith.

NOTES

1. Minear points out that "so effective are the [images] that we hardly need to ask concerning the identity of that reality [to which they all point]. Image after image points beyond itself to a realm in which God and Jesus Christ and the Spirit are at work. It was of that work and of that realm that the New Testament writer was thinking as he spoke of Kingdom or temple or body. The study of images, therefore, reinforces the conviction that the reality of the Church is everywhere Christ." Paul S. Minear, *Images of the Church in the New Testament* (Philadelphia: Westminster, 1960), 223; see also John N. D. Kelly, *Early Christian Doctrines* (New York: Harper, 1959), 190–91; Jaroslav Pelikan, *The Christian Tradition: A History of the Development of Doctrine* (Chicago: University of Chicago Press, 1971), 1:159; G. Berkouwer, *The Church* (Grand Rapids: Eerdmans, 1976), 7; Hans Kung, *The Church* (New York: Seabury, 1980): 266; Avery R. Dulles, *Models of the Church: A Critical Assessment of the Church in All Its Aspects* (Garden City N.Y.: Doubleday, 1974), 126–27; John Mackay, *A Preface to Christian Theology* (New York: Macmillan, 1943), 170; and Charles Van Engen, *The Growth of the True Church* (Amsterdam: Rodopi, 1981), 68-72. 194–202.

2. These include G. Warneck, *Outline of a History of Protestant Missions from the Reformation to the Present Time: A Contribution to Modern Church History*, 7th ed., George Robson, ed. (New York: Revell, 1901), and J. Warneck, *The Living Christ and Dying Heathenism*, 3d ed., Neil Buchanan, trans. (New York: Revell, 1909); see also W. Holsten, "Warneck, Gustav (1834–1910)" in Stephen Neill, Gerald H. Anderson, and John Goodwin, eds., *Concise Dictionary of the Christian World Mission* (Nashville: Abingdon, 1971), 643 ff.

3. For a discussion of what new ideas were at work in the IMC, see Rodger C. Bassham, *Mission Theology 1948-1975: Years of Creative Tension—Ecumenical, Evangelical and Roman Catholic* (Pasadena, Calif.: William Carey Library, 1980), 23 ff.

4. The best volume to date on the history of the IMC is W. Richey Hogg, *Ecumenical Foundations: A History of the International Missionary Council and Its Nineteenth-Century Background* (New York: Harper, 1952).

5. See Steven C. Mackie, *Can Churches Be Compared?* (Geneva: World Council of Churches, 1970); and Steven Mackie, "Seven Clues for Rethinking Mission," *International Review of Mission*, 60 (1971): 324–26.

6. An urgent call for new ecclesiological and missiological thinking about the church has come from a number of Roman Catholic and Protestant Latin Americans like Leonardo Boff, Juan Luis Segundo, René Padilla, and Orlando Costas.

7. David Barrett, "Five Statistical Eras of Global Mission," *Missiology*, 12.1 (Jan. 1984): 31.

8. Winter first presented the idea in "Churches Need Missions Because Modalities Need Sodalities," in *Evangelical Missions Quarterly* (Summer 1971): 193–200. He later elaborated it in "The Two Structures of God s Redemptive Mission," in *Missiology* 2.1 (Jan. 1974): 121–39. The address was subsequently published in booklet form by William Carey Library in 1976.

9. See, for example, Hendrik Kraemer, *From Missionfield to Independent Church* (The Hague: Boekencentrum, 1938).

10. See, for example, Austin P. Flannery, ed., *Documents of Vatican II* (Grand Rapids: Eerdmans, 1975). The recent papal encyclical, "Redemptoris Missio," affirms this new ecclesiology. See *Origins*, 20.34 (31 Jan. 1991).

11. The Church of the Savior in Washington, D.C., the Boston Church of God led by Kip McKean, and the "Community of Communities," a national network of house churches representing a number of denominational backgrounds, are examples of new ways of being the church. See "Called and Committed: The Spirituality of Mission," *Today's Ministry*, 2.3 (1985): 1–8.

12. See Eberhard Bethge, "Foreword," in Dietrich Bonhoeffer, *The Communion of Saints: A Dogmatic Inquiry into the Sociology of the Church.* E. T. (New York: Harper, 1963).

13. For further analysis of these paradoxical perspectives, see Charles Van Engen, *The Growth of the True Church*, "Amsterdam Studies in Theology," vol. 3 (Amsterdam: Rodopi, 1981), 47–94.

14. This issue was raised, for example, by Juan Isais in *The Other Side of the Coin*, E. P. Isais, trans. (Grand Rapids: Eerdmans, 1966).

15. Paul S. Minear, *Images of the Church in the New Testament* (Philadelphia: Westminster 1960), 25.

16. W. Douglas Smith, *Toward Continuous Mission: Strategizing for the Evangelization of Bolivia* (Pasadena Calif.: William Carey Library, 1978), chapter 6.

17. Hendrikus Berkhof, *Christian Faith: An Introduction to the Study of the Faith*, S. Woudstra, trans. (Grand Rapids: Eerdmans, 1979), 345–47.

18. The following questions may help the reader reflect on the way missionary congregations could be stimulated to emerge. At which of the stages above do you look for completion of the translation of the Bible? At which stage do you expect the new church to be self-supporting, self-governing, and self-propagating? At what stage do you begin and end the infusion of outside funds and personnel? At what stage should there be a concentration on theological education? At what stage should national indigenous leaders take over the enterprises originally begun by expatriate missionaries? At what stage do you begin to build the local church as a body, with members variously gifted for ministry? What relation might exist between the stages of congregational development and the church's specialized educational, medical, or agricultural missions? What role should tribal, cultural, and national patterns of structure and organization play in the development and sequence of these stages? What role should the polity of the sending organization play in the subsequent organizational development of the new missionary congregation? What managerial principles are appropriate for missionary congregations?

6

Mission as Prophecy

Michael Amaladoss *

Prophecy is not just one among several possible images of mission, argues Michael Amaladoss. Rather, the notion of prophecy is the theological foundation of mission, especially in our contemporary context. As prophets are called to bear witness to God's covenant in particular situations and call people to conversion and the building of a new future, so the church as Christ's body discovers itself called to share and continue the prophetic service of Jesus to God's Reign. To speak of the church as essentially missionary means that it exists to call people to conversion and change by inviting them to work with God in making all things new.

Both "mission" and "prophecy" are terms that are familiar to us. We use them constantly in various contexts with particular meanings. They have resonances that are often implicit. This may be why it might seem, at first sight, strange to put them together. Perhaps we have never seen prophets as missionaries. Again, prophecy seems quite inadequate to include all the extension that we give to mission.

At least at a popular level, even today mission probably means for many "foreign mission": going out across frontiers to preach the Gospel, preferably in a place where it has not yet been heard effectively. Similarly, the popular meaning of the term prophet will be someone who foretells the future. Of course, understood in this manner, it is difficult to see how mission and prophecy go together.

One could take prophecy as one image, among others, of mission. Thus Stephen Bevans speaks of the various images of the missionary: treasure hunter, teacher, prophet, guest, stranger, partner, migrant worker, ghost, etc.[1] The image of prophecy then highlights a particular aspect of a complex reality.

It is my contention that prophecy is not just one among many images of mission but indicates the essence of mission itself in the contemporary context. David Bosch analyses the many paradigms of mission in the history of the Church and speaks of a postmodern ecumenical paradigm, listing some of its characteristics: the Church-with-others, mediating holistic salvation, quest for justice, evangelism,

* Taken from *Spiritus* 128 (September 1992), pp. 263-75, and reprinted with the permission of the publishers. Michael Amaladoss, SJ, is assistant to the Superior General of the Society of Jesus and is president of the International Association of Mission Studies (IAMS). He is the author of the 1990 Orbis book, *Making all Things New: Dialogue, Pluralism, and Evangelization in Asia.*

contextualization, liberation, inculturation, common witness, witness to people of other living faiths, action in hope, etc.[2] I suggest that the term prophecy could be a useful shorthand to indicate this postmodern ecumenical paradigm, stressing especially the element of challenge to conversion and change.

Since I have indicated that part of the problem in understanding mission as prophecy is the manner in which these terms are popularly understood, it is only fair that I start my presentation looking at the meaning of these terms a little more carefully.

THE MEANINGS OF MISSION

Before the Second Vatican Council, the term "mission" referred both to the *task* (for example, "preaching the gospel is my mission") on which the missionary is sent and to the territory where he/she was sent. The aim of mission was said to be the planting of the Church. The Council widened the context of mission to include the whole history of salvation and spoke of mission as the sending of Christ and the Spirit to realize the plan of God for the world.[3] Mission refers to the process of sending and indicates a global movement. The Asian Bishops indicated rather the tasks of mission when they spoke of it as an ongoing dialogue between the Church and the cultures, the religions, and the poor of Asia.[4] Inculturation, liberation, and interreligious dialogue become integral aspects of mission. Around the Synod of Bishops in 1974 the term evangelization emerges, which focuses not on the Church, but on the Gospel and also points to a process. Paul VI, after the Synod, also broadens the idea of evangelization as "the carrying forth of the good news to every sector of the human race so that by its strength it may enter into the hearts of men and renew the human race."[5] In this sense, the Church itself needs to be evangelized.[6] The other Churches, too, universalize mission both vertically as *missio Dei* (mission of God) and horizontally as being from and to the six continents. Today one speaks of re-evangelization or new evangelization. The broadening of the meaning of mission is perhaps indicated by the frequent use of the term evangelization. Though they are often used one for the other, they are not really convertible: mission can mean sending, while evangelization cannot; on the contrary, evangelizing culture indicates a process in a way that mission to culture does not. Since the meaning of mission has become broad,[7] one specifies it further as mission *ad gentes* (to people who have not yet heard the Gospel) and mission *ad extra* (foreign mission).

Faced with the multiplicity of contexts in which the term mission is used, I suggest that we have to rediscover a basic or core meaning for the term, which can be further specified in different contexts. I think that this core meaning of mission could be well expressed by the term prophecy. I think further that such a core meaning can both keep alive the challenge and dynamism of mission, which may tend to get lost in the process of broadening, and make it appropriate even in the context of postmodern times.

WHAT IS PROPHECY?

Prophecy is a common term both in popular language and in theology. Popularly a prophet is someone who foretells what is going to happen. Prophets have a particular function of being bearers of God's Word in a particular historical situation in the Old Testament.[8] While the pre-exilic prophets called people to conversion and foretold the coming destruction if they did not turn to the God of the covenant, the post-exilic prophets offer an eschatological message of hope based on God's promises.[9] Jesus himself was seen as a prophet, who was also a master who taught. In the letters of St. Paul, prophecy is a charism of teaching and interpretation which has an insight into divine manifestation which others might lack.[10] In theological tradition, Christ is acclaimed as prophet, priest, and king. The Church continues the prophetic role of Christ in proclaiming the Gospel. Every Christian shares the prophetic priesthood of Christ. The Religious have a particular prophetic role in so far as they are, in their lives and work, the symbols of the eschatological Reign of God. Sociologists like Weber speak of prophecy as a charismatic element as opposed to the institutional in religious bodies like the Church.

One can see that the term prophet has a wide spectrum of meaning and manifestation in tradition. I think that in trying to spell out a contemporary meaning for prophecy we need not take a particular model, but rather aim at a composite picture. Prophecy is not a univocal term. In calling mission as prophecy we are using it symbolically or metaphorically. The experience of mission therefore will serve as a horizon within which we try to spell out the meaning of prophecy. Who then is a prophet?

A prophet is some one who feels that one is *called* and *sent*. One speaks in the name of God or even the words of God. One is often sent—missioned—even when one is rather unwilling, either because one feels unworthy of being God's messenger or one foresees that the message will not be welcome. Therefore one does not become a prophet on one's own initiative.

The prophet discovers his/her mission in the *context of a covenant*. God has manifested God's self in the history of a people and they have responded with a commitment of faith and obedience. There has been a personal relationship. People have forgotten or turned away from this relationship. The prophet reminds them of the covenant.

The prophet is *historically rooted*. One is sent into a particular sinful situation, where people have turned away from God. The turning away from God is normally lived as injustice towards and oppression of the other, which is often a manifestation of selfishness and pride. Money, power, and pleasure become idols in the place of God. Injustice takes both personal and structural forms. It might even seem outwardly successful.

The prophet *calls people to conversion*, to turn to God and to turn away from sin. Authentic turning is not merely a mental and spiritual attitude. People are called to do justice: to liberate the captive, to feed the hungry, to restore stolen goods. As sin and oppression have a tendency to be cumulative, conversion also needs to be periodic—another reminder that we are living in history.

Turning to God and turning away from sin is not turning to the past. One is called *to build a new future* in accordance with the promise of God. Even when this looks impossible one is called to hope in the power of God. The prophet lives in the intermediary period—already, not yet—between promise and fulfillment. While the promise is recalled, the fulfillment is assured. The realism of the hope is not of the order of clairvoyance into the future of history—as popular views seem to credit the prophet with—but is based on God, who is faithful to the covenant, even if the time and the manner of fulfillment may not be clear to us at the moment. They "do not *predict*, but *announce* future events as divine interventions in history. That announcement may be of judgement or of salvation."[11] They do not foresee the development of history; rather they imagine the irruption of God's newness into history. That is why they speak in symbols.[12]

The prophet therefore *interprets the signs of the times* from the point of view of God and of God's covenant. Since people are bound to God by the covenant, the prophet does not speak a strange language. The prophet does not proclaim a new God, but challenges the people to go deeper into their own experience and discover and manifest the newness of One who is ever Ancient and ever New.

CHRIST AS PROPHET

While Christ is very much in the prophetic tradition, his prophecy has many special characteristics. It is *universal*. Whereas the other prophets arise in the context of a particular historical sinful situation, Christ's call to conversion is addressed to every one in the context of sin as such. Though the call is localized in time and space, its outreach becomes universal through the disciples sent by Christ. He is challenging the whole structure of sin, not only its particular manifestations.

His *solidarity* with the poor and the oppressed leads him to a *confrontation* with the powerful. The conflicts ends in suffering and death. But his life and experience embody and symbolize *a new way of looking* at others, at power, at sacrifice. He traces a path of humility, love and nonviolence. He spells out a new system of values based on self-gift and solidarity, freedom and fellowship, sharing and justice. Suffering itself, as a manifestation of love and self-gift, becomes creative. He confronts the power of death itself as the ultimate effect of sin. Christ not only announces the coming of God's salvation as many prophets did, but shares its effects. His prophecy is therefore not merely proclamative, but *participative*.

Christ announces the Reign of God, not only as a future, but as a *present reality*. His miracles are symbolic manifestations of the presence of the Reign. His resurrection realizes this new future as its first fruits. The dialectic is not one of promise and fulfillment, but of already and not yet. He not only proclaims the prophetic word. He is himself the presence of the prophetic, which is at the same time the effective, Word. His word not only proclaims, but realizes. The future becomes present. The last times are here.

THE CHURCH AS PROPHET

The prophetic charism takes on a permanent structural and historical form in a community, the Church, and its symbolic actions, the sacraments. In this way it enters the dynamic movement of history. The Spirit is present as the animator of the process of creating a new world, a new heaven and a new earth, a new humanity. The focus of the Church's prophecy is the Reign of God. While it refers back to the paschal mystery as the beginning of the Reign, it looks forward to the future to its complete realization.

All of us are called to share this prophetic charism. The sacraments of initiation are not primarily a passport to salvation, but an anointing to prophecy. It is particularly symbolized by the anointing and/or the imposition of hands that constitute the sacrament of Confirmation. This is certainly the significance of *Confirmation*: a sacrament that *missions*—sends Christians into the world as prophets.

The Church's and the Christian's prophetic charism is a *service* to the abiding prophetic presence of Christ and the Spirit in the world. Sometimes we may have a tendency to put ourselves in the place of Christ. But the Church is a pilgrim. It is as much subject to the prophetic word of God as any one else in the world. As Paul VI said, it needs to be evangelized even as it evangelizes. Its prophetic witness will be the more effective, the more it listens to the word. As symbol and sacrament of the Reign of God, the Church's listening and proclaiming is not that of a mechanical transmitter of a message, but is to become what it proclaims. It witnesses to what it, however imperfectly, experiences. In this sense its prophecy is sacramental. Such sacramentality must not be reduced, as it often is, to ritual, but to symbolic celebration of a lived experience. The awareness of being still on the way will not only keep the Church humble, far from every form of triumphalism, but will also challenge the Church to solidarity with the poor and the suffering in the context of a conflict with the rich and the powerful, thus experientially integrating itself in the paschal mystery of Christ.

To say that the Church is by its nature missionary is to say that Church's essential function is prophecy. The charism of prophecy, understood in this manner, is not just one of the charisms that the Church may have. It is the self-identity of the Church. To be Church is to be prophet. This is its functional identity. There are many other images and models of the Church that look at it as an institution, sacrament, community, etc. But I think that all these are subordinate to its function. It is its prophetic mission that constitutes the Church, which is sacrament, community, etc.

MISSION AS CHALLENGE

The paradigm of our mission is the mission of Christ himself. The missionary proclamation of Jesus has been summarized by St. Mark: "The Kingdom of God is at hand. Repent and believe in the Gospel" (1:14). Mission is a call to conversion, *a challenge to change*, an invitation to realize the Reign of God, an urge to enter into the creative dynamism of God's action in the world, making all things new. This is the focus of mission I wish to capture by calling it prophecy. This specificity will perhaps be seen more clearly if it is compared to other traditional views, implicit or explicit. What I am suggesting here are types that may not be found anywhere unmixed with other perspectives. My only purpose is to clarify the view of mission as prophecy.

Mission as *proclamation* may be considered as a communication of revelation, understood as a creed or a body of truths, to which faith as an assent is demanded. The supposition is that the truth, once known, will lead to appropriate moral behavior. But the focus of mission is communication. The Protestants may concentrate on diffusing the Bible. One conveys a message. One preaches the Good *News*, with the stress on the news. The other aspects of evangelization are seen as consequences. Jesus and the Church are seen as teachers.

It was even more traditional to see mission as the *planting of the Church*. The focus here is on the institution. Missionaries often tried to convert kings and chiefs, with the hope that once the leaders were converted, the people would follow them. Mission compounds with Church, school, convent, and dispensary are concrete manifestations of this focus. A basic instruction—in the form of a simple catechism—was, of course, given, and a certain conformity to moral law, especially in the field of marriage alliances, was demanded. The hope was that once the institutions were in place, people would be progressively christianized. One could examine how far colonial expansion was the model for this type of mission. Belongingness to the Church seems more important than radical conversion of life. The Church becomes a social presence. It is significant that New Religious Movements and Born Again groups find quick adherents in such institutional communities.

Sometimes mission focuses on the needs of the people, especially of the poor and the oppressed. Mission then becomes *development and/or liberation*. Schools, hospitals, and other development projects are established. Conscientization projects are launched. One could note a move from development to liberation in modern times. The liberation that one proposes might overemphasize the economic and the political. The option for the poor and the oppressed may become an exclusive one. Some who are involved in development hesitate to challenge prophetically the rich and the powerful. Sometimes the preaching of the Reign of God may have millenarist overtones. While the move from development to liberation is welcome, liberation needs to be seen as integral. When mission is spoken of as prophecy, one of the reservations that one indicates is the fear that mission may be reduced to liberation, with the further misunderstanding that liberation itself may be reduced to its economic and political aspects. On the contrary, the understanding of mission as prophecy may help a broadening of perspectives and point to positive and creative aspects that help us to shift our focus from liberation-from to liberation-to.

Today one speaks frequently of the evangelization of culture and of *inculturation*. For many young Churches, becoming aware of their identity after a colonial past, inculturation is seen as a priority. The focus here is on building up the local Church. But the local Church is built up precisely to be on mission in its cultural situation. For the local Church to be on mission is actually to be countercultural. Inculturation is a preparation and not the goal. Inculturation is said to be incarnational. The focus of mission would rather be the paschal mystery. Incarnation is only a first step in the process of transformation. The challenge of mission as prophecy is therefore to *transform culture*.

Interreligious dialogue may focus on the removal of prejudices and the promotion of mutual understanding. It may even move to collaboration in the promotion of common human and spiritual values. I think that these are normal consequences of neighborly living in a religiously pluralistic society. One often discusses the relationship between dialogue and mission. The obvious presupposition is that dialogue is not mission and that they have different, perhaps contrary, focuses.

I suggest that mission is not something added on or exterior to the process of dialogue, but that dialogue itself becomes mission when it moves on from mutual understanding, appreciation, and collaboration to *mutual challenge*. This would seem inevitable at some stage if one is loyal to one's faith-perspectives. But we have to be careful that such a challenge is not simply a clash between two cultures in which the religions have been inculturated or, even less, has political and economical overtones.

Mission *ad gentes* (to non-Christian peoples) and mission *ad extra* (in foreign countries), which are often identified, seem to be images based on a division of the world into Christian and non-Christian. When one realizes that this division is also internal to the "Christian" world, one speaks of *re-evangelization*. These images point more to places where mission needs to be done rather than say what it is.

After this very brief survey of various images of mission, which probably each one of us is carrying in our consciousness, I think I can say prophecy is not just another image of mission but the meaning of mission itself. It is its prophetic aspect or thrust that makes every other activity missionary.

A CHALLENGE TO GROWTH

Mission as prophecy points to the qualitative rather than the quantitative aspect of mission. In the popular mind (even of the missionaries), mission still evokes Church extension and growth. One counts the number of Baptisms. One plans for areas that have not yet been evangelized. One thinks of growth in quantitative terms as having more: more numbers, more truth, more grace, more love. The history of salvation is seen as an increasing revelation of truths and the growing extension of the people of God. There is some truth in all this, but I wonder whether we should not think of growth in qualitative terms as deepening rather than extension.

The call to conversion is a call to newness. But this newness is in depth, in the process of dying and rising again. It is something personal, not a matter of number and quantity. The idea of salvation history was developed at a time when history was thought to be a process of continuous progress. Salvation has to do with people. For each one, the challenge of mission is new. Each one is called to conversion. Both the call and the response have to be repeated in each generation. That is why mission is a never-ending task everywhere.

Every authentic growth is from within. This is true of persons, of communities, of cultures. The growth may be facilitated, provoked by outside forces. The growing person may integrate perspectives and materials from the outside. But the seeds and the dynamism are within. In the context of the Reign of God, this interior dynamism is nothing else than the Word and the Spirit which is in every person. Speaking about various images of the missionary, Fr. Stephen Bevans writes:

> Mission, while still needing to be understood as bringing something *more* into a culture, needs to be supplemented with the idea that that *more* is often not the possession of the missionary, but the invitation to an adventure in

which the missionary is an active participant. Mission is not really about transplanting the Church from one culture to another, but about searching for the seeds of that Church that are already hidden in another culture's soil. Mission is the prophetic preaching by word and deed alike that the God who is present in every culture is also the God who calls every culture to perfection in the light of the incarnate Divine Word; often that prophetic task is carried out by being a grateful guest and a respectful stranger.[13]

The missionary therefore is not someone who gives some thing that the other does not have, but some one who conveys a call from God and facilitates a response from the people, thus provoking growth in God-experience. That is the function of a prophet. He is the bearer of the Word of God. The Word has its own power to effect growth and transformation.

TRUE AND FALSE PROPHECY

Some prophets, alas, may be tempted to replace the Word of God with their own words, sometimes without being quite aware of it. They may claim visions that they do not see. They may make promises not guaranteed by God. They are false prophets. We have a twofold check against false prophecy. On the one hand there is the Word of God that comes to us through the Scriptures and Tradition. The prophet's word is, of course, not a repetition of God's Word, but an application of that Word to the present situation. It involves a discernment and an interpretation. Such an interpretation and insight may even be inspired. But it must always be consonant with the Word.

Second, the authenticity of a prophet will be known by his life and action. A tree is known by its fruit.

CALLED TO BE PROPHETS

In the modern world, prophecy seems particularly urgent, and therefore it may be appropriate that we rediscover mission as prophecy. As I had suggested earlier, in the Biblical tradition prophets seem to arise whenever the poor are oppressed, injustice is widespread, and pleasure, money and power become idols. I venture to suggest that we are living in such a situation. The gap between the rich and the poor continues to widen. Consumerism has enslaved people. Ethnic and racial strife is on the increase. Public morality is in crisis. I do not think that I really need to offer an elaborate analysis. Today's world needs prophecy to speak to it in the name of God and in the name of the poor of God.

Second, one of the consequences of modernity is secularization, which means the growing differentiation between the various elements that constitute society. They claim to and enjoy a certain autonomy. Even in a society where such autonomy has not become absolute, the influence of religion is not sociologically mediated. Religion does not any longer provide an overarching meaning system. In an atmosphere of growing individualism it is no longer a social presence. Faith is getting privatized. In such a situation, the impact of religion on society cannot be taken for granted and it is not transmitted through a tradition or socialization.

Religion is called to enter into a prophetic dialogue with the world. Paul VI deplored the growing gap between Gospel and culture. John Paul II keeps calling for a new evangelization. I think that the rediscovery of mission as prophecy will help us to be a continuing countercultural presence in an increasingly secular world.

Third, there is a growing respect for other believers and their faiths and ideologies. The dynamics of prophecy seem to combine the urgency of proclamation with the respect for the other and God active in the other that calls for dialogue.

CONCLUSION

The focus of mission as prophecy is the Reign of God, seen dynamically as an ongoing transformation of society in the power of the Word and the Spirit. The Church discovers that its role is to be the servant of the Reign of God in the world. Its service is sacramental, not exclusive, everywhere and at all times. Its proclamation will be authentic and fruitful only insofar as it becomes transparent to the action of the Word and of the Spirit and, in the process, is itself transformed progressively, and not without pain, into the Reign of God.

NOTES

1. Cf. Stephen Bevans, SVD, "Seeing Mission Through Images," *Missiology* 19 (1991), pp. 45–57. (This article appears in the present volume, pp. 160–71 [eds.].)

2. Cf. David J. Bosch, *Transforming Mission* (Maryknoll, Orbis, 1991).

3. *Ad Gentes*, 2.

4. Cf. *For All the Peoples of Asia* (Manila: IMC Publications, 1984), p. 32.

5. *Evangelii Nuntiandi*, 18.

6. *Ibid.*, 15.

7. Cf. *Redemptoris Missio*, 41.

8. Cf. David L. Peterson (ed.), *Prophecy in Israel* (London: SPCK, 1987).

9. Cf. Rosemary Haughton, "Prophecy in Exile," *Cross Currents* 39 (1989): 420–430; Walter Brueggemann, *The Prophetic Imagination* (Philadelphia: Fortress, 1978); Idem, *Hopeful Imagination* (Philadelphia: Fortress, 1986); George Soares-Prabhu, "Socio-Cultural Analysis in Prophetic Theologizing: A Biblical Paradigm" in Kuncheria Pathil (ed.), *Socio-Cultural Analysis in Theologizing* (Bangalore: Indian Theological Association, 1987).

10. Cf. 1 Cor. 14:1–5.

11. Gene M. Tucker, "The Role of the Prophets and the Role of the Church" in D. L. Peterson (ed.) *Prophecy*, p.168.

12. W. Brueggemann, *Hopeful Imagination. Prophetic Voices in Exile*.

13. *Op. cit.*, p. 56.

7

The Vulnerability of Mission

*David J. Bosch**

David Bosch offers the theology of the cross as a theological foundation for mission. Christians are called to be "victim missionaries" rather than "exemplar missionaries," because the Gospel is preached authentically when its messengers share the lot of those to whom they are sent. This article was completed only a few months before the author's death and reminds us that it is only the blood of Christians that is the seed of the church.

THE STORY OF FR RODRIGUES

One of the most moving and at the same time disturbing novels of our time is *Silence*, by the Japanese author Shusaku Endo. It is based on the 17th-century persecution of Christians in Japan. In 1549 Francis Xavier arrived in Japan and started a missionary venture that was astonishingly successful. Within thirty years there was a flourishing community of some 150,000 Christians, whose sterling qualities and deep faith inspired in the missionaries the vision of a totally Christian country (Johnston 1976:3). It was "the Christian century in Japan" (Boxer 1967). Towards the end of the 16th century, however, opposition began to set in, culminating in the edict of expulsion of the missionaries in 1614. The purpose of the edict was the total eradication of Christianity from Japan. Some missionaries went underground, desperately trying to continue ministering to their Japanese converts. C. R. Boxer claims that the gruesome persecution that followed has been "unsurpassed in the long and painful history of martyrdom" both as regards the infamous brutality of methods used to exterminate the Christians and the heroic constancy of the sufferers (Boxer 1967:336f).

Those who were not executed were given the opportunity to apostatise. Often this took the form of placing the *fumie* before would-be apostates—a bronze image

---

* Originally presented as a talk at the twenty-fifth anniversary of St. Andrew's College, Selly Oak Colleges, Birmingham, England, in November 1991, "The Vulnerability of Mission" was reprinted from *Vidyajyoti: Journal of Theological Reflection* 56 (November 1992), pp. 577-96. Until his death in April 1992, David Bosch was professor and head of the department of missiology at the University of South Africa. He was a scholar of international reputation and the author of many books and articles, chief among which is *Transforming Mission* (Maryknoll, NY: Orbis Books, 1990).

of Christ mounted in a wooden frame. All that was expected of them was to trample on Christ's face, which would then be taken as proof of their having renounced the Christian faith.

Missionaries, too, were arrested and tortured, usually by being suspended upside down in a pit filled with excreta and other filth, which quickly proved to be the most effective means of inducing apostasy. Still, for sixteen years no missionary apostatised. And then the blow fell. In October 1633 Christóvão Ferreira, the Portuguese Provincial and acknowledged leader of the Catholic mission in Japan, after six hours in the pit, gave the signal that he was ready to recant (Boxer 1967:353).

Endo's story is not about Ferreira, however, but about Sebastian Rodrigues, one of Ferreira's former students in Lisbon. With two colleagues he left for Japan to carry on the underground apostolate and also to atone for the apostasy of Ferreira which had so wounded the honour of the Church (Endo 1976:25).

Eventually Rodrigues, too, was captured and tortured. And much of Endo's novel deals with his ordeal and his refusal to renounce the faith. For many months he refused. All along he prayed fervently, prayed to God for guidance, for a clear direction to go. But there was only silence, as though God did not hear him, or was dead and did not exist. Then, one evening, the interpreter said confidently, "Tonight you will certainly apostatise." To Rodrigues this sounded like the words addressed to Peter: "Tonight, before the cock crows you will deny me thrice" (Endo 1976:261).

From where he lay, this fateful night, he could hear a ceaseless snoring, as of somebody sleeping in a drunken stupor. Late that night, as if to add insult to injury, the interpreter returned with Ferreira, who had meanwhile assumed a Japanese name. And it was Ferreira who told him, "That's not snoring. That is the moaning of Christians hanging in the pit" (Endo 1976:263). Then Ferreira explained why he himself had aposatised. It was not because of being suspended in the pit, he said, but because " . . . I was put in here and heard the voices of those people for whom God did nothing. God did not do a single thing. I prayed with all my strength; but God did nothing." (265f). And now once again, with Fr Rodrigues in the same cell, God was doing nothing for those suspended in the pit. Then the official told Rodrigues, "If you apostatise they will immediately be rescued." Rodrigues asked, "But why don't they apostatise?" And the official laughed as he answered, "They have already apostatised many times. But as long as you don't apostatise these peasants cannot be saved" (267). And, of course, all he had to do was to trample the *fumie*, already trampled by thousands of Japanese apostates. It was as simple as that! This was the devilishness of the scheme: while God remained silent he himself would save not only his own skin, but also the lives of many Japanese Christians!

It was this silence of God that has given Endo's novel its title—the silence of a God, a Christ, who did not respond to prayers or to torture. Still, in the end the silence was broken. Christ did speak to Rodrigues—not, however, the beautiful, haloed, and serene Christ of his devotions, but the Christ of the twisted and dented *fumie*, the Christ whose face had been distorted by many feet, the concave, ugly Christ, the trampled-upon and suffering Christ. And what this Christ was saying to the priest shocked him to the marrow, "Trample, trample! . . . It was to be trampled on by men that I was born into this world. It was to share men's pain that I carried my cross" (Endo 1976:271). And the novelist writes: "The priest placed his foot on the *fumie*. Dawn broke. And far in the distance the cock crew" (271).

THE BLOOD OF THE MARTYRS

I shall return to the story of Fr Rodrigues, for certainly there is more here than meets the eye. For the moment, however, I wish to pursue another point. The growth of Christianity was severely impeded by the persecutions in Japan, but not extinguished. The Christians went into hiding until Japan was reopened in 1865, for more than two centuries clinging tenaciously to a faith that ruthless vigilance could not stamp out (Johnston 1975:11f). What happened, then, was another confirmation of the famous saying of Tertullian, the second-century North African theologian: "*Semen est sanguis Christianorum*" (freely translated: "the blood of the martyrs is the seed of the Church"). What happened in Japan has happened in thousands of other places throughout two millennia of Christian history. True Church growth, it would seem, takes place not where Christians call the shots, but where they suffer and perform their mission in weakness. A contemporary case in point is China. Even if China has, since 1989, again begun to wrap itself up in its own cocoon, we now know that a remarkable degree of growth had taken place in the Chinese church during the years of persecution and of the Cultural Revolution. In the wake of the Communist takeover in 1949 the work of *all* foreign missionaries was terminated. There was widespread despair over what was termed the missionary "debacle" in China (Paton 1953:50). Many believed that the events had spelled the end of Christianity In China. And yet, today one has to ask whether China would have had as many Christians as it now has if the missionaries had stayed and been allowed to proceed with their work unhindered. The same story has frequently repeated itself elsewhere. Time and again the blood of the martyrs proved to be the seed of the Church (even if many of us might have grave reservations about the type of Christianity that has emerged in some of these places).

It has even been suggested that the 20th century has witnessed more martyrs for the faith than all previous centuries combined (cf. Hefley 1988). One may think of the genocide of Armenian Christians in Turkey between 1895 and 1915. On one fateful day alone, 24 April 1915, an estimated six hundred thousand were slaughtered (Hefley 1988:3118f). One may also think of those killed in Nazi Germany, in the Soviet Union, in Africa, in Latin America, and elsewhere. Not only *Christians* were the victims, however. We know of the six million Jews annihilated by Nazi Germany, of thousands of Buddhist monks killed in the eastern Soviet Union, and of hundreds of Muslims slain by Christian Phalangists in the Beirut refugee camps of Sabra and Shatila, to mention only a few examples.

We may, therefore, never celebrate only our *own* martyrs. We are profoundly involved in all pain and tragedy occurring anywhere in the world. *Gaudium et Spes*, the Vatican II Pastoral Constitution on the Church in the Modern World, puts it as follows in its opening lines:

The joy and hope, the grief and anguish of the people of our time, especially of those who are poor or afflicted in any way, are the joy and hope, the grief and anguish of the followers of Christ as well.

WHENCE EVIL AND SUFFERING?

There is thus, quite apart from suffering for the sake of one's faith, also the phenomenon of *general* suffering in the world and, more poignantly, the *suffering* of the innocent, the presence of inexplicable evil. This has led to the problem of *theodicy*, that is of justifying God in the face of evil, pain, and tragedy. As far back as the third century B.C. the Greek philosopher Epicurus formulated the problem in classical fashion (quoted in Lactantius, *Liber de ira Dei*, caput XIII):

God is either desirous of removing evil but incapable of doing so, or he is able to do it but unwilling; or he is neither willing nor able, or he is both willing and able. If he is willing to eliminate evil but not able to do it, he is weak—something unheard of in God. If he is able to do it but unwilling, he is malicious—also something foreign to God. If he is neither willing nor able to do away with evil, he is both malicious and weak and, therefore, not God. If he is both willing and able to remove evil—the only posture that befits God—*where then does evil come from? Or why does God not take it away?*

Unde malum? Whence evil and suffering? This is a problem with which all religions wrestle. The commonest—and easiest—response is to explain suffering as the just punishment of God or the gods (cf. Ratschow 1986:169–73). We find it in all religions, including Christianity and Judaism, also in the form of punishment being meted out even to the children of the guilty. According to John 9:2, Jesus' disciples, when faced with a man who had been born blind, asked: "Rabbi, who sinned, this man or his parents, that he was born blind?" And in our own time we often hear that people who contracted AIDS are simply getting their deserved punishment. Sometimes this view becomes a rigid dogma that sees a simple cause-effect relationship between transgression and retribution.

At other times, however, there is a shift away from this: the "solution" is then found in the conviction that the creature can never criticize or even explain what the Creator does. One then flees into the doctrine of inscrutability of God. God has the *right* to do as God pleases. Nobody has the "right" not to suffer. This belief can manifest itself either in the form of resignation or fatalism, as in Euripides, or in the form of acceptance and faith, as in Job (Ratschow 1986:171–73).

The latter view would find its consummation in Martin Luther. He distinguished between the *Deus absconditus*—the hidden, incomprehensible God—and the *Deus revelatus*—the revealed God, whom we know in Jesus Christ. The Christian has to face both God's *opera aliena*—God's strange and inexplicable deeds—and God's *opera propria*—God's proper or salvific works.

Luther's *theologia crucis* (theology of the cross) thus attempts to give us some kind of handle on the theodicy question. I wish to use this as the basis for my reflection on theodicy, but also for what I wish to say about mission in weakness.

First, however, I would like to ask whether it is perhaps not just a bit too neat to attribute the starvation of children in Ethiopia, the "killing fields" of Cambodia, the Holocaust, the occurrence of one natural disaster after the other in the Philippines, the misery caused by racial discrimination in all its many forms during the last few centuries, the tragic history of the Kurds, the plight of the civilian population of Vucovar and Ossijek, and similar atrocious occurrences simply to God's "strange works"? Have we "explained" these horrendous things once we have given them a label? I do not think so. Can we ever "explain" the shattered limbs and broken skulls of the innocent; can we ever, in our theologies, account for houses being reduced to rubble, forced removals, and emaciated children staring at cameras out of hollow eyes? There remains an unfathomable mystery here, and at the same time something so repugnant that we can never find peace with it, never supply it with a tag and file it away into our theological systems.

The Christian faith gives articulation to this mystery by saying that whenever the world suffers God is suffering too, *with* the world (cf. Ratschow 1986:176–79; Triebel 1988:8–15). The profoundest expression of this suffering-with, this *compassion*, is God's *passion*, God's suffering-for. God is not an apathetic being. God is *pathetic*, in the original sense of the word, as one who suffers. Long after the terrible ordeal he had gone through, Fr. Rodrigues was arguing bitterly with Christ, saying to him, "Lord, I resented your silence," to which Christ replied, "I was not silent. *I suffered beside you*" (Endo 1976:297; emphasis added).

A DIVINE BEAUTY CONTEST?

It is this dimension, more than any other, that distinguishes the Christian faith from other faiths. I do not say this by way of cheap comparison, with the aim of scoring points. Too often such interreligious comparisons are nothing but "divine beauty contests," as Koyama calls them. And, of course, in such contests one compares beauty with beauty, strength with strength. We shall not, however, find the Christian gospel's distinctiveness along this road. Rather, its distinctiveness is to be looked for in its *weakness*, in its *inability* to prove itself or to force its way.

Another way of saying this, is to submit that Christianity is "unique" because of the *cross of Jesus Christ*. But then the cross must be seen for what it is: not as sign of strength, but as proof of weakness and vulnerability. The cross confronts us not with the power of God, but with God's weakness. A cross-symbol, above all, of shame and humiliation—cannot feature in a divine beauty contest: who would ever think of suggesting a cross as sign of beauty and strength?

And yet, this is precisely what Christians have often been tempted to do. We have done unimaginable things with the cross and in the name of the cross. Like Constantine and thousands of others since his time, we brandish it as a weapon, as a club with which to clobber our own and God's enemies. Sometimes we try to hide it from the probing eyes of others, for a cross is such an embarrassment in public. At other times we wallow, masochistically, in the pain caused by the cross, since this makes us feel so much more virtuous; we even devise stratagems to make it heavier and more uncomfortable than it already is. Alternatively, we attempt to fit the cross with a handle, so as to make the carrying easier. We can then "whistle and light-footedly follow Jesus 'from victory to victory' . . . if necessary, we can even walk ahead of Jesus instead of 'follow him.' " (Koyama 1976:2).

The gospel picture of the cross, and of a faith based on the cross, is, however, a very different one. Helpless, painracked in body and spirit, a victim of trumped-up charges, taunted by the bystanders, Jesus hung between two thieves. Listen to Luke's description of the crucifixion and the jeering (Luke 23:35–37,39):

> The people stood watching, and the rulers even sneered at Jesus. They said, "He saved others; let him save himself if he is the Christ of God, the Chosen One." The soldiers also came up and mocked him. They offered him vinegar and said, "If you are the king of the Jews, save yourself." . . . One of the criminals who hung there hurled insults at him: "Aren't you the Christ? Save yourself and us!"

According to all the bystanders that day (including Jesus' disciples), Jesus would have saved himself if he truly was the king of the Jews or the Son of God. According to their unassailable logic a strong God would not have allowed his son to suffer the way Jesus did. And so, if Jesus does nothing about the matter, it can only mean one thing: he is *unable* to do anything about it; so he is *not* the king of the Jews, *not* the Son of God. Nobody who can help it would have allowed things such as these to happen. What point is there in worshipping God, in claiming to be God's Son, if God renders no help in one's greatest need? Jesus "had not brought down rulers from their thrones they had brought *him* down instead; he had tried to lift the humble, but had been trampled by them in return; he had on occasion filled the hungry with good things, and sent the rich empty away, but the rich now had their revenge" (Bonk 1991:120).

The logic behind all of this is indeed irrefutable. On Calvary, Jesus failed the divine beauty contest, and he failed it miserably. After all, only the one who is victorious can claim to be divine. And we shall only follow such a lord, for in that way we too shall share in his victory and be successful and triumphant in everything we undertake.

This was, incidentally, also Satan's logic in the story of Job. In the very first chapter of the Book of Job (1:9–10), we hear Satan say to God: "Does Job fear God for nothing? Have you not put a fence around him and his house and all that he has, on every side?"

This, then, is Satan's explanation for the phenomenon of religion. People serve God for what they get out of it. Religion pays dividends. This and this alone is the reason for Job's piety.

Satan's religious logic is not foreign to our own time, even to Christians. Only too often we find that Christianity is marketed in a "things-go-better-with-Jesus" wrapping, that preachers tell us that it pays to be a Christian. I once found the following words on the dust cover of a book by the popular American preacher, Dr. Norman Vincent Peale:

> Let Dr. Peale give you ten simple, workable goals for developing confidence; three proven secrets for keeping up your vigor; thirteen actual examples of how prayer power helped people in need; four words that lead to success;

five actual techniques used by successful men to overcome defeat; an eight-point spiritual healing formula; a ten-point guide to popularity.

In this paradigm, Christianity wins the divine beauty contest hands down. And it is from within this perspective on religion, this definition of what the entire phenomenon of religion is all about, that Satan challenges God (Job 1:11). " . . . [Just] stretch out your hand now, and touch all that (Job) has, and he will curse you to your face."

In other words: the moment religion ceases to pay dividends, it forfeits its very reason for existence. Religion is a matter of give and take: if I pay homage to God, I want something for my trouble in return, otherwise there's no point in it. Why serve God if he does not fulfill his part of the bargain?

CHRIST'S KENOSIS AND THE CHRISTIAN MISSION

The Gospel's reply to this is that, in the suffering Jesus, God embraces the suffering of the world for the sake of humanity (Ratschow 1986:179). Moreover, in Christ, God does not necessarily save us *from* suffering, but *in* and *through* it (Vicedom 1963:13). It also means, as Fr. Rodrigues discovered, that Christ suffers when we suffer. The pain people suffer is the pain of Christ himself. Saul was not only—as he had thought—persecuting the *Church*, but Christ as well (cf. Acts 9:5). Christ identifies himself with his followers; what is done to them, is done to him also (Vicedom 1963:26). Paul even says, " . . . in my flesh I am completing what is lacking in Christ's afflictions for the sake of his body, the Church" (Col. 1:24). He can say this only because Christ himself is suffering in him.

The cross is not accidental to the Christian faith. When the resurrected Jesus appeared to his disciples, his *scars* were proof of his identity; it was because of them that the disciples believed (Jn 20:20). Even so, it belonged to the essence of his life and ministry that he could not force his person and message upon people. Whatever he did was characterized by a complete inability to convince and dominate people by arguments based on the trappings of human culture. His ministry was a manifestation of the complete weakness and helplessness of un-armed truth (cf. Comblin 1977:81f). One New Testament term for this, made famous by Paul's Christological hymn in Philippians 2:5–11, is *kenosis*, "self-emptying" (cf. also Neely 1989). It is only in the way of giving up himself that Christ came to us. In his self-denial he came to us. In his dying for us he came to us (Koyama 1975:73). The broken Christ is the one who heals the broken world. The Japanese character for "sacrament," I am told, is a combination of the characters for "holiness" and "brokenness": "when holiness and brokenness come together for the sake of the salvation of others, we have Christian sacrament" (Koyama 1984:243).

This brings us back to the taunts that were hurled at Jesus on the cross: "He saved others, but he cannot save himself." For the onlookers this meant that he was not what he had claimed to be. And yet, this is precisely the point the Gospel is making: it is *false* gods who save themselves; the *true* God, however, saves others. It is in *not* saving himself that Christ reveals the fundamental character of the true God (cf. Koyama 1984:260).

It is at this point that the missionary significance of the cross emerges. I have said that when we suffer Christ suffers also. But the opposite is equally true: When Christ suffers we suffer. "If any want to become my followers," Jesus says (Mt 16:24), "let them deny themselves and take up their cross and follow me." To those termed a chosen race and a holy people, designated to proclaim the mighty acts of God who had called them out of darkness into his marvelous light, the author of 1 Peter 2:21 directs the words, "For to this you have been called, because Christ also suffered for you, leaving you an example, so that you should follow in his steps." And Hebrews 13:13 exhorts us: "Let us then go outside the camp and bear the abuse he endured." Similarly, when Ananias is sent to the penitent Saul in Damascus, he is given a message from Jesus for Saul, "I myself will show him how much he must suffer for the sake of my name" (Acts 9:17). And years later Paul echoes these words when he says, "I carry the marks of Jesus branded on my body" (Gal 6:17).

The affliction missionaries endure is intimately bound up with their mission. William Franzier (1987:46) refers to the Roman Catholic ritual that usually crowns the sending ceremony of missionary communities, when the new missionaries are equipped with cross or crucifix:

Somewhere beneath the layers of meaning that have attached themselves to this practice from the days of Francis Xavier to our own is the simple truth enunciated by Justin and Tertullian: the way faithful Christians die is the most contagious aspect of what being a Christian means. The missionary cross or crucifix is no mere ornament depicting Christianity in general. Rather, it is a vigorous commentary on what gives the gospel its universal appeal. Those who receive it possess not only a symbol of their mission but a handbook on how to carry it out.

"There is nothing attractive, easy, secure, comfortable, convenient, strategically efficient, economical, or self-fulfilling about taking up a cross" (Bonk 1991:18). And yet, says Dietrich Bonhoeffer in *The Cost of Discipleship* (1976:78):

To endure the cross is not a tragedy, it is the suffering which is the fruit of an exclusive allegiance to Jesus Christ. When it comes, it is not an accident, but a necessity . . . the cross is not the terrible end to an otherwise God-fearing and happy life, but it meets us at the beginning of our communion with Christ. When Christ calls a man, he bids him come and die.

EXEMPLAR OR VICTIM?

Let me now, on the basis of what has been said so far, reflect briefly on missionary communication. Looking at our theme from the perspective of a general theory of religious communication, we find that there are three fundamental and interlocking communicative ingredients in all religions: *myths*, *rites of passage*, and *sacrifice*. It is in the last of these that we may observe the most desperately urgent and dramatic attempt at communication, namely, when destructive violence is unleashed on an innocent victim in sacrificial ritual (Verryn 1983, drawing on Rollo May and René Girard). In the area of missionary communication this has profound consequences, for the missionary can enter the communications process in but one of two possible roles—as a model or as a victim.

Not surprisingly, it is the former that has always been the more popular. But it also has devastating consequences. It almost inevitably creates a master–disciple relationship, with a general loss of freedom among the disciples who must perforce rely on their missionary-masters to lead them every step in the strange and new world they have chosen to enter. They cannot really cope, however, since they have to perform on the missionaries' terms (cf. Verryn 1983:23). The result is what Hendrik Kraemer (1947:426) once described as a relationship of "controlling benefactors to irritated recipients of charity." In a slightly different context, David Paton has portrayed the hearts of many Third World Christians as "the scene of a warfare between gratitude, politeness, and resentment" (Paton 1953:66).

The missionary can, however, also enter the communications process as *victim*. Victim-missionaries, in contrast to exemplar-missionaries, lead people to freedom and community (cf. Verryn 1983:23f). It seems to me that this is what the apostle Paul does, particularly as he comes across in 2 Corinthians (cf. Baum 1977; Bosch 1979; Prior 1988). No one has stressed the fragility and weakness of the missionary more than he does (Comblin 1977:80). He could have laid claim to the loyalty of the Corinthian Christians by virtue of his apostolic ministry, or the fact that he was the founder in mission- and missionary-bashing. I wish to state unequivocally that I endorse the mission enterprise. I say this because I believe that the Christian faith (like Islam, for that matter) is intrinsically missionary, that the Church—as Vatican II put it—is "missionary by its very nature." Christians (again, like Muslims) care what other people believe and how they live. It is impossible to expunge the universalistic dimension from the Christian faith; if you do that, you cripple it. It is truth not only for me, for us; it is, as Polanyi says, a commitment held "with universal intent" (quoted in Newbigin 1989:35). As the World Council of Churches' document *Mission and Evangelism* puts it: "Christians owe the message of God's salvation in Jesus Christ to every person and to every people" (para. 41).

Also, I do not wish to suggest that everything that went wrong in the so-called Third World and in Third World Christianity during the last four centuries or so is exclusively to be blamed on the West. Many Westerners, in their eagerness to exculpate the Third World, may not realize that this, too, may be an expression of paternalism: they do not even grant other people their own guilt but rob them of that as well.

Having said this, I have to go further and point out that much of what went wrong in Third World Christianity (to which I limit myself for the moment) undoubtedly had to do with the way in which the missionary enterprise from the West penetrated other cultures and religious hegemonies. Our scanty information about the Jesuit missionaries who went to Japan in the 16th and early 17th centuries does not tell us whether they entered the communication process as "exemplars" or as "victims." Still, we know that their enterprise coincided with the beginning of the colonial expansion of the West and that within the overall Christendom thinking of the era, it was *natural* for Western nations to argue that where their power went their religion had to go also. In the Catholicism of the time this found expression in the "royal patronage"(*patronato* in Spanish; *padroado* in Portuguese), a ruling of Pope Alexander VI who, in 1493 and 1494, for all practical purposes divided the non-Western world between the kings of Spain and Portugal, on the condition that they would Christianize the inhabitants of the countries they colonized. Where the Spanish and Portuguese colonizers went, Catholic missionaries went also.

It is this close liaison between mission and power that, during the World Parliament of Religions held in Chicago in 1893, prompted Swami Vivekananda to tell the delegates what he heard people in India say about Christian missions (quoted in Neill 1970:6):

> All those that come over here from Christian lands to preach have that one antiquated foolishness of an argument that the Christians are powerful and rich and the Hindus are not, ergo Christianity is better than Hinduism, to which the Hindu very aptly retorts, that is why Hinduism is a religion and Christianity is not; because in this beastly world, it is Blackguardism and that alone that *prospers*; virtue always suffers.

Still, it seems that as long as the Japanese rulers were unaware of the intentions of the Europeans, the missionaries were welcomed and the Church expanded rapidly (cf. Boxer 1967). This was soon to change. Around 1597 the pilot of a stranded Spanish ship, in an effort to impress the Japanese, boasted that the greatness of the Spanish Empire was partly due to the missionaries who always prepared the way for the armed forces of the Spanish king. This was enough to infuriate the Japanese ruler Hideyoshi, who had formerly been on intimate terms with the Jesuits (Johnston 1976:5). The outlawing of Christian mission and the persecutions that would lead to the apostasy of Fr. Rodrigues almost half a century later, can be traced back directly to this incident.

Again, we do not know how the missionaries viewed things and whether they indeed saw themselves as the vanguard of the colonization of Japan by Spain or Portugal. But in the final analysis this made little difference. What David Paton said with reference to China just before the Communist takeover certainly also applied to the Japan of Fr. Rodrigues's time (Paton 1953:23):

> In a country which is being revolutionized by the invasion of the Western world, a Christian missionary who comes from the Western world, be he as harmless as a dove, as unpolitical as Jane Austen, is in himself by his very existence a political fact.

So, even if the missionaries themselves were innocent, they could not help but carry something of the atmosphere of Western colonialism with them, just as the smell of stale cigarettes clings to the clothes even of a nonsmoker coming out of a room full of people smoking.

Thus, Rodrigues and his confreres were by implication colluding with the colonial powers. And in the Japan of the early seventeenth century this was suicidal. It is interesting, though, that throughout the period of persecution, the Dutch continued to trade with Japan virtually without difficulty. But by this time the shrewd Dutch Calvinists, under the influence of the early stirrings of the Enlightenment, had already begun to distinguish between trade and colonization on the one hand and Christianity on the other. In the hostile political climate of Japan they could, therefore, conveniently suspend the idea of getting involved in mission work—even if they did do mission work in the more "congenial" climates of Formosa (Taiwan), Ceylon (Sri Lanka), and the Cape of Good Hope.

"CRUSADING MINDS"

On the whole, however, the Dutch, and later the British and other Western colonial powers, were no different from the Spaniards and the Portuguese. Neither were their missionaries. The military terminology used during and after the 1910 Edinburgh World Missionary Conference betrays much of this. Expressions such as "soldiers," "forces," "strategy," "crusade," "campaign," "tactical plans," "marching orders," and the like abounded. The conference was praised as "a council of war" and John Mott compared to a military strategist. Mott himself lent credence to this when he concluded his final speech at the conference with the words: "The end of the conference is the beginning of the conquest . . . " (references in van 't Hof 1972:28f). It is out of the ambience of this culture that at least till recently we sang hymns like "Stand up, stand up for Jesus" and "Onward, Christian soldiers, marching as to war . . . "

In varying degrees, then—leaving aside, for the moment, the very important exceptions—missionaries from all these countries were guilty of paternalism. It is, of course, a simple fact that the activities of adherents of *any* religion which holds that it has a message of universal validity will invoke images of paternalism. And since the Christian faith, as I have suggested, is intrinsically missionary, it will often *be experienced* as *paternalistic* even where it is not. This is, if you wish, simply an "occupational hazard" of Christian missionaries. The fact that these missionaries often *were* paternalistic, even condescending, and that the general world situation since the 16th century has helped to bring this about, is, however, an entirely different matter. Christianity, says Koyama (1974), exhibits a "crusading mind," not a "crucified mind"; and it suffers from a "teacher complex" (Koyama 1975). In these circumstances it is easy for its missionaries to perceive themselves as "exemplars" rather than "victims." Seventy years ago, Ronald Allen saw this with astounding clarity (Allen [1912] 1956:183f):

We have preached the gospel from the point of view of the wealthy man who casts a mite into the lap of a beggar, rather than from the point of view of the husbandman who casts his seed into the earth, knowing that his own life and the lives of all connected with him depend upon the crop which will result from his labor.

Allen, who was comparing Paul's missionary methods with ours, was actually suggesting the model of the "victim" missionary. So was D.T. Niles, one of the most remarkable Third World Christians of our time, who was wont to depict mission or evangelism as one beggar telling other beggars where to find bread. The point is that we are as dependent on the bread as those are to whom we go. And it is only as we share it with them that we experience its true taste and nutritious value.

There is yet another ingredient to the story of Fr. Rodrigues. William Johnston, the translator of Shusaku Endo's novel, remarks in his preface, "if this Christianity had been less incorrigibly Western, things might have been different" (Johnston 1976:12). This is an important point. Latourette (1971:416-482; see especially 478-481) suggests that the Church has never successfully been planted in a previously alien culture unless there was also profound and extensive communication between the Christian culture from which the missionaries came and the culture to which they went. Throughout the period Latourette surveyed in his multivolume work on the history of the expansion of Christianity, the church remained "largely identified with the culture of Europe" (479). Koyama agrees, and suggests that this has been the case because of Western missionary Christianity's "crusading mind" and "teacher complex." This "one-way-traffic Christianity," as he calls it, has been an "ugly monster" (1975:73), and he adds (74), "I submit that a good hundred million American dollars, 100 years of crusading with 100,000 'Billy Grahams' will not make Asia Christian."

SUFFERING AND HOPE

From what we have surveyed and deduced from the story of Fr. Rodrigues, we have to say, then, that not every persecution the Church suffers is persecution purely for the sake of the gospel. Even our beautiful and moving stories about "Christian martyrs" contain elements that have little to do with dying for the sake of the Gospel.

Whether we have eyes to see it or not, the time of the exemplar-missionary is over—in fact, it should never have been. Fr. Bernard Joinet, a French Roman Catholic missionary, tells the story of how he first went to Tanzania some twenty years ago (Joinet 1972). He had been trained to "take over" the missionary enterprise the moment he arrived in Africa, he said. So he went with the idea that, metaphorically speaking, he would be the chauffeur of the missionary car. It took him some time to discover that what was needed was not a chauffeur, but a spare wheel. The chauffeur takes over the whole show and steers it in the direction he has chosen. The spare wheel's role, however, is merely complementary. It does not foist itself on the missionary "car."

Fr. Joinet had to make the painful discovery that he was not to enter the communications process as exemplar, but as victim. There are numerous other such victim-missionaries in our time. Was it not as such a victim-missionary that Terry Waite went to Beirut and was this not the role he played there during five years of captivity? I suggest that Desmond Tutu is another example of the victim-missionary. I remember 18 October 1977, the day when the South African government outlawed nineteen organizations, several of them explicitly Christian, arrested many of their leaders and served banning orders on others. That same afternoon the leadership of the South African Council of Churches held an emergency meeting to discuss the situation. Speaker after speaker took a strong stand on the need for a confrontational approach, the need for showing the state its muscle. Then

Desmond Tutu remarked, "I fear that we have all been so seduced by the success ethic that we have forgotten that in a very real sense, the Church was *meant* to be a *failing* community."

A Church that follows the model of the victim-missionary is one that is called to be a source of blessing to society, without being destined to regulate it (cf. Verryn 1983:19). It knows that the Gospel ceases to be Gospel when it is foisted upon people. Such a Church will also take upon itself the sins of its own members and of its nation, as Toyohiko Kagawa did when his country had invaded China in the 1930s, as some German Church leaders did in the Stuttgart Declaration of 1945, and as the Dutch Reformed Church in South Africa is beginning to do today, even if only haltingly and ambiguously.

Only if we turn our backs on false power and false security can there be authentic Christian mission. Of course, this will lead to opposition, perhaps even suffering, persecution, and martyrdom. But martyrdom and persecution have always been among the lesser threats to the life and survival of the Church. Moreover, they will not have the last word. Just as the last word in Scripture is not the cross but the resurrection and the triumph of God, so the last word for us is not suffering but *hope*—a hope, to be sure, that does not serve itself from suffering in and for the world, for that would cease to be *Christian* hope. True hope is hope-in-the-midst-of-adversity, and yet anchored in God's coming triumph over his rebellious world (Beker 1978:84). After all, we know and confess that God's final triumph is already casting its rays into our present world—however opaque these rays may be and however much they may be contradicted by the empirical reality of adversity and suffering (Beker 1982:58). Caught, for the time being, in this inescapable tension, oscillating between agony and joy, we nevertheless trust that God's victory is certain. And on this we wager our mission and our future.

REFERENCES

Allen, Roland. 1956. *Missionary Methods—St. Paul's or Ours?* (World Dominion Press (first published 1912).

Baum, Horst, SVD, 1977. *Mut zum Schwachsein—in Christ Kraft*. Theologische Grundelemente einer missionarischen Spiritualität anhand von 2 Kor. St. Augustin: Steyler Verlag.

Beker, J. Christiaan, 1982. *Paul the Apostle. The Triumph of God in Life and Thought*. Philadelphia: Fortress Press; 1987. *Suffering and Hope. The Biblical Vision and the Human Predicament*. Philadelphia: Fortress Press.

Bonhoeffer, Dietrich 1976. *The Cost of Discipleship*. London: SCM Press (first published 1948).

Bonk, Jonathan J. 1991. *Missions and Money. Affluence as a Western Missionary Problem*. Maryknoll, NY: Orbis Books.

Bosch, D. J. 1979. *A Spirituality of the Road*. Scottdale, Pa.: Herald Press.

Boxer, C. R. 1967. *The Christian Century in Japan 1549–1650*. Berkeley and Los Angeles: University of California Press.

Comblin, José. 1977. *The Meaning of Mission: Jesus, Christians and the Wayfaring Church*. Maryknoll, NY: Orbis Books.

Endo, Shusaku. 1976. *Silence* (translated by W. Johnston). London: Peter Owen.

Frazier, William, MM. 1987. "Where Mission Begins: A Foundational Probe," *Maryknoll Formation Journal* (Summer), pp. 13–52.

Hefley, James & Marti. 1988. *By Their Blood. Christian Martyrs of the 20th Century*. Grand Rapids: Baker Book House.

Heisig, James W. 1981. "Christian Mission: The Selfish War," *Verbum SVD* vol. 22, pp. 363–86.

Johnston, William. 1976. "Translator's Preface" to Shusaku Endo's *Silence*, pp. 1–18.

Joinet, Bernard. 1972. " I am a Stranger in My Father's House," *AFER* vol. 14, pp. 243–53.

Koyama, Kosuke. 1974. "What Makes a Missionary? Toward Crucified Mind not Crusading Mind," in *Mission Trends No. 1* (ed. G.H. Anderson & T.F. Stransky). Grand Rapids: Eerdmans, pp. 117–32.

Koyama, Kosuke, 1975. "Christianity Suffers from 'Teacher complex,' " in *Mission Trends No. 2* (ed. G.H. Anderson & T.F. Stransky). Grand Rapids: Eerdmans, pp. 70–75.

Koyama, Kosuke. 1976. *No Handle on the Cross: An Asian Meditation on the Crucified Mind*. Maryknoll, NY: Orbis Books.

Koyama, Kosuke. 1984. *Mount Fuji and Mount Sinai: A Pilgrimage in Theology*. Maryknoll, NY: Orbis Books.

Kraemer, Hendrik. 1947. *The Christian Message in a Non-Christian World*. London: Edinburgh House Press (first published 1938).

Latourette, K. S. 1971. *A History of the Expansion of Christianity*, vol. 7. Exeter: Paternoster Press (first published 1945).

Moritzen, N.-P. 1966. *Die Kirche als Missio* (Das Gespräch, No. 66). Wuppertal-Barmen: Jugenddienst-Verlag.

Neely, Alan, 1989. "Mission as Kenosis: Implications for Our Times," *The Princeton Seminary Bulletin*, vol. 10, pp. 202–23.

Neill, Stephen C. 1970. *Call to Mission*. Philadelphia: Fortress.

Newbigin, Lesslie. 1989. *The Gospel in a Pluralist Society*, Geneva: WCC Publications.

Paton, David M. 1953. *Christian Missions and the Judgment of God*. London: SCM Press.

Prior, Michael, C. M. 1988. "Paul on 'Power and Weakness,' " *The Month*, No. 1451, pp. 939–44.

Ratschow, C. H. 1986, "Ist Gott angesichts der Leiden in der Welt zu rechtfertigen?" in C. H. Ratschow, *Von den Wandlungen Gottes*. Berlin: Walter de Gruyter, pp. 168–81.

Triebel, Johannes, 1988. "Leiden als Thema der Missionstheologie," *Jahrbuch Mission*, vol. 20, pp. 1–20.

Van 't Hof, I. P. C. *Op zoek naar het geheim van de zending: In dialoog met de wereldzendingsconferenties 1910–1963*. Wageningen: H. Veenman & Zonen.

Verryn, T. D. 1983. "What is Communication? Searching for a Missiological Model," *Missionalia*, vol. 11, pp. 17–25.

Vicedom, G. F. 1983. *Das Geheimnis des Leidens der Kirche* (Theologische Existenz Heute No. 111) Munich: Chr. Kaiser Verlag.

8

Ministry and Mission

Christological Considerations

Jacob Kavunkal[*]

Mission is Christocentric, says Jacob Kavunkal, not because its task is to preach dogmatic facts about Jesus but because it continues Jesus' ministry of making God known in word and deed. Jesus' knowledge of God was missionary knowledge that moved him to proclaim God's love and to act with God's healing power. The church's faith in Jesus as Lord invests it with that same power, so it can live with the same openness, joy, and conviction that Jesus did. Genuine faith in Jesus, according to Kavunkal, opens Christians to all forms of the divine presence and calls them to be living sacraments of that presence in their historical and cultural situations. Kavunkal provides a christological foundation for mission that focuses not on exclusive claims but on inclusive witness and action.

Aloysius Pieris begins his book, *Love Meets Wisdom: A Christian Experience of Buddhism*, with the observation: "It is common knowledge that the West *studies* all the world religions, whereas the East simply *practices* them. Religion is a department in many a Western university, just as it has become a 'department' in life. Among us in the East, however, religion *is* life."[1] In this essay I wish to relate this statement to a missiological context. In the Western Church there is a tendency to identify mission with the proclamation of the "Fullness of the Truth." This in turn has been broken down in terms of various dogmas and doctrines about God, Christ, and the Church. Authentic missionary activity, however, "has but one purpose: to serve many by revealing to him the love of God made manifest in Jesus Christ" (*Redemptoris Missio* 2).

I have here no intention of developing an Indian Christology. All I want is to emphasize that in modern times of religious pluralism, the winning characteristic of a religion is the goods it delivers—the quality of life it enables its followers to

[*] Reprinted from *Vidyajyoti: Journal of Theological Reflection* 56 (December 1992), pp. 641–52. Jacob Kavunkal, S.V.D., is an Indian missiologist and the author of many articles in Asian and international periodicals. He is the author of *To Gather Them Into One: Evangelization in India Today—A Process of Building Community* (Sankt Augustin, Germany: Studia Instituti Missiologici Societatis Verbi Divini, 1985).

lead—rather than the doctrines it proclaims. In this context I want to point out that for the Christian, faith in the centrality of the historical person Jesus Christ is not primarily a question of dogmatic expressions to hold, but of the discipleship that one lives in this faith-commitment. In the process, certain new contours of Christology may become sharp due to the particular sociocultural and religious context in which they are expressed.

CHRISTIAN FAITH IS CHRISTOCENTRIC

At the very outset it has to be admitted that Christianity is not Christian if it is not Christocentric. For it is precisely the centrality of Christ that makes Christianity what it is, as Thor Hall has pointed out.[2] Christian faith is essentially faith in Christ. This does not mean any kind of Christo-monism, but it has to do with the perspective, not the purview, of Christian faith. Christian faith sees all things through Christ. Christocentricity does not stand over against theocentricity, rather it says that the Christ-event is the key to the understanding of God. Further, it also says that this faith is inclusive of all revealed truth, God's Word in any form, from beginning to end (Jn 1:1-18). A Christian considers Christ the universal agent in all that God saves and does.

On the other hand, the Christology of the Christian community is historical and contextual. The Christian understanding of Christ is dynamic, it is developed in response to and in the light of the life-situation of the community—that is to say, the Christian community's awareness of the meaning, the implications, and the consequences of its Christocentric faith is in touch with the realities of life. The Christocentric theological reflection has evolved and must continue to evolve in every new context. The Christian community is responsible for advancing its Christocentric perspective in relation to the context in which it finds itself. It need not parrot the past reflections on Christology. But it must learn the dynamic of reflective method from its ancestors.

Just as the Jerusalem Council (Acts 15) made a transition from the Jewish Messiah to a Christ for all the world, and hence, the commitment to Christ remained no longer tied to practices according to the Jewish Law but adapted itself to the new situations, so also a radical inclusive Christology must evolve according to the context of today.

JESUS IS GOD-CENTERED

The New Testament evidence vouches that Jesus himself is God-centered. For Jesus God is the absolute point of departure, the center and the goal. His understanding points to a radical theocentrality, as is obvious from the prayer he taught his disciples (Lk 11:2-4). As Rahner has pointed out, Jesus' understanding of God has a certain unity of tension between God's majesty and the nearness of God, who is intimately addressed as Abba. The sanctification of God's name takes place in the realization of God's reign, the fulfilling of God's will. This is effective in Jesus himself as he appears in the NT. Those who enter into a relation with God must make a decision regarding Jesus and his activity. He contains the human hope for the absolute future. What we perceive in the life of Jesus is his unity with God (Mk 1:35) and the sense of fellow-humanity as a response to the Divine.[3]

Unlike the Synoptics, where the identity of Jesus is unfolded gradually, culminating in Peter's confession at Caesarea Philippi (Mk 8:27–30 and par.), John begins with an absolute high Christology (Jn 1:1ff). In spite of this descending Christology, throughout the Gospel John presents a picture of Jesus whose identity is to be understood in relation to his mission. The sense of having been sent into the world to reveal the Father lies at the very core of Jesus' consciousness. As part of this sense of mission, Jesus acknowledges that his will is not his own, but that of the Father who sent him (4:34; 5:30; 6:38; 8:29). His is not a grudging submission but a glad embrace of God's will. Jesus feeds on it. It is the root of his communion with the Father. It follows that Jesus' words are not his own, but the Father's.[4] The sent One's mouth is filled with the Sender's words, because his ear hears the Father's words. His speaking depends on his hearing (5:30; 8:26.40.47; 15:15). Jesus can speak the words of God, not only because he is at each moment radically attentive to God, but because he knows God (7:28–29; 8:55; 17:25). In fact, Jesus' knowledge is a missionary knowledge to share with others.

Just as his words are not his own but those of the Father whom he reveals, so also his works are not his own but of the Father (4:34; 5:36; 9:4). In fact, the Johannine Christology is a perfect transparency in the sense that Jesus does not draw attention to himself but points to the Father whom he reveals constantly. Jesus is a medium. As the revealer of God, he lets all the light to pass through him. According to John, Jesus' public ministry consists of "signs" and discourses. The two are expressions of his activity as revealer and are closely connected and reciprocally related.[5]

The Gospel is about Jesus, but Jesus is about God. "John was concerned to confront his readers through Jesus with God," comments Barrett.[6] It is God, whom no one has ever seen, who is seen when people look at Jesus, and heard when they listen to his word. Theme after theme is taken up and set in this light: the figure of Christ himself (14:9); his teaching and his works of compassion (14:10.24); his call of the disciples (17:6); the baptism and the Lord's supper, images such as bread (6:32) and the vine (15:1). Commenting on the Johannine text, "The Word was made flesh and dwelt among us" (1:14), George Soares-Prabhu has shown how Jesus is the disclosure of the divine in human history and the real presence of God in material reality. This Jesus accomplishes through "a concrete human life, lived out in radical self-giving and obedience and service. It is this human life that tells us what God is like (that God is love!) because it is the visible expression, the 'flesh,' of the Word that is what God is."[7]

JESUS' IDENTITY, A MISSIONARY IDENTITY

Often we think of Jesus Christ only in metaphysical terms, i.e., as the second person of the Blessed Trinity. However, Jesus himself can be understood only in terms of his vocation and mission, as is often the case with other persons in the Bible. Jesus can be appreciated only relationally, in respect to his mission of realizing the reign of his Father.[8] He was so overwhelmingly charged with this call that he had to make the Father known.

The very name "Christ" means one who is anointed for a ministry. In the Old Testament it was a functional term: one was anointed to do something. This gave rise to the expectation of the Messiah (Christ/anointed one) who would free Israel and usher in the divine reign. The divine Sonship of Jesus was not at the center. "But if it is by the Spirit of God that I cast out demons, then the Kingdom of God has come upon you," declares Jesus (Mt 12:27).9 Similarly speaking about the titles of Jesus, "Christ" and "Son of God," Vellanickal observes that John makes use of the title Son of God almost exclusively in contexts expressing Jesus' mission among the people.10 "The surest thing we know about Jesus is that he positively would not let people define him, would not let them say who or what he was, before they had grasped the values represented in his words and deeds," observes Segundo.[11]

The centrality of Jesus challenges us to develop a ministry-centered approach to Jesus Christ and our own following of his life. In the past the centrality of Jesus had been almost exclusively interpreted as the centrality of the dogmas about Jesus Christ, which, in turn, based themselves almost exclusively on the death and resurrection of Jesus. I am of the opinion that the New Testament evidence does not justify such an approach. What we have in the Gospels is rather a description of the ministry of Jesus. Even the death and resurrection of Jesus are a consequence of his ministry, a result of his ministry.

What was for Jesus the first and central aim can be seen clearly in the reasons for his opposition to the Pharisees, the models of piety among the people (Lk 15:1; Mk 2:15–17). The Pharisees criticize Jesus for eating with "sinners," i.e., people whom the Pharisees regarded as excluded from the people of God because they had broken the Law and its interpretation by the rabbis or had collaborated, as tax collectors did, with pagan powers occupying Israel.

By eating with tax collectors and sinners Jesus accepted them into his community, something abominable to his critics. With a meticulous sense of purity, they kept themselves off from all who did not know the Law or did not keep it. The prophet from Nazareth destroyed this religious structure by tearing down the wall separating the just from the sinners, and this proved to be a stumbling block for the Pharisees. "The fatal antithesis between Jesus and the Pharisees can be seen most sharply in this light."[12] Jesus' active life demonstrated a fundamental denial of the religious principle of separation. Jesus wanted to extend God's mercy to all humankind. This is demonstrated in his prologue quotation of Isaiah 61:1-2 in Luke 4:18–21: he has to proclaim and to take to all people the mercy of God. The rift between Jesus and the Pharisees is based on their respective image of God. As is seen from Luke 18:9–14, the Pharisee made himself God's partner and expected a return from God in response to his own achievement. He wants to tie God down to the plan that he thinks he has come to possess from the Torah.

Jesus accused the Pharisees of a gulf between what they said and what they did (Mt 23:1ff). They claimed they carried out the law of God in its minute details, while failing to carry out the real will of God. They could not tolerate God acting beyond their interpretation of the Torah. They could not tolerate the all-inclusive mercy of God. Mortimer Arias has shown that what angered the Pharisees at the Galilean Synagogue in Luke 4:23ff was Jesus' deliberate omission of one clause from Isaiah 61:2, "the day of vengeance to the gentiles," and the insertion in its place of another clause from Isaiah 58:6, "to set at liberty the oppressed."[13] In their attitude of self-righteousness, they refuse to accept the all-inclusive mercy of God, the characteristic of the Kingdom as it is realized in Jesus. Jesus' concern was that God's real will be done (Cf. Mt 21:31). For Jesus there is unity of love of God and love of neighbor. The Pharisees with their legalistic interpretation, saw the cultic worship, divorced of fellow-humanity, as the sole criterion. The Sadducees too failed to see this connection of one's relation with God and the fellow-humanity. This, in turn, led to the friction between Jesus and the Jewish authorities that ultimately led to his crucifixion and death. The resurrection of Jesus was the vindication, so to say, by the Father of Jesus' ministry (Acts 2:24). Jesus himself was ministry-centered both according to the synoptics as well as according to John.

DISCIPLES SENT TO CONTINUE THE MINISTRY

In the Synoptics, Jesus, having made the announcement of his mission in Galilee (Mk 1:9–14), continues to fulfill it by the call of the first disciples to follow him and to share in his mission (Mk 3:13). Thus, the first actions of Jesus are related to each other: the announcement of the Good News and the gathering of the first disciples. The disciples are called to be with him so that they can be sent out to execute his very same mission (Mk 3:14; cf. Mk 1:39). They are called to be witnesses of Jesus' life and co-workers in his mission. There is a historico-theological continuity between Jesus and the disciples: "By means of his literary composition Mark builds an arch which spans over the call of the first disciples (1:16–20) to the meeting again with the Risen Christ, and rests in the middle on twin pillars of the appointment of the Twelve (3:13–19) and their mission (6:7–17)," comments Eloy Sanchez.[14] The evangelist inaugurates the vocation process of his disciples as witnesses and co-workers. The call is to "follow" him, to be inserted into his mission.[15] Ernest Best has shown how "listen" and "follow" mean the same things and they refer to discipleship.[16]

At the culmination of this ministry of revealing the Father, Jesus sends out his disciples with the same mission: "As the Father has sent me, so do I send you" (Jn 20:21, 17:18). Here we have the transition from the life of Jesus to the history of the Church, something which Luke expressed through the separation of his two books. The Father's sending of the Son serves both as the model and as the ground for the Son's sending of the disciples. They have to continue the Son's mission of revealing the Father, realizing God's reign.

Jesus sent his disciples to continue his mission of realizing the Divine Reign. Christianity is not a set of ideas but a celebration, an actualization, of a historical event, viz., God's self-manifestation and the response to it, made visible in Jesus Christ. Jesus called others as participants and collaborators of his ministry (Lk 10:1; Mk 3:14; Mt 10:7–8; Jn 20:21). Christianity is not primarily a question of believing and professing, but living. We can believe and profess many things that would not make any difference to the context or may even become objects of derision for a later generation.[17] Even theological jargon such as "fulfillment," "ordinary ways," "anonymous Christians," etc., can serve no meaningful purpose for the authentic ministry to which Christians are called nor can this jargon dispense them of their ministry. What we need today more than ever is a Christology of verbs, what Jesus Christ did, rather than a Christology of nouns and adjectives, i.e., what he was.

To be a witness does not primarily mean the verbal proclamation of one's faith, but following the person of Jesus. The Kingdom he announced is his own person, and the realization of the Kingdom is the following of his life-style by his disciples. Every vocation implies the struggle for the realization of the Kingdom. It asks us to be fellow-travellers with Jesus. The only way to know Jesus is to follow his pattern of life. In that the disciples come to learn the Master. In fact the Markan Gospel in particular is a handbook of the discipleship which describes the call and the initiation of the Twelve into discipleship by introducing them to Jesus' mission and his life of suffering and service.[18] The qualification that Peter sets for the one who is to replace Judas is that he must be one who had been with the Lord all through Jesus' ministry beginning with his baptism (Acts 1:21–22).

The disciples have to make it possible for others to experience God as Jesus experienced God and as Jesus revealed that experience. According to Matthew 5:16, for instance, they are asked to shine before people "that they may see your good works and give glory to your Father in heaven." In the parable of the prodigal son (Lk 15:25ff), the elder brother is an example as to how this experience can be blocked. The disciples are to be open to the will of God so that they would hand on God's mercy (cf. Mt 5:20.48). Just as the Kingdom of God was made present in Jesus' person and activity, so also the disciples' attitudes and actions must contribute to the realization of the Kingdom. Jesus' consciousness of "having been sent" is oriented to the consciousness of his mission of realizing the Kingdom (Lk 4:17ff).

The historical person Jesus of Nazareth must be the primary standard for a Christian. In the New Testament, particularly in the Gospels, we have seen how Jesus points always to God. Jesus shows us the way and we are on the way insofar as we follow him. Jesus is the one who accomplished the way. The way is what Jesus taught that must be done. Jesus lived to give glory to God and as a result God glorified Jesus. Jesus did not proclaim himself, but his person and life made God known. To find God is to follow the way of Jesus, observes G. Kelly.[19]

We have come to accept that Jesus is the center of our history because in him we find all Truth. But we have developed this further with all sorts of exclusivistic dogmas often reducing our neighbors in faith to having merely a desire for a divine encounter, in spite of evidence of mystical prayer and meditation among them. Or, we have condescendingly bestowed upon them the status of crypto-Christians. The question is: Have these dogmas in any way helped in the realization of the divine reign, the central message of Jesus Christ? In some cases, they have rather been an obstacle, even if it has to be admitted that dogmatic formulations can have a service-role expressing the faith-experience.

Often our "Christian" vision is too narrow, and we reduce the mission and reality of Christ to the level of what we have understood him to be. Rather than expanding "the Way, the Truth and the Life" as he who enlightens every human being coming into the world, and thus seeing the whole of history as the universal outreach of the Divine, the Divine reaching out to humanity, we have reduced the saving Reality to its historical expression in Jesus of Nazareth. Even though it has to be admitted that Christian faith says that in Jesus of Nazareth we have the perfect revelation of the Divine nature in God's relation to humanity, and that this Jesus of Nazareth is the incarnation of God's Reality, the saving Reality and its mission are not limited to the historical person Jesus. Jesus, as we said, is the perfect revelation of the Divine to humans and the perfect response of the humans to the Divine self-offer. He exemplifies the Divine Reign. He "was anointed by the Holy Spirit and he went about doing good and healing all that were oppressed by the devil, for God was with him," as Peter summarizes the ministry of Jesus (Acts 10:38).

The uniqueness of Jesus Christ has become a key issue of discussion especially in the Western missiological circles. The fact of religious pluralism has created a sense of threat under which thinkers feel obliged to save the Christian faith by defending Jesus Christ. But is it necessary? The dispute over the uniqueness of Jesus Christ smacks of pusillanimity and tribal mentality. The Christian faith says that the Word that was from the beginning and created all things, and enlightens all human beings coming into the world, became flesh and dwelt among us (Jn 1:1-14). This faith tells us that all religious values have a common source, which Christian tradition names the Logos/Christ.

The Christian is called to make Jesus Christ the center of his/her life by following his life and thereby making God's love present for the people of our space and time that they may be converted to this Divine Presence.

In the Indian religious scene there are two leading factors: on the one hand, there is a sense of the Mystery; on the other hand, there is also a rejection of an exclusive claim of any religious tradition as far as ultimate truths are concerned. The sense of Mystery is the ontological basis for tolerance, as S. J. Samartha has observed.[20] Our Christology must leave sufficient theological elbow-room for Christians to live with followers of other faiths, without sacrificing the authentic New Testament evidence.

Christ is the sign of communion, not of division and dissipation. Our faith in Jesus Christ as the fullest revelation of God possible for human beings (*Redemptoris Missio* 6) is not so much a claim to be made at the expense of other religions but a mission, a commitment to live that revelation in our own personal life. Thus, our faith in the centrality of Jesus should not drive us to condemn others out of a sense of superiority but must move us to lose ourselves in service, to remind them (and ourselves) of the divine presence among human beings, to become conscious of the "God who dwells among us" (Jn 1:14). This type of mission is neither offensive nor distasteful to others. Our commitment to Christ does not involve that we save him from other religions or other saviours. Jesus Christ will take care of himself! What we are asked to do is to live his life, to follow him. As Samartha writes, "Christian identity has been distorted by emphasizing a Christology from above and getting it mixed up with dogmas about his person and doctrines about his work."[21] What appeals to an average Indian is not so much the dogmas about Christ, but the person of Jesus of Nazareth, his life and work, words and deeds, his sufferings, death, and resurrection. This must be ever actualized in the lives of Christians, not necessarily through sophisticated and carefully worded dogmas. What I am suggesting is that the Church has to become a contrast society that fulfills its mission through presence and attraction, the corner stone of an oriental missiology. This is something congenial to the Indian tradition too. The Gospel is not "something" to be believed, rather it is a way of life, a message to transform life. In the parable of the Good Samaritan, Jesus gave a perfect paradigm for mission and asked us to "go and do likewise" (Lk 10:37).

Discipleship is a well-understood religious expression in India. All religious leaders, ancient and modern, attracted and attract disciples. In fact, the religious maturity of a person is to be gauged by his/her ability to draw disciples. The very name Sikhism is a derivative of "sisya"—disciple. Many renowned Hindus, including Gandhi, considered themselves disciples of Jesus Christ in their own ways.[22]

A Christology that is blind to the sufferings of the Indian masses cannot be faithful to the Jesus of the Bible. In the midst of the struggles of the millions of India to recover their human identity and dignity, our Christology will be characterized by its prophetic role that will offer hope for the hopeless, that will be a source of courage for the present and inspiration for the future. What do the poor care for the niceties of a Nicaean or a Chalcedonian Christology when survival itself is a luxury for them! What they need is the Jesus who actualized the concreteness and this-worldly dimension of the acceptable year of the Lord (Lk 4:21), who can bring about the biblical Jubilee in their own immediate social and economic circles.[23] Through his disciples, the poor of India must experience a Jesus who put forth his power to heal and to feed. Thus, Christology becomes a process of participation and a process of doing.[24]

CONCLUDING REMARKS

In every religion there is the experience of a "Mystery" described differently. Christian faith enables us to see this as the fruit of a divine revelation. Each religion is the response to this experience of the divine, though each religion may perceive this in different degrees and may even respond differently. Each religion, however, has its place and role in salvation history, for God is the Creator of all and the Lord of history, leading all to their destiny and fulfillment in Him.

In the Gospels, Jesus stands in continuation with this general revelation insofar as he is the Word through whom God created everything and who enlightens every human being (Jn 1:1–9). Jesus' own identity is relational, in relation to his Father and in relation to his ministry of making him known. Thus, Jesus is ministry-centered, his aim being to realize the reign of his Father. This ministry, in turn, led him to his death and resurrection. The cross is the paradigm of a twofold love: God's love for humans and the human response to that love. Jesus was Word made Flesh and Flesh made Word.

The community of his disciples is sent to continue that ministry of making the divine presence actual and challenging people to respond to the divine in their personal and social life. Jesus' person and life are to be seen as the revelation of God's being-in-relation to the world. Jesus is the pattern of a true humanity, insofar as he was the perfect response to the divine self-offer. Jesus' life is seen as the most sublime example of authentically humanizing life. Active love for those whom he called "the least of my brethren" is shown by Jesus to be the criterion of the final judgment (Mt 25), not any particular profession of doctrines and dogmas, in spite of their relevance and role in human situations. Thus, in the final analysis the distinguishing characteristic of Christian faith is the ministry of Jesus, which a Christian must re-enact in his/her own life.

NOTES

1. Aloysius Pieris, *Love Meets Wisdom*, New York, 1988, p. 3.
2. Thor Hall, *The Evolution of Christology*, Abingdon, 1982, p. 26.
3. Karl Rahner and Wilhelm Thuesing, *A New Christology*, London, pp. 123–24.
4. Cf. 7:16–18; 8:28; 12:49; 14:24; 17:18.
5. Cf. Stephen S. Smalley, *John: Evangelist and Interpreter*, Exeter, 1979, pp. 87–89, for a description of the Johannine structural arrangements of the words and deeds revealing the Father.
6. C. K. Barrett, *The Gospel According to St. John*, London, 1978, p. 97.
7. George Soares-Prabhu, "The Sacred in the Secular: Reflections on the Johannine Sutra: 'The Word was made Flesh and Dwelt among us' (Jn 1:14)," *Jeevadhara* 18 (1987), p. 133.
8. Cf. Mt 7:21ff; Mk 3:31–35; Lk 8:19–21; Jn 14:14.
9. Cf. also Lk 11:18–15; Mt 11:4ff.
10. Matthew Vellanickal, *Studies in the Gospel of John*, Bangalore, 1982, p. 7.
11. Juan Luis Segundo, *The Historical Jesus of the Synoptics*, Orbis, 1985, p. 16.
12. Rahner and Thuesing, *ibid.*, p. 128.
13. Mortimer Arias, "Mission and Liberation," *IRM* 63 (1984), p. 44.
14. Eloy Sanchez Roman, "Follow Me: How Jesus Calls a Disciple (Mk 1:16–20)," in *Images of Jesus*, Frizleo Lentzen-Deis (ed.), Bombay, 1989, p. 85.
15. "To Follow" is found 18 times in Mark; 17 times it is used with the meaning of following Jesus. Cf. Sanchez, *ibid.*, p. 177.
16. Ernest Best, *Following Jesus, Discipleship in the Gospel of Mark*, Sheffield, 1981, pp. 57–58.
17. Thus the Council of Florence (1438–45) solemnly declared: "The holy Roman Church believes, professes and proclaims that none of these who are outside the Church—not only pagans, but Jews also, heretics, and schismatics—can have part in eternal life but will go to the eternal fire." J. Neuner and J. Dupuis (eds.), *The Christian Faith*, Bangalore, 1973, p. 265. Less than 500 years later, Vatican II asserted: "Those also can attain everlasting salvation who through no fault of their own do not know the Gospel of Christ or His Church, yet sincerely seek God . . . " (*Lumen Gentium*, 16).
18. Cf. Carlo Martini, *L'Itinerario Spirituale dei Dodici nel Vangelo di Marco*, Roma, 1980, p. 5.
19. Cf. Joseph G. Kelly, "Lucan Christology and the Jewish Christian Dialogue," *Journal of Ecumenical Studies*, 21/4 (1984), p. 693.
20. S. J. Samartha, *One Christ, Many Religions, Toward a Revised Christology*, Maryknoll, 1991, p. 83.
21. Cf. Samartha, *ibid.*, p. 118.
22. Cf. Jacob Kavunkal, "Jublilee, the Frameword of Evangelization," *Vidyajyoti*, April 1988, pp. 181–91.
23. Cf. Hans Staffner, *The Significance of Jesus Christ in Asia*, Anand, 1985.
24. Cf. George Soares-Prabhu, "The Spirituality of Jesus as a Spirituality of Solidarity and Struggle," in *Liberative Struggles in a Violent Society* (A Forum Publication), Hyderabad, 1990, pp. 135–64.

Part II

HISTORICAL BACKGROUND

9

From Wheaton to Lausanne

The Road to Modification of
Contemporary Evangelical Mission Theology

Efiong S. Utuk *

Missiology's "new fact of our time," argues Efiong S. Utuk, is that there is not a growing gulf between evangelical and conciliar missiology but an emerging consensus on many issues. Evangelicals have been influenced by conciliar missiological thought, and ecumenicals are becoming more evangelical. While the article does not include reference to the most recent congress in Manila (1989), it does point to a movement among evangelicals that Manila confirmed and continued (see New Directions in Mission and Evangelization 1, *pp. 292–395 for a number of evangelical Protestant mission statements).*

Contrary to popular thought, it is not only the conciliar movement which has experienced rapid modification of its mission theology. The evangelical movement also has undergone the same process. If one assumes, as Glasser and McGavran (1983) did, that the contemporary conciliar, missiological perspectives took several years to unfold and that, during those years, the evangelical perspectives were largely unchanged (pp. 83–99), then the modification process the evangelical perspective underwent between 1966 and 1974[1] was even more swift and uncharacteristic of evangelicals.

Equally revealing and telling of the rapidity of this modification process is, surprisingly, the tiny number of evangelicals who perceived the wind of change that was blowing in and around evangelical gatherings in the 1960s and 1970s.

Few took the unexpected and the unplanned seriously. Fewer still thought through the implications of summoning worldwide conferences. Not surprisingly, even today, there are those evangelicals who are oblivious to this "new fact of our time"—the modification, reconceptualization, or abandonment, as some would

* Reprinted from *Missiology* 14 (April 1986), pp. 205–20, with the permission of the publisher. Efiong S. Utuk is an ordained minister of the Presbyterian Church of Nigeria and is doing research in the United States on questions having to do with African missions. He is author of *From New York to Ibadan: The Impact of African Questions on the Making of Ecumenical Mission Mandates, 1900–1958* (New York: Peter Lang, 1991).

incautiously dub it, of "classical" evangelical missiological positions. To such evangelicals, the mere idea of modification would strike them as bizarre; and the very fact that this has, indeed, taken place without their awareness or assent, can be a hard pill to swallow.

Yet we know that whether many churched people are aware of it or not, whether evangelicals themselves admit it or not, evangelical mission theology has not remained stagnant. Like its conciliar counterpart, it has not been very successful in warding off modernist ideas. Rather, it has sought to respond to them, albeit in its own peculiar way.

PURPOSE AND PROCEDURE

This paper zeroes in on this oft-neglected aspect of evangelicalism. It seeks to go beyond the form the movement projects or how its deans want us to think it is. The central thesis is that, like its conciliar counterpart, the evangelical missionary motivation has not remained a constant. Within it has been a continual, painful process of shifting, testing, reformulation, and even discarding. Beneath this thesis lies the assumption that, because of the urgent demands posed by secularization, nationalization, and rapid social change, evangelicals have been compelled, like their conciliar counterparts, to take a hard look at what it means to confess Christ across national and confessional boundaries.

Because this paper is not so ambitious as to cover all the issues fully, the main focus is on discernible changes—from Wheaton to Lausanne—in evangelical missiology vis-à-vis conciliar missiology. Conscious that evangelicals have almost always prided themselves as biblicists, the presentation revolves around four key missiological questions about which evangelicals like to waver. They are (1) church-mission relations; (2) evangelism and social action; (3) Christianity and other religions; and (4) unity in the church and in the world.

With this approach, it is immediately clear that matters that concern the theological or philosophical basis of mission *per se* are outside the purview of this study. Nevertheless, this does not mean that they are altogether sidetracked. Actually, references are made to them where they illuminate the analysis. It means, however, that I do not dwell on them, because, although both some conciliarists and evangelicals have attempted to show how their basic philosophical bases of missions differ from each other (cf., for instance, McGavran, 1977), I consider both schools as soul mates, not antagonists.

Our intellectual journey, therefore, begins at Wheaton, Illinois, and proceeds to Lausanne, Switzerland, by way of Berlin, Germany.

WHEATON

When evangelicals met at Wheaton (1966), certain currents and undercurrents had led to its organization. Among the currents was the growing uneasiness in the evangelical community with the conciliar missiology. And among the undercurrents was the gradual awareness that the evangelical viewpoint cannot attract the mass media, if that viewpoint remains fragmented and provincial. Accordingly,

Wheaton was billed as a Counter-World Council of Churches (WCC) movement. Its primary objective, according to "The Call to the Congress" was to enable "evangelical leadership to make plain to the world their theory, strategy, and practice of the church's universal mission" (Lindsell, 1966:3). Not only did this avowed goal presage how defensive the Congress' organizers wanted it to be, it also indicated how they wanted it so badly to stand in the tradition of New York (1900) and Edinburgh (1910).

But Wheaton's dream of recapturing New York and Edinburgh was wishful thinking. Neither the world New York knew nor the one from which Edinburgh drew its buoyant confidence was there anymore. Failing to recognize this historical fact, Wheaton remained largely in the comfortable world of idealism and make-believe. While, like the WCC's New Delhi Assembly, the issues before her required radical change of perspectives, not piecemeal reformism, and surgical operation, not palliative or conservative medicine, Wheaton responded largely negatively. The result was that its pronouncements were replete with ambiguities, inconsistencies, and indifference.

Its position on church-mission relations, for example, saw the possibility of tying the two together when it opined that "In obedience to the Great Commission, the Church has a continuing responsibility to send missionaries into all the world." But this was later rendered ambiguous with the tagging on of the following statement: "We recognize a continuing distinction between the church established in the field and the missionary agency" (Lindsell, 1966:40). Whereas New Delhi formally baptized with no apology Hoekendijk's favorite brain-child—the God-world-church formula of missions—into the conciliar rubric, Wheaton, because of the nature of its sponsor's organizational structure, left the issue of church-centric or cosmos-centric missions hanging in the air.[2]

With regard to the correlation between evangelism and social action, Wheaton also displayed an unwillingness to situate the two on equal footing or even to consider them as indissolubly linked, biblical motifs. Forced by some delegates to make a straightforward declaration on this, Wheaton succeeded only in acknowledging the biblical origin of the two missiological motifs. But that its accent lay unequivocally on evangelism was never disputable. A similar fate followed the challenge of religious pluralism in the world. Wheaton was loud in labeling the conciliar position vis-à-vis interreligious dialogue as a sellout. It was quick to condemn what it called "Romanish tendencies" in the conciliar movement, but slow to recognize that "forever gone is the day when one could confine his preparation for the religious encounter to mastering a few Bible texts, to be quoted to all and sundry with a 'that-settles-it' finality" (Lindsell, p. 210).

Wheaton's main suggestion as to the Christian response to the menace of non-Christian religions consisted only of a strong warning not to succumb to the approach, which many of the delegates felt the conciliar movement was espousing: a syncretistic and neo-universalist approach.

Wheaton's attitude toward questions of unity also demonstrated the ambiguities and uncertainties that characterized the Congress. Conscious that its very nature and distinctiveness can be preserved by fulfilling the task of "an opposition party," Wheaton moved sharply to the right of the missiological stage. It vehemently opposed any form of organic unity which it believed the WCC stood for. To further rebuff the WCC-affiliated churches, it urged its constituency to disavow unitive sentiments that suggest a visible superchurch structure.

Yet Wheaton could not wholly dispense with unitive concerns. One aspect of the declaration was a pointer to this irresistible quest. Thus, although organic unity was out of the question, residues of unitive sentiments punctuated the final report and pronouncement:

> We will encourage and assist in the organization of evangelical fellowships among churches and missionary societies at national, regional, and international levels. . . . We will encourage evangelical, mission mergers when such will eliminate duplication of administration, produce more efficient stewardship of personnel and resources, and strengthen their ministries (Lindsell, p. 232, cf. passim).

This, then, unquestionably expresses the kind of motivation that was operative at Wheaton. On the one hand, there was this self-conscious desire to differ from the conciliar movement. On the other hand, there was a compelling force to move beyond traditionalism, posturing, and wars of semantics to face the crucible of the changing context of mission. So, are there discernible signs that Wheaton was, even though unconsciously, engaging the evangelical party in the inevitable process of refinement and modification? Obviously, there are such signs in the debate that ensued between those who believed evangelicals must endorse social action programs enthusiastically, and those who defended the *solus evangelismus* position. But to attempt such a blanket answer is to miss the point about Wheaton. Wheaton was not called to undo or modify evangelical doctrines but to reaffirm them. Moreover, it must be remembered that Wheaton was the evangelicals' first experiment with a worldwide conference. Up to this time (1966), evangelicals had never undertaken or risked such a conference with such a comprehensive agenda. Ignorant of what to expect and with a missiological framework that was still largely Christendom-bound—even though the notion of *Corpus Christianum* was long shattered by the two world wars, what they accomplished was insignificant, compared with what the very idea of the Congress symbolized.

Wheaton must, therefore, be seen in this light and as the *terminus a quo* for evangelicals to begin to worry about, not just the *praxis*, but also the *theoria* of missions. Prior to Wheaton, there was the tendency in the evangelical camp to prioritize pietism and downplay well-thought-out strategies. Now, at Wheaton, they discovered how difficult it is to reach agreement on missiological issues, even if conference participants have Abraham as their father and appeal to the same version of the Bible. Nevertheless, the central thing that Wheaton exhibited about evangelicals is precisely the very fact or idea that the gathering could take place and under the auspices of two autocephalous associations, with diametrically opposed organizational structures.[3] In the words of one of the insiders:

> The very fact that we gathered at all, on such a scale and under the sponsorship of these two groups, seemed almost a miracle in itself. For there

have been among us strong differences in conviction that have kept us apart—in spite of the basic theological unity we have claimed. It seems safe to say that five years ago such a congress could not have taken place (Fenton, 1966:477).

To be sure, prior to Wheaton, evangelicals did not take the political clout associated with worldwide movements seriously. Neither did they recognize that evangelicalism in and of itself is not immune to spatial factors, theories of mass movements, and the social dynamics that come into play at any international, intercultural assemblies. With Wheaton, the first test toward remodeling evangelical mission theology was passed. Cherished doctrines were, for the first time, partially criticized at a globe-sized forum. Debates were intense and perplexing. Discordant notes, hitherto mute in evangelical circles, surfaced. More than that, these antithetical notes even became chronicled side by side with the Congress' theses. At last, historical critical method had found its way into bastioned evangelical missiology. Now, the evangelical movement cannot escape its positive and negative effects, its constructive prodding and its crippling debilitation.

BERLIN

The first opportunity to expand on Wheaton's mandates came with the Berlin Congress on Evangelism (1966). Held approximately five months after Wheaton, Berlin was burdened with a docket far more comprehensive and ambitious than Wheaton. According to its sponsor, *Christianity Today*, Berlin was tasked, among other things, to define biblical evangelism, study the obstacles to biblical evangelism and to propose the means of overcoming them, and discover new methods of relating biblical evangelism to our times.[4]

Although the siting of the Congress in a divided city was consciously designed to indicate how prepared the evangelicals were to confront and engage a revolutionary world, the desire to let the world know how distinct the evangelicals were from the WCC was still present. Thus, in addition to specifying the Congress' objectives, *Christianity Today* also took pains to editorialize:

In contrast to other recent ecumenical conferences, such as Vatican Council, World Council of Churches assemblies, and the conferences on Faith and Order and on Church and Society, [the Berlin Congress] assumes both the Reformation principle of the final authority of the Bible and apostolic emphasis on the evangelization of mankind as the primary mission of the church.[5]

Accordingly, because the outcome of the Congress seems to have been predetermined by its sponsor, Berlin, like Wheaton, found itself oscillating perilously between tradition and modernism. Papers were not altogether penetrative. Rather, like sermons, they were largely inspirational and hortatory. Yet, there were signs that unresolved missiological questions had received some intellectual attention.

In the first place, Berlin appropriated for itself the Student Volunteer Movement's watchword—evangelization of the world in this generation—as its goal and aim for missionary strategy. Without any overt acknowledgement, Berlin dumped Wheaton's ambiguous position on church and mission relations. Berlin's participants largely "assumed the place of the church in the total process of evangelism," despite the regrettable fact that there were no outstanding treatises on ecclesiology at the Congress. This notwithstanding, most delegates probably nodded in agreement with Kunneth's theological presuppositions concerning the church when he asserted unequivocally that "Gospel and Church . . . stand in an indissoluble relationship. The Gospel points to the Church, and the Church derives from the Gospel" (Henry and Mooneyham, 1967:173). Indeed, they did, for the Congress' statement declared that mission and church are coterminous.

However, there was a sign of uneasiness on the part of some delegates when some Asians, Latin Americans, and Africans urged the Congress to be explicit on the status of the emergent churches. In the end, those who voted for an implied rather than stated recognition of the unique locus of the emergent, national churches carried the day.

In the second place, Berlin's position on the connection between evangelism and social action was indicative of the gradual shift evangelicals were making from a one-dimensional mentality to a double one. It was theoretically easy to affirm that evangelism and social action should not be separated, but very difficult to spell out what this indissolubility entails. It was easy to accept that the two ideas are, in the light of the Protestant principle of holism, mutually modifying, but nerve-breaking to come to a declaration that won unanimous support. It was common to hear denunciations of opinions judged to be inverting "the New Testament accent on evangelism." But few heard that the same New Testament could be used to justify "evangelism as social action only."

In the third place, Berlin was obsessed, like Wheaton, with denouncing interreligious dialogue projects that even tacitly bordered on "accommodation" with non-Christian religions. Instead of a forceful and positive proposal for dialoguing with other religionists, Berlin regressed from even Wheaton's minimal accomplishment on this matter. It ignored Wheaton's double signal of triumphalism and sympathetic study of non-Christian religions, and suggested only triumphalism. By so doing, Berlin failed to achieve even minimally item five of its charge: "to study the obstacles to biblical evangelism and to propose the means of overcoming them."

Perhaps, as compensation for its lack of clear direction on the Christian/non-Christian encounter, Berlin made bold strides on unitive questions. Although, like Wheaton, Berlin's litmus test for unity was, "What kind of unity?" noticeable attempts were made to counteract the image that evangelicals thrive on bickerings and squabbles. A case in point is the fact that the need for unity in shared beliefs was a recurring theme at the Congress. Speaker after speaker admonished evangelicals to come together, at least, for the sake of holding the conciliar movement in check. And it was shown that the ideal of evangelizing the world in this generation lies squarely in unitive projects, and in the incorporation of the laity into the movement. Ironically, while the Congress itself represented another historic landmark for the evangelicals, in their quest to construct an alternative missiological road map vis-à-vis the conciliar perspectives, the Congress' sponsor and chairman Billy Graham emphatically tried to downplay its unitive suggestions. Denying that organizational unity was in the offing, they preferred, instead, to describe the Congress as an "evangelical ecumenical gathering" brought about by shared creeds.

A final observation about Berlin is that it avoided, despite its church-centric propensity, addressing itself fully to proposing "new means" through which cross-cultural missions can be effectively carried out. On the other hand, in both institutional and theological senses, the Congress could not avoid the danger of becoming introverted. Still, while Berlin was supposed to indicate evangelicals' willingness to discuss "global evangelism in the context of nuclear, space, and mass communications era," no frantic search for relevance was evident. Unable to untether itself from its ideological captivity, it was satisfied to pose questions that had pregiven answers. Where there were searching and disturbing questions for which there were no acceptable or pregiven answers, the Congress retreated into ambiguity.

Yet, when the pluses and minuses, the assets and liabilities, and the strengths and weaknesses of Berlin are assessed, without any escape into familiar kinds of circumlocution and double talk, and without the arguments not consciously weighted on either side, Berlin represented a leap and a triumph for the construction of contemporary evangelical mission theology. A significant move forward was made, despite uncertainties, on such questions as church-mission relations and evangelism and social action. As a matter of fact, the Congress reminded the delegates and their constituencies that evangelicalism need not translate into quietism. Some increased awareness was in the making when Black American evangelicals provided a telling criticism of any evangelical movement which declares, on the one hand, "that morality cannot be legislated" and, on the other, revels in calling Lord Shaftesbury and William Wilberforce its fathers. "Law did for me and my people in America," one was reported as saying, "what empty and high-powered evangelical preaching never did for 100 years" (Bassham, 1979:227).

That Berlin epitomized a high point for the evangelicals was clear. However, that it also embodied the unresolved nagging problems was equally salient. As rendered by one man who, because of his incomparable role at the Congress, had an insider's view of what the gathering managed to pull off:

Evangelical Christianity has not only received new prominence through the [Berlin] World Congress on Evangelism, but it has also gained new perspective and promise for the near future. But this same turn of events has brought the evangelical movement to a brink of decision over three major concerns that impinge upon its evangelistic task in the world. These concerns are theological, socio-political and ecumenical (Henry, 1967:1).

The next opportunity to come to terms with these concerns was Lausanne. There evangelicals had to decide whether their movement was at a brink of crisis, as asserted by Henry,[6] or at a turning point, as the vicissitude of ecclesiastical history would suggest.

LAUSANNE

If good organization is an index of maturity and decisiveness an index of self-confidence, Lausanne, to be sure, represented these. By the way it was conducted and from the *testimonium* that came out of it, there existed very little doubt that Lausanne was to the evangelicals what New Delhi was to the conciliarists—a turning point.

But before we delve into this turning point, we should take a brief glance at the context in which Lausanne gathered. The unfinished business inherited from Berlin demanded attention. This means that Lausanne had to decide whether to toe Berlin's line of reasoning—of splitting evangelists from theologians, carry on Wheaton's reactionary mandates, or build on or seek to explicate what both Wheaton and Berlin left implicit. More than this, Lausanne had to confront the conciliar threat, especially Bangkok (1972/73) where the conciliarists dealt with the theme "Salvation Today," and where the controversy this theme provoked began. As with some WCC constituencies, especially the Orthodox churches, who were concerned about the meaning of Bangkok's declaration, the evangelicals had to do something. Fortunately, the Lausanne Congress (1974) was their best platform.

Despite its attempt to roll back some mistakes of the past, Lausanne essentially continued the process initiated at Wheaton and Berlin. The fruit of its deliberations came in the form of a fifteen-point Covenant. But it would be wrong to think that this Covenant was actually manufactured at Lausanne as such. As the man who had much to do with it has said, the Covenant actually took its present form precisely because a greater part of its formulation was done prior to and outside of Lausanne (Stott, 1975a:l). While not a binding document, because Lausanne, like other evangelical gatherings, had no legislative mandate, the Covenant expressed "a consensus of the mind and mood of the Lausanne Congress." More important, it certainly represented an authoritative statement of the evangelical position on many contemporary missiological questions as the Lausanne delegates saw them. Still, it can be said without any fear of exaggeration that the Covenant is still perceived by some evangelicals as the culmination of their attempt to counterbalance the conciliar missiology, and, therefore, to establish the evangelical movement as the "bearer of biblical evangelism."

In what ways did the Covenant represent a turning point for the evangelical mission theology? What salient features indicate that they had succeeded in modifying some of their extremist and hard-line positions?

First, for a figure such as John R. W. Stott, who is at home both with the evangelical orthodoxy of his biblical faith, and in the wider circles of the conciliar movement, Lausanne produced "some marked changes in evangelical mission theology." Evangelism, for instance, was no longer considered as the only focus of the Congress, but was placed in the wider context of the whole life and mission of the global church.

Second, ecclesiological questions were pressed with great urgency. The Radical Discipleship group challenged the Congress to face the implications of discipleship concerning the total needs of humanity. Other "interest" groups did not soften their lobbying pressure. Instead, some combined their efforts with the Radical Discipleship group to produce a Covenant that, for the first time in the evangelical movement, affirmed in unambiguous tone "that biblical evangelism is inseparable from social responsibility, Christian discipleship, and church renewal" (Padilla, 1976:11).

Third, the Congress, through a candid reversal of Berlin's refusal to recognize mission "as everything the church is sent into the world to do," provided a balanced biblical understanding of the connection and the disconnection between social action and evangelism. In this regard, it was John Stott's frank rejection of his Berlin position that spurred the Congress to abandon both Wheaton's and Berlin's uncertainties on this matter. Stott had acknowledged that, at Berlin, many evangelicals, including himself, argued for a radical disconnection between social action and evangelism.

> Today, however, I would express myself differently. . . . I now see more clearly that not only the consequences of the commission but the actual commission itself must be understood to include social as well as evangelistic responsibility, unless we are to be guilty of distorting the words of Jesus (Stott, 1975:23).

On the basis of this new understanding and awareness of the "Last Command," Stott let it be known that the relationship between evangelism and social action is not a question of biblical indicative vis-à-vis imperative:

> Social action is a *partner of evangelism.* As partners the two belong to each other and yet are independent of each other. Each stands on its own feet in its own right alongside the other. Neither is a means to the other, or even a manifestation of the other. For each is an end in itself (Stott, 1975:27).

What a difference in thought a few years can make!

Fourth, there was a sustained effort to grapple with the thorny issue of church-mission relations. Howard Synder's "insightful" and "unconventional" paper on "The Church as God's Agent in Evangelism" integrated the several diverse elements of evangelical theology, namely, the emphasis on personal witness of Christians, the need for quantitative and qualitative church growth, with an appreciation of the indispensability of the charismatic gifts necessary for church leadership. Snyder also posited that the church is the only divinely appointed means for spreading the gospel. Most significantly, he suggested what evangelicals had earlier condemned at Berlin, the necessity of regarding the world as the focus for mission. Later, the Covenant echoed his concern for the world, not just the church, although it was hesitant, understandably, to embrace cosmos-centric missions wholesale. In any case, "it was clearly recognized that the initiative for evangelization in the (so-called) Third World is being transferred to the church and that the mission must now serve in a subordinate role. . . . "[7]

Fifth, Lausanne, by asserting in paragraph 8 of the Covenant on Churches in Evangelistic Partnership that "a new missionary era has dawned," managed to kill two birds with one stone. First, it directly acknowledged the inevitability of cultural pluralism and debunked the old position which clearly tied Christianity primarily to Western culture. Second, it indirectly affirmed that the issues it had had to struggle with were not different from the WCC's problems. Hence, by covenanting on "Partnership," the Congress signalled to the evangelical community that the WCC's "Partnership in Obedience" strategy was not, after all, an unreasonable missiological parameter to emulate. Similarly, paragraph 10, "Evangelism and Culture," enjoined evangelicals to recognize the bipolar attitude Christianity ought to have toward cultures: naturalization and overagainstness. Paragraph 11 confessed that evangelicals no less than conciliarists have been too slow to recognize when their "baby-churches" in the Southern Hemisphere need weaning and *rites de passage* to puberty and adulthood.

Sixth, Lausanne's approach to the perennial question of Christianity's relationship to other faiths revealed, at least in part, the positivistic spirit that dominated and permeated the Congress. Not only did it endorse dialogue "whose purpose is to listen sensitively in order to understand" (paragraph 4), it also went out of its way to do what was hitherto considered taboo in some evangelical circles: a thoroughgoing probe into specific non-Christian religions in relation to the task of Christian evangelism.

On the question of unity, Lausanne also moved beyond mere tokenism. At least three papers addressed the thematic and theoretical aspects of this question: Henri Blocher's "The Nature of Biblical Unity," Jonathan T'ien-en Chao's "The Nature of the Unity of the Local and Universal Church in Evangelism and Church Growth," and Howard Snyder's "The Church as God's Agent in Evangelism." In contradistinction to Wheaton or Berlin, the Roman Catholic Church received a much more positive evaluation at Lausanne. Vatican II theologians Rahner, Küng, and Schillebeeckx were recognized and appreciated for their theological contributions. The Congress also performed the usual ritual of confession for past evangelical failures in relation to unity. It admitted that disunity mars and undermines the gospel and called for international missionary frameworks for carrying out the church's *raison d'être*. Like Edinburgh (1910), a Continuation Committee was set up.

Yet, in fairness to Lausanne, it must be said that although its strength canceled out its weaknesses, the weaknesses were there, nonetheless. While it sought to show that evangelicals harbor no fear with regard to unitive questions, what the Congress had in mind in paragraph 7's affirmation that "the Church's visible unity in truth is God's purpose" is not both immediately and entirely clear. The same vagueness is noticeable in the Congress' affirmation of the inseparability of church and mission as well as social action and evangelism. At any rate, Lausanne's lacuna was not caused by its failure to specify in transparent terms what social action, for example, means or what "one Lord, one faith, one baptism" means in concrete historical situation—these and other questions were secondary. Contrariwise, it stemmed from a much more basic and primary question: What precisely is evangelical ecclesiology? The Congress never really confronted this question. Therefore, it is not out of place to say that, if ecclesiology is the acid test of a sound missiological proposal, as suggested by even one of the Congress' active participants, Howard A. Snyder, Lausanne certainly failed on that subject,[8] in spite of its ability to achieve "a passing grade" on other related subjects. All things considered, Lausanne was and is unmatched by any other evangelical gathering.

SUMMARY OBSERVATIONS

On the basis of this historical survey, I shall venture some general observations about evangelical mission motivation vis-à-vis the conciliar one. First, are there discernible changes that have occurred between Wheaton and Lausanne?

Although there continue to be some evangelicals who have refused to admit the changes even within their own ranks, it is safe to say that there are clear-cut changes on some missiological questions. Prior to Wheaton, few had hoped that evangelicals would come to grips with a turbulent and increasingly escapist world. Yet they did in a manner few would have predicted. Similarly, few would have thought that as a group the evangelicals would come to rely on ecumenical gatherings to define their missiological position or even to entertain the notion of "doctrinal unity." Yet, through Wheaton, Berlin, and Lausanne, and, indeed, many other mini-conferences, evangelicals have gradually moved into the center stage of missiological discussions. Put schematically, the following can be said as representative of the most salient changes in post-Lausanne evangelicalism:

1. Except for some phrasing problem, the trinitarian motif for mission is now *a priori* both for the evangelicals and the conciliarists. *Missio Dei*, once considered anathema by some evangelicals, is now assumed in some post-Lausanne evangelical thought.

2. The same attitude can be said to be applicable to the evangelical approach to church-mission relations. In general, it is now theoretically acceptable to some "moderate" evangelicals, such as John Stott, that the two should be integrated and that they are coterminous.

3. Mission and unity is now generally assumed to be a "good idea." Yet the mere fact that at Lausanne it was possible to affirm that "the church's visible unity in truth is God's purpose," is significant, though ambiguous. Through regional agencies as well as international ones, mutual cooperation is now part of the watchword (Cf. Keyes, 1983).

4. On Christianity and other faiths, clearly, no drastic change is discernible. Yet, there is an increased recognition that the intra-Protestant debate has been based on a particular reading of official statements, misinterpretation, and hearsay. Thinkers like Glasser and Winter have put forth new models for cross-cultural encounter, and dialogue between Christians and non-Christians was endorsed, in principle, at Lausanne.

5. Perhaps the most visible change involves the definition of evangelism and social change or action. Up to Lausanne, evangelicals were still uncertain. Mixed signals were the rule rather than the exception. At Lausanne, new ground was broken. Lausanne affirmed a two-mandate view of the warrant for discipling (Matt. 28: 18-20). God was affirmed as the God of justice as well as the God who demands *metanoia* and discipleship. In short, Lausanne made it clear that evangelicals are not averse to evangelism and social action, provided the former is seen or inter-

preted ontologically and the latter teleologically. In other words, calling people to Christ and His Church is logically prior, while social concern is a primary task of the Kingdom or rule of God in its earthly setting. Again, put differently, Lausanne said that *being* precedes *doing*. Most indicative of the new attitude to this question is the increasing number of mini-consultations which take their root from Lausanne's handiwork: The Evangelical Fellowship of India's Madras Declaration on Evangelical Social Action (1979), The Evangelical Commitment to Simple Lifestyle (1980), Consultation on Theology of Development (1980), and Evangelism and Social Responsibility (1982).[9]

It must also be mentioned that the evangelical movement, consciously or unconsciously, has also come to terms with our revolutionary age. Prior to Wheaton, evangelicals tended to condemn the WCC's attempt at proposing a missiological strategy that took into account the reality of a "post-Christendom" world. The summoning of evangelical congresses with representatives from different countries and from different sociopolitical contexts brought about a remarkable "revolution" in evangelical thought. We can see, therefore, that the same nontheological factors that have affected the conciliar movement have, similarly, affected the evangelicals. Moreover, it cannot be denied that directly or indirectly the conciliar movement itself has had a determinative effect on the modification path the evangelical movement has taken since 1966. Conversely, the conciliar movement has had to recognize the presence of the evangelical movement since that same year.

Consequently, we hazard that neither the conciliarists nor the evangelicals can claim to possess a special *gnosis* concerning how the Church is to carry out her missionary burden. Neither the conciliar nor the evangelical versions of Reformed thought can claim a privileged access to the will of God. Both are still searching, groping, and dependent on the Spirit of God, who is not always on the side of popular thought or the majority's wishes.

There is good evidence to show that both movements are, like all movements, tempted to promote a certain understanding of the Gospel, a certain view of cross-cultural missions, and a certain concept of what other non-Christian religionists are like. The danger that the church may confuse its institutional ideology with sound missiological strategies is, therefore, what should concern us (Verkuyl, 1978:391f), not minute points of theology which are not going to go away insofar as we are situated in different status positions, bred in divergent cultures, and socialized to perceive biblical reality (or other realities, for that matter) from a certain perspective, not others.

Viewed from this angle, the real problem missiological thinkers have to resolve is whether they can overcome the lurking epistemological temptation to verge more to the left or right of the religiopolitical spectrum. It is, therefore, not a question that concerns only one movement in Protestantism, but a question Protestants and non-Protestants must face. It does seem that, in fairness to the main issue on the missiological agenda (such as the philosophical justification for cross-cultural evangelism, and, therefore, proselyting), we should begin to move away from the mistaken view that the evangelical mission theology is the *locus classicus* for "authentic evangelism" (McGavran), while strategies that receive their imprimatur from the WCC are "novel" and "inauthentic." Missiology's "new fact of our time," of course, is not the widening gulf between evangelicals and conciliarists that Horner (1968:9) saw developing or the one Glasser and McGavran (1983) depicted. It is, rather, the fact that there is an emerging consensus on many missiological questions (Bassham, 1979:331–67 Costas, 1984:135–61) as well as the fact that "evangelicals" are becoming more "ecumenical" than ever, while "ecumenicals" are becoming more "evangelical" (Anderson, 1985:226). This development was simply unthinkable prior to Wheaton, Berlin, and Lausanne. Today, it appears destined to be taken for granted. Given time, would it not be possible to resolve most of the unresolved questions such as the Christian attitude toward non-Christian religionists?

It is my considered opinion that it is not impossible. The real question is whether the rapprochement will last long or whether the nature of our kaleidoscopic world will force or necessitate another round of aggressive, hostile conduct between the two movements. Both movements, therefore, have their work cut out for them.

NOTES

1. Evangelicals are sometimes referred to by others as "conservative evangelicals." For the purpose of this paper, the word "evangelicals" will refer to that wing of the Protestant party, without denying that there are evangelicals within the conciliar circles or vice versa. Notice also that the evangelical congresses all happened so suddenly. Within a period of eight years, the face of evangelicalism was changed for the better!

2. Wheaton's sponsors were the Evangelical Foreign Missions Association and the Interdenominational Missionary Association. Structurally, the former has "a mixed constituency of independent and denominational boards," while the latter "is composed of independent mission boards which do not have any denominational affiliation." Rodger Bassham, *Mission Theology 1948-1975. Years of Creative Tension* (Pasadena: William Carey, 1979), p. 214.

3. *Ibid.*

4. The journal actually listed a seven-point objective. For the other objectives, see "Good News For a World in Need," *Christianity Today* 11.1 (Oct. 4, 1966), p. 34.

5. *Ibid.*

6. Notice that Henry's work is titled *Evangelicals at the Brink of Crisis.* His is a post-Berlin reflection which gives a very good focus on the central missiological dilemmas with which evangelicals have had to grapple.

7. Carl F. H. Henry and W. Stanley Mooneyham (eds.) *One Race, One Gospel, One Task, World Congress on Evangelism, Berlin, 1966* (Minneapolis: World Wide, 1967), p. 524. Cf. pp. 201, 341–42, 501–3, 508–23.

8. Cited in Padilla, *The New Face of Evangelism* (Minnesota: World Wide 1976), p. 131. Cf. p. 138.

9. A brief historical overview of all these mini-consultations on evangelism and social action is given by Ronald Sider in his *Evangelicals and Development: Toward a Theology of Social Change* (Philadelphia: Westminster (1982), pp. 9ff.

REFERENCES

Anderson, Justice C. 1985 *Review of Contemporary Theologies of Mission* by Arthur F. Glasser and Donald A. McGavran. *Missiology* XIII, 2 (April): 225–26.

Bassham, Rodger C. 1979 *Mission Theology 1948-1975. Years of Creative Tension.* Pasadena, CA: William Carey.

Costas, Orlando E. 1984 *Christ Outside the Gate: Mission Beyond Christendom.* New York: Orbis.

Douglas, J. A. *Let the Earth Hear His Voice: International Congress on World Evangelism, Lausanne, Switzerland.* Minneapolis: World Wide Publication.

Fenton, Horace L. 1966 "Debits and Credits—the Wheaton Congress" *International Review of Missions* 55.220, 477–79.

Glasser, Arthur F. and Donald A. McGavran. 1983 *Contemporary Theologies of Mission.* Grand Rapids: Baker Book House.

"Good News for a World in Need," *Christianity Today* 11,1 (Oct. 4, 1966) 34.

Henry, Carl F. H. and W. Stanley Mooneyham (eds.). 1967 *One Race, One Gospel, One Task. World Congress on Evangelism, Berlin, 1966.* Minneapolis: World Wide Publications.

Henry, Carl F. H. 1967 *Evangelicals at the Brink of Crisis.* Waco, Texas, Word Books.

Horner, Norman A. (ed.). 1968 *Protestant Crosscurrents in Mission: the Ecumenical Conservative Encounter.* Nashville, TN: Abingdon Press.

Keyes, Lawrence E. 1983 *The Last Age of Missions: A Study of Third World Mission Societies.* Pasadena, CA: William Carey.

The Lausanne Continuation. 1982 *Evangelism and Social Responsibility.* Grand Rapids: Committee for World Evangelization.

Lindell, Harold (ed.). 1966 *The Church's Worldwide Mission: Proceedings of the Congress on the Church's Worldwide Mission, 4–16 April, 1966, at Wheaton College,* Waco, Texas: Word Books.

McGavran, D. A. (ed.). 1977 *The Conciliar-Evangelical Debate: the Crucial Documents 1964–1976.* Pasadena, CA: William Carey.

Newbigin, Lesslie. 1978 *The Open Secret.* Grand Rapids: Eerdmans.

_____. 1982 "Crosscurrents in Ecumenical and Evangelical Understanding of Mission," *International Bulletin of Missionary Research* (Oct.), 146–55.

Padilla, C. Rene (ed.). 1976 *An International Symposium on the Lausanne Covenant.* Minneapolis, MN: World Wide Books.

Rooy, Sidney. 1979 "Righteousness and Justice," *Evangelical Review of Theology* 2, 166–74.

Scott, Waldron. 1980 *Bring Forth Justice.* Grand Rapids: Eerdmans.

Sider, Ronald (ed.). 1982 *Evangelicals and Development: Toward a Theology of Social Change.* Philadelphia: Westminster.

Stott, John R. W. 1975 *Christian Mission in the Modern World.* London: Falcon.

_____. 1975a *The Lausanne Covenant: An Exposition and Commentary.* Minnesota: World Wide Publications.

Verkuyl, J. 1978 *Contemporary Missiology: An Introduction.* Grand Rapids: Eerdmans.

10

Changes in Roman Catholic Attitudes
toward Proselytism and Mission

Robert J. Schreiter *

The foundations of Roman Catholic theology of mission today can be understood only by tracing the dramatic changes in missiological thinking during the 20th century. This survey of these changes begins with the "period of certainty" (1919 until the beginning of Vatican Council II in 1962) and explains how shifts in theological thinking during the Council brought about a "period of missionary crisis" in the 1960s and 1970s. Since 1975, however, in the opinion of Father Schreiter, the Catholic Church has been experiencing a "rebirth of the missionary movement."

When examining claims to exclusivity and patterns of proselytism, the Roman Catholic Church provides material for a particularly useful case study. For until quite recently, it not only held strongly to the Christian exclusivist claim on truth, but also went even further in maintaining that it alone represented the true form of Christianity. Roman Catholicism has maintained a long history of proselytizing efforts as well. With the beginning of the so-called voyages of discovery at the end of the 15th century, it mounted an extraordinarily large mission effort, something sustained more or less down to the present time.

Yet significant changes have come about in both the claims to exclusivity and in the understanding of proselytism and mission within the Roman Catholic Church in the past twenty-five years. These changes in both official position and in attitudes appeared in the course of the Second Vatican Council, held in Rome from 1962 to 1965. Some dramatic shifts took place. While Roman Catholics still saw their form of communion as the best manifestation of the church of Jesus Christ, it was no longer to be considered the sole or the complete manifestation of that church. The other Christian churches were accorded a new respect, a respect extended to other

---

* Taken from Martin E. Marty and Frederick Greenspahn, eds., *Pushing the Faith: Proselytism and Civility in a Pluralistic World*, copyright © 1988 by University of Denver-Colorado Seminary, reprinted by permission of the Crossroad Publishing Company, New York, NY. Robert J. Schreiter, C.PP.S., is Professor of Doctrinal Theology at Catholic Theological Union, Chicago. He is the author of numerous articles and books, including *Constructing Local Theologies* and *Reconciliation: Mission and Ministry in a Changing World* (Maryknoll, NY: Orbis Books, 1985 and 1992), and is the General Editor of the Orbis Faith and Cultures Series.

forms of religious faith as well, especially to Judaism. And that respect went further than general esteem; these religions were seen as possible ways to the salvation preached heretofore as the exclusive property of Catholicism.

The missionary movement went into a ten-year decline immediately following the Council. Many factors contributed to this downswing. Part of it was due to the exodus from religious orders. But more importantly, there was the most profound questioning of the missionary movement, both in its principles and its practice, that the Catholic Church had ever undergone. While the number of missionaries coming from First World countries has declined, there is a growing population of missionaries coming from Third World countries.

Why have all of these shifts taken place? What has been their effect on Roman Catholic self-understanding? And what might they teach us about the themes under examination here? This presentation will try to trace these shifts in understanding of mission and proselytism through the twentieth century. The question of exclusivity will not be addressed directly, but will be viewed from the perspective of mission and proselytism. The question of Christianity's relation to other religions is probably the most thorny and important theological question before the church today, but a full examination of that would take us too far afield. Rather, how understandings of exclusive claims to truth affected the sense of mission will be the window upon this vexing problem.

The presentation here will divide the history of these changes in attitude into four periods: (1) the period prior to the Second Vatican Council (1919–62); (2) the period of the Council itself (1962–65); (3) the period of the missionary crisis (1965–75); and the period of the rebirth of the missionary movement (1975 to the present). In examining this history, we will want to attend not only to official pronouncements and statements by theologians, but also some of the social factors that were at play. Having done this, I will then try to distill out of this history any salient points that might prove useful for our discussion here. Given the compass of this presentation, the overview of that history must be rather summary, touching only the high points of these periods. But I hope that even with this the contours of a remarkable history will be evident.

THE PERIOD OF CERTAINTY (1919–62)

Roman Catholics experienced the same surge in missionary activity during the 19th and early 20th centuries as did Protestants. Although the Catholic Church had kept a high level of missionary commitment since the mid-16th century, the 19th century nonetheless represented a significant increase. New religious orders were founded exclusively for mission work. National missionary societies were founded in Europe and North America (the United States missionary society, Maryknoll, was founded in 1911), and missionary patronage societies were developed on the national and international levels.

The popes, too, encouraged missionary activity in the lands outside Europe throughout this period. But the history we wish to trace here can be dated from 1919, when Pope Benedict XV issued the encyclical letter *Maximum Illud*, subtitled "On Spreading the Catholic Faith throughout the World."[1] This was to be the first of five encyclicals issued on missionary work between 1919 and 1962. Pius XI issued *Rerum Ecclesiae* in 1926; Pius XII issued *Evangelii Praecones* in 1951 and *Fidei Donum* in 1957; and John XXIII issued *Princeps Pastorum* in 1959.[2]

Remarkable about all of these letters is that virtually no attention is given to the theological foundation of missionary work. Generally, Christ's commission to the apostles to go out, preach, and make disciples of all nations (Matt. 28:20) sufficed. This commission to the apostles was now passed on to the successors of the apostles, the bishops. These were to go out and rescue those lost in darkness and the shadow of death (*Maximum Illud*, 6; *Evangelii Praecones*, 16). Standing behind the commission to go out and preach was God's will that all be saved. When addressing the more specific purpose of mission, the encyclicals revert to the two classic formulations of purpose: the winning of converts (*conversio animarum*) and the establishing of the local church (*plantatio ecclesiae*). Benedict XV and Pius XI emphasize the former; Pius XII and John XXIII, the latter. The bulk of these encyclical letters, however, are taken up with methods in mission: problems of education, financing, roles of bishops, and the like.

One theological question starts to figure more prominently, though still indirectly, in the letters of Pius XII, namely, the value and status of local customs. In his letter, Pius reiterates the principle, going back to Pope Gregory the Great, that whatever is good should be preserved, purified, and elevated by its contact with the Christian religion. He sums up the principle thus: "Although owing to Adam's fall, human nature is tainted with original sin, yet it has in itself something naturally Christian; and this, if illumined by God's grace, can eventually be changed into true and supernatural virtue."[3]

Direct reflection on the nature, purpose, and methods of mission also begins more or less with this period. The first chair of Roman Catholic missiology was established at the University of Muenster in Germany in 1911, and the first handbook of missiology appeared in 1919.[4] The author of that handbook, Josef Schmidlin, devoted approximately sixty of its 460 pages to the question of why engage in mission. Typical of the period, it is cast in apologetic form.

Throughout this period, the theological grounding for mission was devoted to expanding the two basic principles of the *conversio animarum* and the *plantatio ecclesiae*. The former focused especially on God's universal salvific will; the latter on the church as the concrete manifestation of that will. German missiologists emphasized the former; Francophone missiologists in Belgium and France, the latter. And the two principles provided the foci around which a closed ellipse could be created. The more fundamental question of why mission at all was not being asked; or, when asked, was responded to with the universal salvific will of God. If one looks to the last great handbook to appear before the Council, Thomas Ohm's *Machet zu Jüngern alle Völker*, which appeared in 1962,[5] a great deal more space was devoted to mission theory. But that additional space represented the elaboration of the familiar principles, rather than any advancement on them. The questions that were to become so important in the next period—the meaning of the church, the meaning of salvation in other religions—still found no place here.

This period prior to the Council, then, was a period of certainty, at least in the public positions of church magisterium and of the theologians. In the mission fields, however, things were beginning to change. The nascent struggles for independence from colonial rule were to reverberate in the mission stations in Africa and Asia. When this combined with the impact of the Second Vatican Council, the effect would be seismic. We need to turn now to the work of that Council.

THE PERIOD OF FERMENT (1962–65)

In 1962, the first session of the Second Vatican Council convened. Already in 1960, a Preparatory Commission had been established under the chairmanship of Cardinal Agagianian, the Prefect of the Propaganda Fide, for the purpose of preparing a schema for consideration by the Council, with the working title *De Activitate Missionali Ecclesiae*. The commission included a considerable number of people with missionary experience. The initial draft presented to the commission followed the traditional lines of the papal encyclicals, dealing primarily with the governance of missions and missionaries, with little about the theology of mission. This first draft was composed mainly by people resident in Rome rather than those engaged in the ferment of the current missionary scene. It met with little approval by the Council Fathers and a fundamental revision was undertaken. This and a subsequent revision were considered unacceptable to the great majority of the Council Fathers. The reasons, it seems, were that it did not reflect the contemporary mission experience and did not take adequately into account other theological developments that were happening in the Council.

It became apparent that the Council Fathers wished a more substantial and theologically weighty document. The commission preparing the document reorganized itself, with Cardinal Agagianian gracefully moving into the background. The figure who emerged as the effective leader in preparing a new draft was Father Johannes Schütte, the Superior General of the Divine Word Missionaries. In fact, it is to him that we owe the draft which was approved by the final session of the Council in 1965.

What elements emerged in the final draft that made it acceptable and which reflect the changes in an understanding of mission? It would go beyond the scope of this presentation to discuss those doctrinal elements in detail. It might be more helpful to focus upon three major developments that, in their own way, define the tensions that were to surround Catholic understandings of mission in the following two decades. The three elements are: (1) a trinitarian locus for the origin of mission; (2) an expanded understanding of the church; and (3) a new understanding of the nature of other religions.

The first part of the "Decree on Missionary Activity in the Church," known by its opening words in Latin, *Ad Gentes*, locates the origins of missionary activity in the Trinity itself, in God's eternal plan of salvation for all seen in the sending of the Son and the Holy Spirit into the world. Now the idea of grounding missionary activity in the Trinity itself had been gaining considerable current among theologians prior to the Council. In itself, this is not entirely new. But the implication of making the Trinity the locus of the origin of mission, rather than the great commission of the Gospel ("Go out and preach to all nations"), is that mission is no longer simply a duty incumbent upon Christians, but becomes part of the very nature of being a Christian. The decree is quick to pick up on this implication and to show where this leads. While one can continue to define certain activities of the church as specifically missionary, on a more fundamental level the church has to come to see itself as missionary by its very nature. Thus, the church goes from "having missions" to "being missionary." This was to be the most fundamental shift that theology of mission and proselytism was to experience. Mission became, therefore, more than an extending of the perimeters of the church, it was to be something motivating the very heart of the church, not because some command had been laid upon the faithful, but because by being missionary the church was drawn into the life of the Trinity itself. For this reason, Roman Catholic theologies of mission since that time tend to speak of missionary activity as "mission" (in the singular), rather than "missions" (in the plural), to emphasize the unity of mission in the Trinity—albeit the plural usage does survive in some official usages.

What have been the implications of this shift in theological basis from the great commission to a trinitarian basis? Perhaps the most significant has been a change in the metaphors used to describe missionary activity. Prior to this shift, Roman Catholic missiological language shared with the Protestant missiology of the time (still to be found in some conservative evangelical circles) a predilection for military metaphors. Referring to Matthew 28 as "the great commission" is already indicative of that. Since the trinitarian foundation in *Ad Gentes* uses primarily the language of love, the whole tone of what constitutes missionary activity changes. To be sure, some of the more military language remains, but the tone of confrontation with the nonbeliever moves away from conquest to invitation, dialogue, and sharing. Effective proselytism, then, is not so much marked by conquest and submission, but is a more complex process that acknowledges the work of the Holy Spirit already active in the life of the potential convert long before he or she actually hears the Gospel. And the act of conversion itself is seen to be only the beginning of a long, complex process of growth away from sinfulness into the full life of grace. While proclamation is not played down in this approach, it clearly had to make room for a more "dialogical" approach, mirroring the intimate communication between those who love. For again, the purpose of missionary activity it not just to convert, but to bear witness to the trinitarian life, to bear witness to the very life of God. When one begins to think in these terms, one begins to feel a new set of tensions in missionary activity. Whereas previously missionary activity was the specialized and clearly defined task of winning converts and establishing the church, it now became the general task of all believers, involving a more complex combination of proclamation, witness, dialogue, and service. It had become at once more fundamental and less well-defined.

To understand the full implications of what this was to mean in the succeeding periods, we need to turn to the second element that emerged in the Council, namely, a shift in the understanding of the nature of the church itself. This shift is best seen in another document of the Council, the "Constitution on the Church," known as *Lumen Gentium*. In that document, two differing (although not necessarily contradictory) understandings of the nature of the church are juxtaposed. The first is a more refined form of the sense of church that had been formulated at the First Vatican Council in 1869, refined by subsequent popes, especially Pius XII in his

1943 encyclical *Mystici Corporis*. This ecclesiology had its roots in the Catholic Reformation, notably in the work of such theologians as the sixteenth-century Jesuit Robert Bellarmine. The dominant image of this understanding of church was that it was a *societas perfecta* or "perfect society," mirroring the celestial society surrounding the throne of God. It was hierarchical in nature and represented on earth the most complete possible presence of God. This self-understanding of the church was the basis for the policy it was to follow subsequent to the First Vatican Council in trying to create an alternate, self-sufficient culture against the onslaught of modernity. Pius XII was to begin the softening of the harder edges of this image with his theology of the church as the mystical body of Christ, taking up the Pauline imagery. However, while this enriched an understanding of the church as *mysterion* or manifestation of the divine reality, it kept with it a firm sense of hierarchy, considerable self-assuredness, and confidence in its mirroring of heaven.

Juxtaposed to this understanding of church, we find in the second chapter of *Lumen Gentium* the presentation of the church as the pilgrim people of God. It was to be this image that captured the imagination of so many of the bishops at the Council and of others who saw the need to create a new relationship with the world. Instead of being an already perfected society, the church as the pilgrim people of God saw itself perhaps as the vanguard of that perfect society, but in highly modest and provisional terms. The image of the pilgrim people was dominated by the story of the Exodus, of a people indeed liberated from their captivity, yet far from the Promised Land. The image came to evoke for many the idea of the church as a collection of people engaged in a common quest for the fulfillment of the kingdom of God. No longer could the church be identified as the kingdom of God; it would be seen rather as pointing to that kingdom. To be sure, the constitution would continue to see the current presence of God's kingdom as "subsisting" in the church; but the compromise of using the word "subsisting" rather than the simple copulative verb "is" already opened up considerable latitude where virtually none had existed before. The real charter for mapping out the implications of this shift was to be the "Constitution on the Church in the Modern World," *Gaudium et Spes*. This document, like no other in the history of the Catholic Church, called for a positive and constructive dialogue with the world (or more specifically, with the industrialized and secularized West).

What were the more specific implications of the introduction of this considerably different understanding of the church for the sense of mission and proselytism? Most notably, it had a profound effect on one of the two great motives for mission, the *plantatio ecclesiae*. The establishment of the church, although still important, no longer in and of itself was the be-all and end-all of mission. And the reason was that the church itself was but a herald, an envoy of the kingdom of God, not the kingdom itself. That would be only realized in heaven, when the church as such would pass away. To be sure, the Council documents continue to speak of the necessity of the church and membership in the church as the visible sign of the fullness of salvation to which we might attain here on earth. But in almost the same breath, speaking of the church as pilgrim and provisional necessarily opened up the question of just how necessary the church was—really—to salvation. Might not conversion to a better life along the lines one's life had already taken be a better task for the missionary rather than insisting upon formal membership in the church? And what was to come into greater evidence in the succeeding period was that the boundaries of church itself, once so clear and secure, were now beginning to appear considerably more vague.

When this shift of awareness of what constitutes the church is paired with the aforementioned shift in the understanding of the nature of mission, a new kind of paradox is set up. On the one hand, the missionary task of going out and imparting the message of the Good News of salvation becomes something of the very nature of the church and of the individual Christian. But on the other hand, what one is witnessing to (at least as regards the visible community of Christ) has become considerably more vague. The conjunction of this paradox set the stage for the missionary crisis in the next period. Before turning to that period, however, we need to take into account the third element that was to emerge from the Council, namely, a new understanding of other religions.

In many ways, the Council's understanding of other religious traditions was not new. As the text goes to great pains to show, its understanding was rooted in patristic thinking and a theology of creation. Since the patristic period, there had been a strain of thought which held that there were indeed noble elements in non-Christian religion that served as a *praeparatio evangelica*, a preparation for reception of the Gospel. These elements were not to be abolished or set aside in the evangelizing process, rather they were to be purified, transformed as needed, and elevated to the realm of divine grace. While there had always been a great deal of controversy in Western Catholic Christianity as to what those elements might be and how they were to be engaged (for example, the 17th-century "Rites Controversy" in China), this was a principle that had remained part of the tradition. The encyclicals of the 20th-century popes had reaffirmed these principles, especially those of Pius XII and John XXIII. What we find in *Ad Gentes* essentially reaffirmed the principles of those encyclicals without going beyond them in any special way.

The catalyst here was yet another Council document, the "Declaration on the Relation of the Church to Non-Christian Religions," *Nostra Aetate*. Originally intended to address Catholic relations with the Jews (which was to remain its principal purpose), it was extended to include all the great religious traditions. *Nostra Aetate* builds upon that tradition and in so doing takes it a step further. The document goes to great pains to reaffirm the positive value of Judaism, Buddhism, Hinduism, and Islam, noting the parallels in these traditions to Christian faith. The call found in *Nostra Aetate* was not so much to conversion as to dialogue. And the point of dialogue with other religious traditions was not only to come to understand those traditions better; its purpose was also to come to learn religiously from them about pathways to God. The stance of the Christian believer in approaching people of other faiths was to be one of humility and hospitality rather than superiority.

Nostra Aetate was one of the most hotly contested documents of the Council. It opened up new pathways by posing the question most seriously about the role of salvation in other religions. It continued to affirm that all people were redeemed in Christ, but the way the question of other religions was raised carried with it the possible implication that the church was not the sole agency through which that salvation might be realized. This, therefore, takes the redefinition of the nature of the church discussed above one step further. Not only is the church seen as a provisional sign of the coming kingdom of God, the very nature or purpose of the church is also challenged by this new relationship to other religions.

With twenty years of hindsight, it is now clear that the Council rarely spoke univocally on any subject and that it raised more questions than it provided answers. In the matter of mission and proselytism, selective readings of the Council documents can provide support for a considerable variety of interpretations. Yet if one looks at the changes that the missionary movement underwent in the years following the Council, it seems clear that the frontiers pointed to by questioning the nature of mission, the church, and the relation to other religious traditions marked out the territory that would need to be explored. And with that we turn to the third period of this history.

THE PERIOD OF THE MISSIONARY CRISIS (1965–75)

Missionaries in the field and leaders of missionary orders were quick to catch the implications present in the conciliar documents. The fact that many of their concerns had finally been heard in the drafting process of *Ad Gentes*, albeit interpreted still in a somewhat conservative manner, gave many the impetus to explore more deeply the implications of what the Council had said. And indeed, in the initial period following the Council the number of missionaries entering the field continued to rise until 1968. Thereafter, the numbers moved into a steady and often precipitous decline. Much of this can be attributed to the large-scale exodus of priests, sisters, and brothers world-wide in those years. But the growing insecurity about what was the exact nature of mission in a post-Vatican II church surely fueled this development as well.

By the late 1960s the implications that could be drawn from the Council documents and the exodus of many missionaries from the field had set the stage for reflection on the profound challenge that traditional mission was facing. While mission was to be at the very heart of the Christian vocation, what was to be its acceptable form, given the new understanding of the church and of non-Christian religions? The old motives of the *conversio animarum* and the *plantatio ecclesiae* no longer exercised the same attraction, yet could not be relegated to the dustbin of history. Where was the acknowledgment of the good conscience of the non-Christian to be located in missionary strategies aimed at conversion? (This had been something affirmed in the "Declaration on Religious Liberty," *Dignitatis Humanae*.) And how was the new stress on dialogue to be related to evangelization?

A landmark attempt to deal with these dilemmas occurred early in 1969, in the form of a theological conference sponsored by SEDOS (Servizio di documentazione e studi), an association of the mission-sending orders of men and women.[7] This conference gathered together some of the most able minds reflecting on mission at that time. The conference took the most radically neuralgic point in the missionary crisis as its theme: why mission at all? The collected papers from that conference represent perhaps the single best attempt to grapple with the theological foundations of mission in that period.

The most cohesive and persuasive paper is that of Johannes Schütte, the man responsible for the final draft of *Ad Gentes*. The very title of his paper set forth the question: "Why Engage in Mission Work?"[8] Schütte frames the dilemma by using theologian Karl Rahner's phrase "anonymous Christian." Put simply, the idea is that if God wishes the salvation of all and Christ is the source of that salvation and if those who live uprightly according to the best dictates of their conscience do therefore experience that salvation, they are Christians, although "anonymously." Schütte sets forth the question directly: If God through unfathomable mystery is leading these upright non-Christians to salvation along other ways, what right do we as Christians have to disturb them? Having said this, he proceeds to develop a theological answer that is to serve as a foundation for motivation to mission.

What Schütte does is develop the eschatological aspect of mission; that is, following the early Christian vision that all things are ultimately to be brought together in Christ (Eph. 1:10), the task of mission is to help build up that *pleroma* or plenitude in Christ. This is to be achieved by continuing to proclaim that Christ stands at the center of human history. Secondly, the task of mission is to carry further the incarnation of Christ into every culture. And thirdly, the task of mission is to work toward peace and reconciliation, since such peace and reconciliation are to be signs of the imminent return of Christ and the establishment of his sovereignty.

To my knowledge, Schütte's paper remains the best articulation of a theological response to the missionary dilemma of that period. Its influence is evident in the concluding statement of the conference, where the motivation to mission is seen as helping people discover the mystery of God at work in their own lives and in their own situations. The statement also emphasizes the place of development within the missionary enterprise. But no real headway was made on the question of relation to other religious traditions. One finds in the concluding statement the same juxtaposition of the exclusivity of salvation to be found in Jesus Christ with an affirmation of the authentic values of other traditions.

The eschatological argument for establishing the motivation of mission remains probably the most effective one available to Catholics to this day. Seeing God at work in mysterious and hidden ways and helping to make that more explicit through the proclamation of Christ have become a standard part of contemporary Catholic missiology. It would generally be seen as a more convincing motivation than the trinitarian argument used in *Ad Gentes*. Such an approach, as we shall see, leaves room for dialogue within mission, but it does not address sufficiently the role of other religious traditions within the scheme.

What this period presents in terms of our understanding of mission and proselytism is a consolidation of some of the implications suggested by the positions taken during the Council. For proselytism to fit within a different understanding of the church, a church more provisional and exploratory in its nature and more vague in its boundaries, the motivation has to be shifted from a clear point of departure to a more anticipatory vision of a future. That allows for considerably more change and development than does the more deductive style of the trinitarian argument. This extra leeway has the advantage of at least buying time to construct a more ordered approach. The anticipatory approach also has the advantage of tying in dialogue and development more closely to the motivating factors for mission.

Dialogue and development need not be grounded only in the general love of neighbor; they are part of bringing about the incarnation of Christ in every culture and in heralding the fulfillment of all things in Christ.

This approach, then, goes some way to meet the challenge of plurality without exactly addressing pluralism itself. To carry it a step further, we need to turn to the fourth and final period of this history.

THE REBIRTH OF THE MISSIONARY MOVEMENT (1975—)

The fourth period of this history is marked at the beginning by the publication by Pope Paul VI of his apostolic exhortation *Evangelii Nuntiandi* in 1975. This document grew out of the synod of bishops held in Rome in 1974, which took up the question of mission and evangelization in the modern world. The synod itself was not able to agree on a concluding statement and turned its material over to the pope, who then issued it as an apostolic exhortation. It has often been remarked that *Evangelii Nuntiandi* is the document that *Ad Gentes* was intended to have been. It remains to this day the subject of close study in Catholic missionary groups around the world.

For our purposes here, the most important section of this document is the second chapter, which deals with the nature of evangelization. Paul VI begins by noting the complexity of the evangelizing process. Although the direct proclamation of Christ is central to evangelization, there is much more involved, and to deny this runs the risk of distorting the meaning of evangelization. Evangelization, Paul maintains, involves the renewal of humanity in all its aspects, both individual and collective. It involves, too, the evangelization of cultures, by which he means a creative encounter between the Gospel and cultures. He assigns a certain priority to the witness of life as a form of evangelization alongside direct proclamation. He sums up evangelization as "a complex process made up of varied elements: the renewal of humanity, witness, explicit proclamation, inner adherence, entry into the community, acceptance of signs, apostolic initiative."[9] In the related matter of relationships to non-Christian religions, Paul VI reaffirms the teaching of the Council, attesting to the dignity of these traditions while reasserting the right to missionary activity of Christians among them. Thought on the issue is not advanced further, although Paul recognizes that the issue "raises complex and delicate questions that must be studied in the light of Christian tradition and the Church's Magisterium, in order to offer to the missionaries of today and tomorrow new horizons in their contacts with non-Christian religions."[10]

In 1981 SEDOS again convened a seminar to assess developments in mission.[11] The editors noted that there had been considerable development in thinking about mission since the 1969 conference. If the question then was the *why* of mission, six years after *Evangelii Nuntiandi* it was the *how* of mission. In its concluding statement, the seminar saw four principal directions in the *how* of mission: proclamation, dialogue, inculturation, and liberation of the poor. In the matter of proclamation, two differing but complementary models were presented: one of extending the visible communion of the church, and the other of recognizing and furthering the values of the kingdom. Participants in the seminar saw the second model as gaining prominence in mission over the first.

In many ways the concluding statement of the 1981 SEDOS seminar remains the charter of the contemporary missionary movement in the Catholic Church. In its fourfold emphasis on proclamation, dialogue, inculturation, and liberation, it continues themes that were first consolidated in the documents of the Second Vatican Council. The question of relation to non-Christian religions arose in the seminar but did not achieve much prominence in the discussions.

It is with a brief examination of this last point that we conclude this survey. Two church documents deserve mention here. The first is the so-called Venice Statement of 1977, actually a paper presented by Professor Tommasso Federici to a meeting of a liaison committee between Roman Catholics and Jews.[12] While the document does not have official status, it has been widely recognized as reflecting official Vatican thinking. This document rejects "any action aimed at changing the religious faith of Jews." In subsequent official documents this position has been reiterated. This was certainly the first time that the Catholic Church abdicated any right to evangelization among a given group.

The second document was issued in 1984 by the Vatican Secretariat for Non-Christians, entitled "The Attitude of the Church toward the Followers of Other Religions: Reflections and Orientations on Dialogue and Mission."[13] In the section on mission and conversion (arts. 37-40), the document reaffirms the Christian's right to proclaim the Gospel and to seek the conversion of others, as long as this is not forced upon the unbeliever. In the same breath, it reaffirms also the primacy of conscience, especially in religious matters.

The document does not break new ground but consolidates once again the thinking of the period since the Vatican Council on the nature of mission and the complexity of the dialogue process. Following out the title, the document can be said to be rather long on reflections and short on orientations.

A number of theologians have pointed out the ambivalences of the Catholic Church in facing the implications of the two differing sets of principles it holds: the necessity of mission and the integrity of other religious traditions. Methodist missiologist Gerald Anderson raised the question forcefully a number of years ago in responding to a paper by then-Secretary Pietro Rossano of the Secretariat for Non-Christians.[14] More recently, Catholic theologians Paul Knitter and especially William Burrows have raised this question.[15] The problem comes down essentially to this: How can the church retain its absolute claim to exclusive possession of the truth and of salvation and at the same time affirm the goodness and even validity of other religious traditions? What both Knitter and Burrows have said in effect is that the Catholic Church has yet to grapple seriously with this. It wants to have it both ways and ends up in a great deal of confusion or vagueness. I would have to concur with their challenge. The question of the relation of the church to other religious traditions is, to me, the single most important question facing us today. This is the case not only because of missionary activity; it has to do with the very identity of the church itself.

CONCLUSION

What conclusions might be drawn from this history of the Roman Catholic church's attitude toward proselytism and mission? The history relates a considerable change of opinion in the course of this century. Let me suggest a few things that strike me as useful.

First of all, proselytism works best when there are only two parties within the purview of the proselytizer: the proselytizer and the one to be proselytized. When the one to be proselytized fragments into a plurality, there are more possibilities of challenge to the proselytizer. In other words, the world of that other comes at the proselytizer in many different ways, and so raises more questions than would otherwise have been the case.

Second, proselytism requires that the proselytizer have a firm sense of his or her own identity. That identity must have clearly established boundaries so that one can tell quickly and simply when one is or is not a member of the group. When that sense of identity or the boundaries of the identity become porous or vague, proselytism becomes more difficult. As we saw in this history, when the meaning of the church shifted during the Second Vatican Council, the conversion aspect of mission came into difficulty.

Third, when competing groups give priority to acknowledging their similarities over their differences (usually this is done to assure some peaceful coexistence), proselytism loses much of its energy. Thus, when the Catholic Church affirmed the positive values in other great religious traditions in *Nostra Aetate* and emphasized the value of dialogue, this necessarily undercut more straightforward proselytizing efforts. Put another way, when the post-Vatican II church opted for a more inclusive approach to other traditions, it became more difficult to say exactly why one should switch from one tradition to another.

Fourth, when boundaries surrounding identity became unclear, the complexity of the conversion process comes more into evidence. As Paul VI noted in *Evangelii Nuntiandi*, not to acknowledge this distorts the very process itself. And missionaries have become more aware of how long conversion takes, even after the primary symbols of Christianity have been embraced. This seems to take the urgency out of proselytism in one kind of way, since conversion is always a more gradual process than it might seem on the surface.

Fifth, if the proselytizer wishes to acknowledge pluralism and not simply plurality (i.e., the existence of many different forms as legitimate), then the proselytizer will have to shift the values involved in mission and proselytism to a broader context. In terms of our discussion here, the shift was made from rescue from damnation to "renewal of humanity" (Paul VI) or "furthering the values of the kingdom" (SEDOS, 1981). The values attained are no longer the exclusive property of the proselytizer; they are open, at least in principle, to others. The proselytizer participates in the realization of these values rather than claims to have exclusive right to them. This allows some form of mission to continue, but under considerably different auspices.

And finally, the identity of the proselytizer will tend to be more anticipatory than participatory in the ideal. This allows for sufficient ambiguity to permit the considerable and largely unforeseen kinds of change that are likely to come upon the proselytizer in the course of interaction within the pluralist framework. We saw a general shift in the motivation for Catholic mission away from a deductive trinitarian argument toward the anticipatory eschatological argument. This provides a reasonable amount of firmness in the identity of the proselytizer without foreclosing the possibility of changes. There is a good deal more flexibility in a church as "pilgrim people" than there is in a church as "perfect society."

Much more, no doubt, could be said about the changes that the Roman Catholic Church has undergone. They are indeed remarkable. What is noticeable today in the Catholic Church is the large proportion of missionaries now coming from Third World churches. This seems to grow out of a deep sense of the missionary nature of the church itself.[16] Whether they will teach us something new about mission and pluralism as they have in so many other areas remains to be seen. Suffice it to say for now that great challenges still lie ahead, especially in the more direct confrontation of how the salvific role of other religions is really to be assessed.

REFERENCES

1. *Acta Apostolicae Sedis* 11 (1919) 440–55.

2. *Rerum Ecclesiae, ibid.*, 18 (1926) 65-83; Evangelii Praecones, Ibid., 43 (1951) 497–528; *Fidei Donum*, ibid., 49 (1957) 225–48; *Princeps Pastorum*, ibid., 51 (1959) 833–64. For an overview of the contents of these encyclicals, see René-Pierre Millot, *Missions in the World Today* (New York: Hawthorn Books, 1961).

3. *Evangelii Praecones*, 55–60.

4. Josef Schmidlin, *Katholische Missionslehre im Grundriss* (Münster: Verlag der Aschendorffsche Buchhandlung, 1919).

5. Freiburg: Erich Wewel Verlag, 1962.

6. The two best histories of the preparation of this document may be found in Suso Brechter, "Decree on the Church's Missionary Activity: Origin and History of the Decree," *Commentary on the Documents of Vatican II*, ed. Herbert Vorgrimler (New York: Herder and Herder, 1969) IV: 87–111; Saverio Paventi, "Étapes de l'élaboration du texte," *L'Activité missionnaire de l'Église*, ed. Johannes Schütte (Paris: Éditions du Cerf, 1967), 150–77.

7. The proceedings of this meeting were published as *Foundations of Mission Theology* (Maryknoll, NY: Orbis Books, 1972).

8. *Ibid.*, pp. 39–50.

9. Article 24. I cite here from the edition issued by the United States Catholic Conference in 1976.

10. *Ibid.*, art. 53.

11. The proceedings may be found in *Mission in Dialogue*, ed. Mary Motte and Joseph Lang (Maryknoll, NY: Orbis, 1982).

12. "Study Outline on the Mission and Witness of the Church," SIDIC 11 (1978) no. 3.

13. To be found in the *Bulletin* of the Secretariat, no. 56 (1984) 126–41.

14. At a conference held at Union Theological Seminary in Richmond, Virginia, in 1979, the proceedings of which were published as *Christ's Lordship and Religious Pluralism* (Maryknoll, NY: Orbis Books, 1981). The Anderson response is on pages 110–19.

15. Paul Knitter, "Roman Catholic Approaches to Other Religions: Developments and Tensions," *International Bulletin of Missionary Research* 8 (1984) 50-54; William Burrows, "Tensions in the Catholic Magisterium about Mission and Other Religions," *ibid.*, 9 (1985) 2–4; "Mission in the Context of 'Conscientized Action' and Dialogue," *Missiology* 13 (1985) 473–86.

16. See Omer Degrijse, *Going Forth: Missionary Consciousness in Third World Churches* (Maryknoll, NY: Orbis Books, 1984).

11

Evangelism in the WCC

From New Delhi to Canberra

Priscilla Pope-Levison *

The World Council of Churches (WCC) has been accused of being indifferent to evangelism, but for its own part the WCC has steadfastly maintained that evangelism lies at the core of ecumenical activity. In this analysis of WCC assembly and conference statements, Priscilla Pope-Levison demonstrates that confusion about ecumenical evangelism results in part from the inter-changeablity of key terms in ecumenical documents. The essential key to ecumenical evangelism, however, is that it is wholistic—the "whole church" brings the "whole Gospel" to the "whole world,"—and comprehensive—involving both word and deed. The article traces WCC efforts to restate the evangelistic mandate at meetings from New Delhi in 1961 to Canberra in 1991.

In the assembly reports and study documents of an organization like the World Council of Churches it is possible to glean insight into the meaning and importance of words. One can look at such factors as: frequency of use, omissions, word associations or substitutions, developments in definitions, and alterations in themes. In this study of the word "evangelism" in the WCC assemblies and reports since New Delhi,[1] the attempt has been to evaluate what the texts say at face value. As Orlando Costas once suggested, "Yet since everyone sees reality through his own 'grid,' it is imperative that the conference first be allowed to speak for itself through its official documents."[2] In light of this statement and because of the limitations of space, the focus of this article is the texts and not the historical and theological context. Thus the aim is to consult WCC documents in this time period in a chronological fashion in order to interpret the WCC's understanding of evangelism as it appears in these texts.

* This chapter is an abridgement of a two-part article in *International Review of Mission* 80 (April 1991), pp. 231–41, and 81 (1992), pp. 119–25. Priscilla Pope-Levison received her doctorate from the University of St. Andrew's in Scotland and serves as assistant professor of contextual theology at North Park Theological Seminary, Chicago. She has published *Evangelization from a Liberation Perspective* (New York: Peter Lang, 1991) and, with John R. Levison, *Jesus in Global Contexts* (Louisville, KY: Westminster/John Knox, 1992).

A clarification of terminology is pertinent at this point. The word "evangelism" is scarcely used in these documents. For the most part, "witness" is the favored word. For instance, the report of the Uppsala Assembly, *Renewal in Mission*, uses the word "evangelism" only once, whereas "witness" appears eight times. At four of the conferences (New Delhi, Mexico City, Melbourne, and Vancouver), "witness" appears in the titles of the reports; "evangelism" is never used in a title during the time period of this survey. In addition, just as there is a preference for the word "witness" rather than "evangelism," the same is true of "mission" instead of "evangelism." As Philip Potter notes, "One finds in ecumenical circles and also among those involved in the work of the WCC a preference for "mission" over against "evangelism."[3] Potter then offers a further observation about terminology. "In fact, ecumenical literature since Amsterdam has used 'mission,' 'witness,' and 'evangelism' interchangeably."[4] It appears, however, that it is more than the words being interchangeable; both "witness" and "mission" are used instead of "evangelism." With at least two words given preference over evangelism, it is not surprising that it rarely appears in WCC writings.

Another confusion in terminology is evident. Evangelism is difficult to distinguish from mission. Philip Potter lists the relationship between mission and evangelism as an aspect "about which there is much debate and even disagreement."[5] He then proffers the following statement, thus attempting to clarify their relationship: mission is defined as "the Church's total involvement in Christ's ministry among men in life and service," and evangelism is defined as "the calling of men to faith in Christ."[6] In this same article he exhorts the WCC to distinguish between these terms. Yet, after twenty years, his statement remains one of the few places where this question is addressed. The thesis is that evangelism is present, though in a limited way, and it is a wholistic evangelism that the WCC puts forth in these documents.[7] With these preliminary remarks in mind, the survey of evangelism in WCC documents from New Delhi to Canberra will begin.

NEW DELHI AND MEXICO CITY

The assembly at New Delhi in 1961 and the CWME (Commission on World Mission Evangelism) conference at Mexico City in 1963 are similar in their discussion of evangelism. At both of these meetings evangelism is defined by the phrase, "commission given to the whole Church to take the whole Gospel to the whole world."[8] The "whole Gospel" is concerned with reconciliation of the "whole world" to God; this reconciliation affects persons, institutions, and structures at every level. Along with this, the "whole Gospel" must witness to all realms of life—physical, social, economic, and spiritual. As the report from New Delhi states, "Witness to the Gospel must therefore be prepared to engage in the struggle for social justice and for peace; it will have to take the form of humble service and of a practical ministry of reconciliation amidst the actual conflict of our times."[9]

And it is the "whole Church" that is to bring the "whole Gospel" to the "whole world." This "whole Church" refers, first of all, to the role of the laity in evangelism. Lay witness is an integral part of evangelizing the "whole world." Second, the "whole Church" also refers to the entire Christian church in an ecumenical sense.

Their one mission of bringing the "whole Gospel to the whole world" necessitates this unity. Thus, at New Delhi and Mexico City, evangelism is understood as bringing the "whole Gospel" of reconciliation by word and deed, to the "whole world" of structures and individuals and to the sociopolitical and religious realm, by the "whole Church," composed of the laity and every Christian denomination.

At New Delhi, the Holy Spirit has a central role in the church's evangelism.[10] An example of the search for new ways of evangelism is the study on congregational structures. This study, commissioned at New Delhi, placed under the auspices of the Department of Studies in Evangelism, and published in the late 1960s, is called, "The Missionary Structure of the Congregation." This study is designed to address the question of whether the congregational structure aids or hinders the congregation's witness to Jesus Christ. "Evangelism" is used only twice in the documents of the working groups, and these two references critique evangelism in its "traditional" form. Traditional evangelism is declared to be proselytism since it is interpreted as "a call on the part of insiders to outsiders inviting them to come into the inside."[11] Whereas traditional evangelism calls people in conversion to leave the world, a new evangelism should call people in conversion into the world where God is actively at work. The world, in this study, is portrayed as a positive place where God is at work, rather than a negative place from which to rescue sinners.[12]

The pattern of relationship between God, the church, and the world is changed from the earlier model of God-Church-World to God-World-Church. The congregational study explains the pattern in these words: "That is, God's primary relationship is to the world, and it is the world and not the Church that is the focus of God's plan."[13]

What then is the role of evangelism in the world? The study does not address the question, but comments from Hans Margull, the WCC secretary for Studies in Evangelism who was responsible for initiating and coordinating this study, are helpful.[14] The role of evangelism, then, is to discern where God is active in the world and to promote God's plan, the *missio Dei*, in the world. "God's plan," however, is not defined in this study, which leaves evangelism with an undefined role. More clearly defined is what evangelism should *not* be; the action of rescuing persons from an evil world. What evangelism is and what it should do remain ambiguous.

In the report of the Uppsala Assembly in 1968, entitled "Renewal in Mission," the idea of the new humanity dominates. The new humanity is the goal of God's mission, and it is also a gift of God that is received by faith. Evangelism is that which enables people to respond to this gift of the new humanity. As the report reads, "Our part in evangelism might be described as bringing about the occasions for men's response to Jesus Christ."[15] When one receives the new humanity offered by God, conversion occurs. As background to conversion in the Uppsala report, there was a WCC study on conversion by Dr. Paul Löffler, completed just prior to the assembly. Several of the highlights of this conversion study are present in the Uppsala report. First, conversion entails a turning to God and a turning away from the old self . . . to form "the nucleus of a new humanity,"[16] which will be both a sign of and a force for society's becoming the new humanity.

In addition, integral to the conversion process is the Holy Spirit. It is the Holy Spirit who is active in the evangelistic process and who brings about conversion. The report states this in these words: "The Holy Spirit offers this gift to men in a variety of moments of decision. It is the Holy Spirit who takes the Word of God and makes it a living, converting word to men."[17] To summarize evangelism in the assemblies and documents of the WCC in the 1960s, it is necessary to point out that "evangelism" appears more in New Delhi and Mexico City than in the study on congregational structures and at Uppsala. Towards the end of this decade, evangelism is rarely addressed directly except for a few scattered references. When the concept of evangelism does appear in these documents, it is obscured under various names. Perhaps if the WCC would address evangelism directly, bring it out from hiding and call it by name, then the WCC could correct the "traditional" connotations of evangelism, which the ecumenical movement tries desperately to avoid.

Where evangelism is discussed, it emerges as a concept that unifies aspects that are often separated. Several examples can be cited. First of all, conversion is not reserved solely for the individual and his/her turning to God *and* to neighbor. Second, evangelism promotes the "whole Gospel," which reconciles individuals as well as structures and the socioeconomic and the religious realms of life. Third, the "whole Gospel" is presented through proclamation and action. Proclamation and action, together, encourage a breadth of evangelistic expression. Bringing together seeming opposites as integral parts of evangelism promotes wholistic evangelism.

BANGKOK

Bangkok, 1973, was the next conference, a meeting of the CWME. "Salvation Today" was the theme of Bangkok, and naturally the topic of salvation pervaded the conference. Salvation is part of evangelism. As the Bangkok document states, "It is our mission—to call men to God's salvation in Jesus Christ."[18] Conversion was again a topic of importance at Bangkok, as it was at Uppsala. However, the Bangkok report on conversion differs substantially from that of Uppsala, which is based on the study done by Paul Löffler. This is apparent in several ways. At Bangkok, no mention is made of a conversion that begins or even includes a turning towards God. Bangkok simply states: "The Christian conversion relates to God and especially to his son Jesus Christ."[19] "Relates" is an ambiguous word at best, but it certainly is not interchangeable with "a turning to," a *metanoein*. Second, Löffler had shown the inseparability of conversion and social action,[20] but he precedes this assertion with these words: "Conversion . . . is a theologically identifiable, independent entity which must be distinguished from the personal and social action which results from it."[21] So Löffler maintains that conversion is an act that can be separated from social action, but, simultaneously, that it cannot be separated and must result in social action. Bangkok did not preserve any sense in which conversion is an act all its own, a "theologically identifiable, independent entity." Therefore, conversion at Bangkok appears more restrictive than it was at Uppsala.

At the Bangkok Assembly, evangelism seems to be understood as proclaiming

God's salvation in Jesus Christ and calling people to salvation. The mission of the local church is expressed in these terms. As the Bangkok document says, "The *local* church in action should be an expression of the impulse of the *whole* church to further the proclamation of the Gospel of Jesus Christ to all the world so that, by responding to him, persons and their situations may be saved."[22] Yet, this statement stands on its own, because, for the most part, evangelism is unexpressed at Bangkok.

NAIROBI

Interest in evangelism since New Delhi and Mexico City had been waning until the Nairobi Assembly in 1975. At Nairobi, evangelism reappears as a crucial task in the report, "Confessing Christ Today." An unavoidable summons to confess Christ is issued in these words: "We do not have the option of keeping the good news to ourselves. The uncommunicated gospel is a patent contradiction."[23] Even a sense of urgency is present; evangelism is to be done *now*.

Evangelism in the Nairobi report is reminiscent of New Delhi and Mexico City with the return to the phrase, "the whole Gospel for the whole world by the whole Church." In its explanation of this phrase, the Nairobi document distinctly and without hesitation brings together evangelism and social action as integral parts of the "whole Gospel." These two are one in the "whole Gospel," according to the Nairobi document.[24] The unity of evangelism and social action should be a part of the Christian life even from the time of conversion. If one or the other is missing, the conversion is void of potential or meaning. In an effort to define the "whole Gospel," the Nairobi document lists every aspect that is included.[25]

Throughout Nairobi's call to confess Christ, the role of the Holy Spirit is highlighted. It is the Holy Spirit who bears witness to Christ. It is the Holy Spirit who prompts the church to evangelize. The centrality of the Holy Spirit in evangelism is similar to that at New Delhi. This resurgence of interest in the Holy Spirit is probably influenced by a document written by a Joint Working Group of Roman Catholic and WCC participants entitled, "Unity and Common Witness." This study was commissioned for the purpose of offering insights to the Nairobi Assembly. One of its contributions to the report, "Confessing Christ Today," centers on the Holy Spirit.[26]

In the 1970s there is a divergence in the two assemblies in their attention to evangelism. At Bangkok evangelism rarely appears, while at Nairobi evangelism emerges as an important and an inclusive entity. Nairobi links evangelism with social action and underscores its wholistic nature with the phrase: "the whole Gospel for the whole world by the whole Church." A statement from Paul Löffler summarizes the WCC approach to evangelism at this point:

> Ecumenical study and action have rediscovered the close links of evangelism to other dimensions of Christian faith and life. They have thereby helped to overcome a narrow concept of evangelism witness while preserving its specific character.[27]

It is true that evangelism's connection with other aspects has been underscored in these assemblies, and evangelism in ecumenical circles is wholistic, not restrictive. Still, it is unclear in what way the WCC has preserved the "specific character" of evangelism. The danger, of course, is that in broadening evangelism to avoid a narrowness, almost anything can be classified as evangelism. This is precisely the fear that Mortimer Arias expressed in his speech at Nairobi.[28]

MELBOURNE

In the report from the Melbourne Assembly of the CWME in 1980 entitled, "The Church Witnesses to the Kingdom," proclamation is given a position of substantial importance. The report commences with this statement about the significance of proclamation:

> The proclamation of the word of God is one such witness, distinct and indispensable. The story of God in Christ is the heart of all evangelism, and this story has to be told, for the life of the present church never fully reveals the love and holiness and power of God in Christ. The telling of the story is an inescapable mandate for the whole church.[29]

Proclamation of the good news is comprised of three parts: 1) the announcement that the kingdom of God is at hand; 2) a challenge to repent; and 3) an invitation to believe. Under the first part, announcing the kingdom of God, the church is commanded to announce the kingdom of God to the poor. Melbourne offers two reasons for the church's evangelization of the poor. First, God's kingdom has a preference for the poor. Jesus exemplifies this preference in his earthly ministry. Today, in this time, the church must announce the preference for the poor. Second, the poor and the poor churches have a decisive role in evangelism. The poor bring to evangelism unique qualities not possessed by other evangelizers.[30] This new dimension of the poor evangelizing has grand potential for world evangelization.[31]

In addition to these three parts, Melbourne mentions two other characteristics of proclamation: it is contextual and it denounces injustices. Proclamation is contextual: it should never be a general, universally applicable message. It is related to the particular context or culture in which it finds itself. Also, proclamation denounces injustices. Denouncing injustices accompanies a contextual proclamation, for injustices vary depending on the context. Proclamation must know the concrete situation and discern the specific wrongs being done in order to be effective. In this way, proclamation is aware, up to date, and trustworthy.

Melbourne continues the emphasis on Jesus Christ as the pattern for evangelism that began at Uppsala. At Melbourne, Jesus Christ is the example for the church, especially for the church's evangelism. Jesus announced the kingdom: the church must do the same. Jesus evangelized the poor, so must the church. Jesus was consistent between word and deed, and the church must follow his example. The example of Jesus is the basis of evangelism.

In 1982, a document was published by the WCC entitled, *Mission and Evangelism: An Ecumenical Affirmation*. The purpose of the study was "to prepare a document containing the basic convictions of the ecumenical movement on the topic of mission and evangelism."[32] Since its publication, this study has found wide acceptance as an important and timely document.

Found in this document are the prominent themes of recent WCC assemblies, with little variance. First of all, the document continues in the Melbourne tradition by giving to the poor an important place in evangelism, both as the evangelized and as the evangelizers. As the evangelized, the poor are primary beneficiaries. As evangelizers, they are primary doers. This document goes beyond Melbourne by stating that announcing the good news to the poor requires simultaneously working to make the good news a reality in the lives of the poor. When the church labors on behalf of the good news for the poor, the poor will see the good news becoming a reality, as well as hear it being proclaimed. Proclamation and action, together, are essential in evangelism.

Second, this affirmation on mission and evangelism testifies to the unity of evangelism and social action, a familiar theme in ecumenical documents. And, third, conversion is another common theme, frequently discussed. In this study, the interest in conversion, unlike in other documents, is primarily in personal conversion. In one paragraph alone, ten references to the individual's conversion are found. The last sentence in that paragraph reads: "While anonymity and marginalization seem to reduce the possibilities for personal decisions to a minimum, God knows each person and calls each one to make a fundamental personal act of allegiance to God and to God's kingdom in the fellowship of God's people."[33] Of course, the corporate aspect of conversion is also present; however, personal conversion is encouraged in an uncharacteristically forthright manner.

In these three themes, the document is reminiscent of other assemblies, especially Melbourne and Nairobi. However, a "new" idea is present, one revived from yesteryear. This study includes planting churches as a foundational part of the church's mission.[34] Unfortunately, this study, in its discussion of mission and evangelism, does not clarify their relationship. Philip Potter's exhortation of twenty years ago to do just this remains unheeded. In another contemporary document, a Roman Catholic study entitled, "Memorandum From a Consultation on Mission," a brief yet important explanation of mission and evangelism is written in these words:

> *Mission, evangelization and witness* are nowadays often used by Catholics as synonymous. Though each of these terms has its own history and special meaning they are all used to designate in a comprehensive way the one complex mission of the Church.[35]

Such a procedure in the WCC document on mission and evangelism would have clarified this question of several decades.

VANCOUVER

The fifth WCC assembly took place in Vancouver in 1983. Its report, "Witnessing in a Divided World," deals with issues related to evangelism.

Towards the end of the document, witnessing is defined as

those acts and words by which a Christian or community gives testimony to Christ and invites others to make their response to him. In witness we expect to share the good news of Jesus and be challenged in relation to our understanding of, and our obedience to, that good news.[36]

Witness hopes for a response to its message. The document continues by addressing the relationship between witness and dialogue, another dilemma needing to be solved. Dialogue is then defined as:

that encounter where people holding different claims about ultimate reality can meet and explore these claims in a context of mutual respect. From dialogue we expect to discern more about how God is active in the world, and to appreciate for their own sake the insights and experiences people of other faiths have of ultimate reality.[37]

Putting dialogue alongside witness underscores their deviation in motive. Witness "invites" a response to the good news; dialogue is not interested in a response. Dialogue is merely an opportunity for learning and exploring, whereas witnessing speaks of Jesus Christ. With these varying goals, dialogue and witness appear to be opposed to each other; yet, the Vancouver report maintains their interrelatedness. Are dialogue and witness related to each other or in opposition to each other? Again, there is a confusion in terms. One hopes that the WCC will face this challenge in the proposed future study on the relationship between witness and dialogue.

Vancouver does not contribute anything new to the WCC discussion of evangelism. Even its presentation seems weak and diffuse. Perhaps this can be explained by the prior publication of the study on mission and evangelism, which left Vancouver with nothing more to say.[38] Or perhaps, as is most likely, it can be explained by the fact that the document was rushed through with a hasty approval at the end of the assembly.[39]

SAN ANTONIO

The 1982 WCC statement, *Mission and Evangelism* (ME), and section I of the San Antonio report are salutary indications of a shift in the locus of evangelism in the WCC. In these documents, evangelism finds its home in ecclesiology and, in particular, at the very center of the church's life—worship.

This integration of evangelism into ecclesiology did not characterize former documents of the WCC. In a study entitled, "The Missionary Structure of the Congregation," published in the late 1960s by the Department of Studies in Evangelism, evangelism was centered in the world, not the church. This study contended that the church mistakenly understood itself as being at odds with the world, and mistakenly understood evangelism as its way of rescuing people out of the world and bringing them to safety within its walls.[40] In order to change the church's perception of the world, the study presented the world as a positive place where God was primarily at work. In other words, "God's primary relationship is to the world, and it is the world and not the Church, that is the focus of God's plan."[41] The role of evangelism, then, was to discover and become involved at the very place where God's plan, *missio Dei*, was being implemented in the world. This study relocated evangelism within the context of the formula, GOD–WORLD–CHURCH, from the church to the world.

Subsequent assemblies reflected relatively little on the relationship between ecclesiology and evangelism. A few scattered references, nevertheless, did fore-shadow the relationship between ecclesiology and evangelism that would later characterize ME and San Antonio—for example, in the Nairobi document.[42] A similar statement appeared in the Melbourne document in 1980: "The whole life of the Church is oriented towards this witness in its total sacramental life—in prayer, proclamation, service and liturgy."[43] These statements were not developed; they were rather intimations of a shift soon to occur.

These intimations are fully developed into affirmation in ME and section 1 of the San Antonio report where evangelism becomes firmly rooted in ecclesiology. The church is the Body of Christ and as such shares "in the ministry of Christ as Mediator between God and His Creation" (ME 6). Its mediation is two-way: from God to the world and from the world to God. On the one hand, the church makes known God's love to the world. In fact, it is God's love that provides the motivation, the "urgency to share the gospel incitingly in our time . . . " (SA I:7). On the other hand, the church in solidarity with the world offers up the world's pain and suffering to God in the context of its worship, specifically in intercessory prayer and the eucharist (ME 6).

This ecclesiological emphasis on the church's mediatorial ministry renders inadequate the previous formula, GOD–WORLD–CHURCH. The church now is called to live between God and the world. Therefore, I suggest that the ecclesiological formula for ME and San Antonio should be, GOD–CHURCH–WORLD. This ecclesiological shift has two profound implications for evangelism. First, the church is the primary evangelist: "The church [is] God's chosen instrument for proclaiming the good news of the reign of God . . . "(SA I:33, see also ME 6). The church's role in evangelism is to proclaim the good news of the crucified and risen Jesus. "It is this Jesus that the Church proclaims as the very life of the world because on the cross he gave his own life for all that all may live. . . . Evangelism calls people to look towards that Jesus and commit their life to him . . . " (ME 8). The ME document highlights the invitation to respond to the proclamation in a personal way through conversion (ME 10,11). The San Antonio document lacks a corresponding emphasis on the personal dimension of evangelism perhaps because its call to repentance is solely focused on "those who are involved in this mission," rather than those to whom the gospel is proclaimed as in ME (SA I:6).

Second, integral to evangelism is the church's nurture of those who respond to the proclamation. The church nurtures the evangelized through worship, celebration of the sacraments, education, prayer, and Bible study. Thus, evangelism is intimately related to these other activities of the church. "Christian communication does not end with the proclamation of the message, but continues in an unending process directed to the education and formation of persons in the Christian life, helping them to grasp more deeply and to enter more fully into the Christian story" (SA I:35; see also ME 6, 21, 47).

The church must maintain a balance between these two dimensions of primary evangelist and nurturing community. As evangelist, it must continue to cross frontiers to proclaim the gospel to those who have not yet heard or not yet responded. In this way, evangelism brings persons into the nurturing worship of the church that is, itself, a witness to the good news of the gospel. As nurturing community, its worship encourages persons to evangelize and transform individuals and society. Thus, the church is exhorted to "hold together this witness of the worshipping and serving community united in love, with that of its evangelistic task of sending persons to proclaim the word to those who have not yet heard or realized its fulfilling and saving grace" (SA I:33). Raymond Fung, in a 1989 *Monthly Letter*, confirms the perspective of ME and San Antonio as an ecclesial evangelism when he outlines the WCC's approach to global evangelism.[44]

In addition to this ecclesiological shift, another observation about evangelism at the San Antonio conference needs to be noted. Whether knowingly or not, San Antonio focuses on God's love as the motivation for evangelism and thus complements the past emphasis on Jesus as the example of evangelism. Now evangelism has both as motivation and example. Beginning at Uppsala, the WCC documents lifted up Jesus as the example for evangelism. This was most evident at the Melbourne Assembly.[45]

The San Antonio report complements the pattern of Jesus with an exploration of the motivation for evangelism. Evangelism is done simply because of God's unconditional love for humanity and the world. "The love of God for the world is the source for our missionary motivation. This love creates an urgency to share the gospel incitingly in our time" (SA I:7). And the "source and sustained" of the church's proclamation is the Triune God (SA I:1). Thus, the example of Jesus for evangelism is set within a Trinitarian framework.[46] From these observations, evangelism would seem to be a central issue at San Antonio. Indeed, Raymond Fung enthusiastically endorses the attention that San Antonio gives to evangelism when he writes:

A psychological barrier has been broken through—the feeling that in WCC circles and meetings, one simply does not talk the language of evangelism, or that one does it only at the risk of confrontation, and that even if one does talk about it, one should so load it with qualifications, ("balance" is the ecumenical word), that it no longer soars. That barrier has been broken through.[47]

Section I of the report is the only one of four sections that takes evangelism seriously. The word "evangelism" appears only three times in the remaining three sections. Its absence from other sections is disconcerting because the impact is to isolate evangelism from the other sections' issues, such as justice, stewardship, and participation in struggles. Then, in two of the instances where the term is used, evangelism is viewed through the negative effects of cultural imperialism (SA

II:16) and colonialism (SA IV:5). This juxtaposition further caricatures evangelism as having little positive to contribute. However, the established ecclesiological foundation for evangelism has the potential to bring evangelism into relationship with other sections of the church as it works for justice, as it cares for the earth, and as it participates with those who are struggling for life. This potential for a wholistic, ecclesial evangelism needs to be explored.

CANBERRA

Writing in 1989, Raymond Fung anticipates that Canberra "will also witness the breaking of the psychological barrier."[48] His expectation is based on Canberra's preparatory material, *Resources for Sections*, particularly section II, issue 1, "The challenge to be free in order to struggle." He includes all the preparatory material on this issue in *A Monthly Letter on Evangelism*, and instructs his readers that this is "the assigned location for the discussion on evangelism . . . So if you wish to major in evangelism at the assembly, you want to be part of section II, issue 1."[49]

Fung's expectation is well founded because all the elements for a wholistic evangelism are present in the preparatory material. The paragraphs devoted to this issue discuss topics related to evangelism, including personal conversion, liberation, inner freedom, transformation of history, and the church's "evangelistic vocation."[50]

There is, however, a striking discrepancy between the preparatory material for section II, issue 1, and the Canberra report, which does not, in fact, "major" in evangelism. The only possible reference to evangelism occurs in the first sentence: "Both as individuals and as churches we have often forgotten our communal vocation and task to render an authentic witness to the gospel."[51] Evangelism is absent from the rest of the section and from the six recommendations that follow the section. These recommendations call for action on spirituality, a laity department, communities of justice, and the gifts of the differently-abled, but not evangelism.

This absence on the subject of evangelism continues throughout the entire final report. Discussions and references to evangelism are difficult to locate. The word itself occurs three times throughout the four sections. On two of those occasions, the term "evangelism" is followed immediately by a reference to the word "proselytism." This juxtaposition suggests a purposeful caution attached to the concept of evangelism lest it become too pronounced, or to ensure that it remains "balanced." Like sections II, III and IV of the San Antonio document, the Canberra report implies that what intrigues the WCC are the negative effects of evangelism.

The most positive reference to evangelism appears in section IV, where evangelism is set in the context of the church's worship, which reflects the ecclesiological foundation of ME and section I of the San Antonio document. One sentence brings together evangelism and other activities of the church into the context of worship: "Worship in its richness has a variety of dimensions and implications: it relates to evangelism, spirituality, social justice, human values, integrity of creation, unity and peace, even as it celebrates salvation."[52]

Along with the absence of evangelism in section II, issue 1, another discrepancy between the preparatory material and the Canberra report is the discussion of the inner freedom, or personal liberation, brought about by evangelism. In *Resources for Sections*, evangelism and liberation are set alongside each other as complementary rather than mutually exclusive entities. On the one hand, the inner freedom that evangelism awakens provides "the right motivation" and encourages involvement "in concrete struggles to transform history in the perspective of the kingdom of God." On the other hand, the commitment to work for liberation is the "test of the reality of our inner freedom in Jesus Christ."[53] In this way, personal liberation, awakened by evangelism, leads to actions that transform the world to reflect God's reign. Although the preparatory material lifts up evangelism and personal liberation, the Canberra document presents this personal experience in a negative context. The report cites the "exclusively internal and personal experience" of the Holy Spirit as the reason why witnessing to the gospel is forgotten.[54] There is no suggestion that inner freedom and social liberation can enhance each other.

This last discrepancy is tempered somewhat by the "theological perspective," which precedes issue 1 of section II in the Canberra document. This theological statement avers that freedom does encompass the personal and the communal. Interestingly, though, it assumes that personal freedom will of necessity be "individualistic, 'spiritual,' other-worldly freedom."[55] What is lacking is the wholistic outlook of the preparatory material, which states that inner freedom is the "right motivation" for involvement in the liberation of society and the whole creation.[56] In addition, the theological perspective, which includes the individual's inner freedom, is not integrated into issue 1, with the result that there is a split between theology and practice.

From these observations, I would suggest that, with respect to evangelism, Canberra took one step forward and two steps backward, while San Antonio took two steps forward and one step backward. The momentum for evangelism leading up to Canberra, produced by section I of the San Antonio report and the preparatory material for Canberra, moved evangelism forward a step. Expectations were raised that Canberra would move even further forward to dismantle the WCC's "psychological barrier" about evangelism. Instead, the references to evangelism are not substantial enough to warrant much comment, except that a few appear in contexts that caution against its potential negative effects. This is reminiscent of evangelism in the 1960s, in the study on "The Missionary Structure of the Congregation," in which evangelism is mentioned only to be criticized as being proselytism.[57]

In San Antonio, evangelism took two steps forward into an integral relationship with ecclesiology. The document unequivocally lifted up the church as the primary evangelist. In addition, the document cited evangelism and the church's nurture through education, worship, prayer, and celebration of the sacraments as mutually inspirational activities. Still, the WCC took a step backward at San Antonio by isolating evangelism from other ecumenical issues.

Perhaps the WCC will, in future conferences, strengthen its "evangelism agenda" by following the recommendation of the Stuttgart Consultation on Evangelism in 1987. This consultation specifically advised the WCC to "stimulate theological reflection on the nature of evangelism and its relationship to the nature of the church."[58] Such reflection would advance significantly the ecclesiological foundation for evangelism initiated by the *Mission and Evangelism: An Ecumenical Affirmation* and San Antonio documents.

REFERENCES

1. Because of the historical importance of the integration of the International Missionary Council into the World Council of Churches in 1961, this survey begins with the New Delhi Assembly where this occurred.

2. Orlando Costas, *The Church and Its Mission: A Shattering Critique from the Third World*. Wheaton, Illinois: Tyndale House Publishers, Inc., 1974, p. 267.

3. Philip Potter, "Evangelism and the World Council of Churches," in *The Ecumenical Review* 20 (April 1968), p. 176.

4. *Ibid.*

5. *Ibid.*

6. *Ibid.*

7. Martin Lehmann-Habeck affirms the thesis that the WCC presents a wholistic evangelism in an article entitled, "Wholistic Evangelism: A WCC Perspective," in *International Review of Mission*, vol. LXXIII, no. 289 (January 1984), pp. 7–16. His article approaches the subject from a different vantage point to this present one, and uses a different methodology. His vantage point is primarily theological. He cites and explains several theological concepts of wholistic evangelism, such as: conversion, the pattern of Jesus, the vocation of the church, and evangelism as the good news to the poor. His methodology is to investigate these aspects of wholistic evangelism within their historical context in the WCC. This present study bases its findings on the documents themselves whose contents are analyzed and set in chronological order. Despite varying purposes and methodologies, it is important to note that both studies come to a similar conclusion about evangelism in the WCC.

8. W. A. Visser't Hooft, ed., *The New Delhi Report*, The Third Assembly of the World Council of Churches, 1961. New York: Association Press, 1962, p. 85.

9. *Ibid.*, p. 86

10. *Ibid.*, p. 78.

11. Department on Studies in Evangelism, *The Church for Others*. Final Report on a Quest for Structures for Missionary Congregations by the Western European Working Group and North American Working Group. Geneva: World Council of Churches, 1968, p. 76.

12. Thomas Wieser, ed., *Planning for Mission*. Working Papers on the New Quest for Missionary Communities. New York: The U.S. Conference for the World Council of Churches, 1966, p. 9.

13. Department on Studies in Evangelism, *op. cit.*, pp. 16–17.

14. Hans J. Margull, *Hope in Action: The Church's Task in the World*, trans. Eugene Peters. Philadelphia: Muhlenberg Press, 1962, p. xi. Margull defines evangelism in this way: "Evangelism as 'expectant evangelism' is solely participation in the activity of God with a view to his great deed at the end." Also, p. xx.

15. Norman Goodall, ed. *The Uppsala Report 1968*. Geneva: World Council of Churches, 1968, p. 28.

16. World Council of Churches, *Drafts for Sections*, prepared for the Fourth Assembly of the World Council of Churches, Uppsala, Sweden, 1968. Geneva: World Council of Churches, p. 36.

17. Goodall, *op. cit.*, p. 28.

18. World Council of Churches, *Bangkok Assembly 1973*, Minutes and Report of the Assembly of the Commission on World Mission and Evangelism of the World Council of Churches, 31 December 1972 and 9-12 January 1973. Geneva: World Council of Churches, 1973, p. 99.

19. *Ibid.*, p. 76.

20. There is, therefore, on the other hand, absolutely no dichotomy between "conversion" and its realization in social action.... There exists a constant interrelation, which reveals the underlying unity of God's purpose for the world and the church." Paul Löffler, "The Biblical Concept of Conversion," in *Study Encounter*, 1 (No. 2, 1965), p. 99.

21. *Ibid.*

22. World Council of Churches, *Bangkok Assembly 1973*, p. 99.

23. David M. Paton, ed., *Breaking Barriers, Nairobi 1975*. The Official Report of the Fifth Assembly of the World Council of Churches, Nairobi, 23 November–10 December 1975. Grand Rapids: Wm. B. Eerdmans, 1975, p. 52.

24. Paton, *op. cit.*, p. 44.

25. *Ibid.*, p. 52.

26. Joint Working Group between the Roman Catholic Church and the WCC, "Unity and Common Witness," in *Study Encounter*, no. 3 (1975), p. 1.

27. Paul Löffler, "The Confessing Community. Evangelism in Ecumenical Perspective," in *International Review of Mission*, vol. LXVI, no. 264 (October 1977), p. 341.

28. Mortimer Arias, "Contextualization in Evangelism: Towards an Incarnational Style," in *Perkins Journal* 32 (Winter 1979), p. 16.

29. World Council of Churches, *Your Kingdom Come*, Mission Perspectives. Report on the World Conference on Mission and Evangelism. Melbourne, Australia, 12–25 May 1980. Geneva: World Council of Churches, 1980, p. 193.

30. *Ibid.*, p. 219.

31. *Ibid.*, p. 219.

32. Emilio Castro, "Editorial," *International Review of Mission*, vol. LXXI, no. 284 (October 1982), p. 421.

33. Jean Stromberg, ed., *Mission and Evangelism: An Ecumenical Affirmation*. A Study Guide for Congregations, USA: Division of Overseas Ministries, National Council of the Churches of Christ in the USA, 1983, p. 18.

34. *Ibid.*, p. 28.

35. Secretariat for Promoting Christian Unity, "Memorandum From a Consultation on Mission," in *International Review of Mission*, vol. LXXI, no. 284 (October 1982), p. 460.

36. David Gill, ed., *Gathered for Life*, Official Report of the Sixth Assembly of the World Council of Churches, Vancouver, Canada, 24 July-10 August 1983. Grand Rapids: Wm. B. Eerdmans, 1983, p. 40.

37. *Ibid.*

38. There is a striking absence of references to that study: it is mentioned only once and at the very end of the report under "Recommendations to member churches." In contrast, the study, *Baptism, Eucharist and Ministry*, receives attention throughout the report on unity. This lack of input from the study on mission and evangelism was a criticism made by assembly participants. See *Ibid.*, p. 31.

39. *Ibid.*, p. 31.

40. Thomas Wieser, ed., *Planning for Mission*, p. 9.

41. Department of Studies in Evangelism, *The Church for Others*. Final Report on a Quest for Structures for Missionary Congregations by the Western European Working Group and North American Working Group. Geneva: WCC, 1968, p. 75.

42. David Paton, ed., *Breaking Barriers, Nairobi 1975*, p. 53.

43. World Council of Churches, *Your Kingdom Come*, p. 198.

44. Fung, *Monthly Letter* 10/11 (Oct./Nov. 1989), p. 1.

45. See p. 131 above.

46. See Norman Thomas, "Ecumenical Directions in Evangelism: Melbourne to San Antonio," in *Journal of the Academy for Evangelism in Theological Education* 5 (1989-1990), p. 55.

47. Fung, *Monthly Letter* 6/7 (June/July 1989), p. 6.

48. *Ibid.*, p. 5.

49. Fung, *Monthly Letter*, 9/10/11 (Sept./Oct./Nov. 1990), pp. 1, 4.

50. World Council of Churches Seventh Assembly 1991, *Resources for Sections: The Theme, Subthemes and Issues*, Geneva: WCC, 1990, p. 29.

51. Michael Kinnamon, ed., *Signs of the Spirit*, Official Report Seventh Assembly, Canberra, Australia, 7–20 February 1991. Grand Rapids, Eerdmans, 1991, p. 74.

52. *Ibid.*, p. 120.

53. WCC, *Resources for Sections*, p. 29.

54. WCC, *Signs of the Spirit*, p. 74.

55. *Ibid.*, p. 73.

56. WCC, *Resources for Sections*, p. 29.

57. See Department of Studies on Evangelism, *The Church for Others*, p. 75.

58. "Statement of Stuttgart Consultation on Evangelism," in Fung, *Monthly Letter* 10/11 (Oct./Nov. 1987), p. 9.

Part III

MISSIONARY PRAXIS

12

Missionary Myth Making

Anthony J. Gittins *

*Theological foundations for mission can take the form of a largely uncon-
scious web of meanings that make up what Anthony Gittins calls a "missionary myth" (in the positive sense of the word myth). As Gittins sees the issue,
Roman Catholic missionaries before Vatican Council II took their identity
from just such a myth. In it, they were instruments of God, whose faithfulness
to the Great Commission enabled them to bear the burdens of missionary life
for the sake of the Gospel. Because of the social and theological transformations of the 20th century, however, that myth has come unraveled. Along with
this, numbers of missionary personnel and the intensity of their esprit de
corps have decreased. Gittins points to movements and ideas that can become
the stuff of a new missionary myth, one that can serve as a foundation for
missionary activity in a new world.*

In this paper, rather than isolating the putative shortcomings of the past and
contrasting them unfavorably with the putative strengths of the present, so as to
create a false sense of security and purpose, I will examine the self-image of
19th-century missionaries and compare it with the self-image that seems characteristic of today's missionaries, and then make a diagnosis of certain conditions
and hazard a prognosis for the healthy future of mission. I will speak particularly
of Roman Catholic missionary experience, and with explicit reference to Sierra
Leone, West Africa, though comparisons with other places—and with both Roman
Catholic and other perspectives—can be made by the reader.

BUILDING THE PAST: MISSIONARY MYTHOLOGY

There were three striking convictions in the lives of 19th-century missionaries.
In the first place, they were sure that they were instruments of God, chosen to bring

* Taken from *Verbum SVD* 27 (No. 2, 1986), pp. 185–211, abridged and reprinted with permission of
the publisher. Anthony J. Gittins, CSSP, is an anthropologist and has served as a missionary in Sierra
Leone. Professor of Theological Anthropology at Catholic Theological Union, Chicago, Father Gittins
lives and works among the homeless on that city's north side. Among his books are *Gifts and Strangers*
(Paulist, 1989) and *Bread for the Journey: The Mission of Transformation and the Transformation of
Mission* (Orbis 1993).

all people to acknowledge God the Trinity by embracing Christianity (as modelled, naturally, by the denominational faith and practice of the missionary). Second, knowing that carrying the Gospel to "pagan lands" was a hazardous undertaking, they were prepared for the ultimate sacrifice of their lives. With these twin convictions about the nature of their lives—that they had received a Divine mandate and that they had to be ready for death—was associated a third, about the purpose of those lives. This was that their personal fidelity to the missionary undertaking, specifically through the priesthood or some form of Religious Life or community living, was their response to the Great Commission (Mt 28:19–20) and could not be other than permanent; the fruits of this fidelity were the widespread planting of the (Catholic) Church and the individual salvation of the missionary. Since the attainment of eternal life was the explicit aim, through personal sanctification, of the Christian, and *a fortiori* of the dedicated missionary, and since altruism, evangelization, and martyrdom were the classical means to that end, missionary endeavors provided a lifestyle, the epitome of Christian living and the effective guarantee of salvation to the humble and persevering missionary. This kind of thinking and especially the fundamental convictions outlined, were the weft and warp out of which was woven or created what I call the "missionary myth."

Though missionaries implicitly believed that ultimately their work could not fail since it was inspired by God and commissioned by Christ, nevertheless the early history of 19th-century mission—and this penetrated well into the present century—was characterized by reversals, difficulties, opposition, tribulations of all sorts, and the hardest of all burdens to bear, premature or accidental death. If death seemed to stalk everyone and pick off most, the enterprise itself was bound to suffer, and so it became necessary for the missionaries to be able to accommodate apparent inconsistencies and paradoxes—such as, on the one hand a loving, caring God, and, on the other, a missionary "defeat" at the hands of a pagan or Muslim leader, or again, the early, gratuitous deaths of some missionaries and the long lingering of others, years after their "useful" life was over—without becoming disillusioned or neurotic.

The more missionaries were united as a community or group with a strong moral identity and common symbols, the more they would be able to be a sign to others of hope and salvation. And not only did other people need a beacon, the esprit de corps was vital to the missionary enterprise, and this itself necessitated the present perseverance of individuals and the future recruitment of replacements. Standardization and conformity were deemed necessary, and indeed the whole of the long resocialization process which prospective missionaries experienced in the seminary or religious community was adapted to this end. Heroes were eulogized, battles were refought, victories were celebrated, and defeats rationalized, so that missionaries became bonded in a common quest. Prayer and preparation were the ingredients of mission, but they were mixed in laboratory conditions; conformity was extolled as necessary for the undertaking, and if individualism suffered, the evangelizing machine, like an army, was trained to the optimum through the common life and common discipline. Individual differences and social distinctions were levelled out and the vow of obedience was invoked by authority and undertaken by individuals, as particularly conducive to facilitating God's will for the unevangelized.

In the course of seven years or more of preparatory training, missionaries came to share many fundamental viewpoints, attitudes, and beliefs not only about theology and faith, but about the psychology and philosophy of vocations. Not surprisingly, given this long period of "basic" and a lifetime of "in-service" training, patterns, and traditions, a rationale developed among missionaries, serving both to create boundaries and frontiers around their experience, and walls or categories within it. Life's challenges could be and were met by the offensive and defensive armaments which missionaries could thus deploy. Tradition might be invoked for an appropriate response; *ad hoc* solutions would sometimes be required. But the rationale would be actively invoked and articulated to defend and sustain positions and personnel. This activity, in its many forms, is what I call "missionary myth-making," and the rationale itself is the "missionary myth."

THE MISSIONARY MYTH

"Myth" is used here, not in a technical—anthropological or folklorist—sense (though I do not exclude elements of understanding from both these fields), but rather as a portmanteau term embracing the explanations, projections, and rationalizations shared by missionaries explicitly or implicitly, and serving to bind them together as a unitary group with common work, aims, and understanding. By reference to this orally transmitted, informal charter-for-action-and-reflection, missionaries were bonded, sustained, and filled with hope, in frequently hopeless situations.

Second, during the period of assimilation into the world of the "real missionary," one was also very effectively assimilated into the mentality of the missionary myth. After a couple of months the process was complete—and on the rare occasions where it was not, the newly arrived became the newly departed; solidarity was crucial, and nonconformity was simply intolerable.

The missionary myth can thus be understood as the web of relevancies which, largely unconsciously, missionaries wove around themselves and each other, and within which they survived and grew, despite and sometimes because of other worlds of meaning or patterns of relevance which abutted or threatened theirs. Through the myth-making process, missionaries could be sustained in a world of unfairness and rivalry, often amid blatant contradictions and even scandal, and emerge simon-pure and refreshed after skirmishes or setbacks which would have daunted the boldest explorers or soldiers of fortune. What to outsiders might have appeared futile, illogical, or indefensible, was, when referred to the missionary myth with its characteristic logic and theology of Providence and patience, found to be tolerable and often to carry the potential for growth. What to many people would have been regarded as insufferable, discouraging, or just plain stupid, could, by application of the spirit of faith engendered by the missionary myth, be not only accepted but embraced. In fact the missionary myth functioned as a transformer or filter, through which an input (perceived inequities, and so on) could be purified and refined, so as to issue in an enriched and enriching output, a wisdom hidden from the wise and available only to the childlike (Lk 10:21).

The missionary myth—or whatever one calls it—was current and vibrant in real situations and in real people's lives; that is a matter of historical record and of personal experience. In fact the missionary myth was, we may say, a social fact. It should be possible, therefore, by examining the historical context in which the missionary myth flourished, and comparing it with a situation in which it does not, to determine the optimum conditions for its growth. When the conditions change, then presumably the missionary myth will tend to attenuate. And then one will at least know whether a rediscovery of the missionary myth is desirable, and if so, possible. Under the next three sections, we will see some of the conditions under which the myth was palpably thriving; later we will shift the focus and see what has changed.

A View of the Church, Then

The world beyond one's immediate horizons was, in the middle of the last century, very different from the way it appears now. Even within Europe there were national and linguistic barriers, and historical rivalries, all of which facilitated cultural and religious isolationism. Beyond Europe was largely unknown, assumed to be inferior, and known to be dangerous. Social evolutionism would soon become the secular creed, and conveniently overlook many "high civilizations" and cultures beyond Europe and before the 19th century. There had, of course, been missionary endeavors before, and all continents had been reached, but there remained enormous tracts, isolated and otherwise dangerous places, where the Gospel had not been preached and the Church had not taken root.

Fevers and other sicknesses thus abounded, and poor diet was often standard. Against this kind of background the 19th-century missionary movement undertook the ground-breaking work of evangelization, braving hostile climates, unknown languages, and the removal of many comfortable points of reference. As long as the missionary myth provided answers to the many problems, as long as communication between missionaries provided adequate support in distress and reversal, and as long as the missionary myth was not breached or undermined from without, the enterprise was assured, and in fact the myth became an unremarkable fact or part of life, rather like breathing, or air. It might take an unconscionably long time for the Church to be planted and for the harvest to grow; it might be tedious and bloody to pry "superstitious" hands from "idolatrous" practices; it might take generations for the "one true Church" to be brought to the benighted pagans who had little morality and less religion—but it would, it was steadfastly believed, be done, because it had to be done. Quite simply, God wanted all people to be saved, and that meant baptized and incorporated into the Church. Though the laborers were few, the harvest was great, and God would give the increase and extend the Church throughout the world, through the instrumentality of missionaries.

A View of the Community, Then

To emphasize the importance of missionary *esprit de corps* is not to deny the reality of missionary self-consciousness and individuality. Personalistic answers and explanations ("why me?") are demanded by each of us at some time in our lives and the missionary is not exempt. So, particularly when one's companions died or one suffered personal tragedy or bereavement, an explanation was sought and mere statistics or etiological explanations—in terms of which origins or causes were assigned—were deemed insufficient; teleological explanations—in terms of which the purposefulness of events in relation to a (Divine) plan was specified—were also required. While some missionaries died almost as soon as they arrived and others lived and prospered for half a century, it was necessary to be able to reconcile these facts with a loving God who loved *all* missionaries and commissioned them to be "fishers of men." If one could accept the dictum that "Man proposes, God disposes," acknowledge that the missionary was an instrument whose effectiveness was a function, not of longevity nor of intelligence but of dedication and holiness, and live with the fact that God's ways are mysterious; and further, if one acknowledged that "the blood of martyrs is the seed of the Church," that God alone gives the increase, and that the missionary should not worry about the morrow (Lk 12:22–32), but live in faith and trust (Lk 17:10), then, whether one lived or died was acceptable and accepted as compatible with a loving God and a personal salvation.

Yet equally clearly, it was not easy, having perhaps waited for years for new personnel, freshly trained over long years, to see them arrive, healthy and highly motivated, and meet at their funeral only weeks or months later. Yet the missionary myth could bear this enormous weight, for if the individual was thereby liberated for heaven, then the community could only bow to what was seen as God's will for the deceased; the survivors prayed for courage and strength. Situations in which death was a real possibility, though different for the community of survivors, could nevertheless be apprehended by faith-filled disciples as potentially good and therefore even desirable. Just as to die in the cause of the good is happiness, so to live out of self-interest is to the missionary a betrayal of one's vocation and destiny. Death itself thus became a preferential option.

The missionary myth, as can be seen, was flexible yet tough; it could be referred to as a court of appeal, and it could be invoked to calm fears, and through it a wide variety of missionary undertakings could be welded into one. So long as the principles of the primacy of the apostolate and the legitimacy of the authority of duly constituted superiors were upheld, even relatively disparate lifestyles could be seen as unifying rather than as isolating the personnel. A missionary, settled into an administrative or teaching post thousands of miles from the "front line," could still feel very much part of a team, since fidelity to an uncongenial job through "holy obedience" freed others for more active "front line" duty. Similarly a person actually stationed, say, in Africa, building churches and schools, could feel fulfilled as a missionary, even though never having trekked from village to village or having explicitly preached the gospel. The missionary myth supported this pluriformity of work, and insofar as individualism was subordinated to the common good and accepted as such by both the individual and the person charged with discerning that good, then a situation obtained, relative to which one can identify and speak of "missionary ideas" or "missionary policy" or even "missionary work" in a unitary way. Missionary endeavor, in such a climate, was unstoppable.

Martyrs and Others, Then

From the earliest days of Christianity, when the faithful accepted implicitly that it was simply impossible for a true believer to deny Jesus, martyrdom has been the epitome of heroism. Through the kind of adversity that would have demoralized and destroyed armies, the Christian community grew from the earliest years, with indefectible faith in the risen Lord, and convinced that the gates of Hell would not prevail. Missionaries throughout the 19th century and halfway through the 20th may be said to have been at one with the early Christians in their commitment to what Victor Turner, in a sociological analysis, has called the Christian "root-paradigm of martyrdom," the commitment to "underlining the ultimate value of a cause by laying down one's life for them" (*Dramas, Fields and Metaphors*, Ithaca, NY: Cornell University Press, 1974, p. 69 and chapter 2). This theme is worth pursuing for its own merits, but I want to note here that "laying down one's life" need not only be a single, dramatic gesture. Sometimes a willing martyr may find no one willing to bring about that blessed condition; certainly for every massacred missionary there were dozens—hundreds—left behind. Martyrdom, then, may have many faces, at least from the perspective of the recipient.

That the missionary enterprise was sustained by what I call the "missionary myth-making process" seems palpably clear, but just as the myth was capable of reconciling or at least tolerating apparent opposites or paradoxes, so it seems it was responsible for the kind of rationalizing by missionaries, which may have led to some apparently gratuitous deaths. Self-denial was a "little death," very acceptable to Christian piety, and extreme self-denial—a fruit of an essentially pessimistic and neo-Manichaean spirituality which saw the world as a "vale of tears" and people as "poor banished children of Eve"—might lead, indirectly and heroically, to death. As the cowardly suicide surrenders to death, so the heroic martyr embraces it; the believing community would adjudicate on the demise of a missionary as much closer to martyrdom than to suicide; in fact the latter was simply not considered. Certainly missionaries aspired at least to die "on the missions" and to be buried there, as a sign that even if they had not literally shed their blood, nevertheless they had "given their life" to the Apostolate, for the future success of the Mission.

When missionaries were actually killed, it was rarely on direct account of the faith they professed, and more likely to have been because they were a nuisance or a negotiable asset to their killers, as, for example, during the Hut Tax War of 1898 in Sierra Leone, in which several missionary families were killed, probably because, like the government, they were British or perceived as British because white skinned (even though actually North American), and also because mob rule does not conform to cold logic. Nevertheless, not only did the missionary myth facilitate the near apotheosis of those killed, but other missionaries too, accepted the appropriateness of the designation "martyr," both in their panegyrics and thence in their folklore. Further, the positive connotation of the word "martyr" may arguably have eased the period of transition and bereavement, and helped cement ruptured relationships through appeal to a sense of community pride.

Missionaries whose death could be directly linked to the environment (and even some who did not qualify) were buried to the emotive language of martyrdom, receiving respect and status, ascribed rather than acquired; those left behind kindled their common idealism in the fires of the deceased person's zeal, and the work went on. But even though such deaths could be explained as related to the environment, I would like to suggest that the missionary myth-making process and the temperament of some missionaries might have subtly encouraged another form of self-actualization: carelessness or recklessness about personal safety or hygiene, which slowly and not surprisingly led to a death which could be described as not entirely unexpected and even to some degree willed by the missionary.

Do we have here a *prima facie* case for arguing that some of the early deaths in missionary circles were at least preventable? I think we do, and simply quote here a remarkable letter from as early as 1827, written by one outside the missionary ethos but one who was certainly very perceptive. K. Macaulay, Acting Governor of the Colony of Sierra Leone, writing long before Catholic missionaries worked there permanently, but speaking generally, said:

> I cannot help attributing much of the more recent mortality among missionaries in the first two years of their residence in the Colony, to a morbid state of mind. Other men go out filled with the hope of realizing a little property and returning home; that occupies their thoughts; sickness is never found until it comes; and then the natural buoyancy of youth and the ardent expectation of the individual do more towards recovery than all the medicines or doctors in the Colony.
>
> Very different are the feelings of the missionary; his mind is strongly infused with a dread of the Colony; he looks on himself as sent on a forlorn hope; he considers sickness and death in a few years a certainty: by brooding on the subject he often brings on a slight indisposition which his imagination exaggerates into a serious illness, when a man of more ardent temperament and a more elastic turn of mind would throw it off with facility. When to this desponding [sic] state of mind are added the enervating and enfeebling effects both mental and bodily, of severe fever, I have no doubt that many of the sufferers secretly wish the struggle were over and their course were run. And instead of the least attempt to rally their fainting spirits, they quietly resign themselves to the arms of death" (Governor's Letter Book for 1827, Government Archives, Fourah Bay College, Freetown, Sierra Leone. See also *Anthropological Review* 3 [1865], pp. clxiii ff. for further classic examples in a paper entitled "Efforts of Missionaries among Savages.").

What, to Macaulay, was both inexplicable and silly, was precisely the missionary myth operating in all seriousness! If the blood of martyrs is the seed of the Church, and the unbloody sacrifice of one's life was acknowledged as a form of martyrdom, then not only was the Church well-seeded but the missionary myth was eminently reinforcible.

BUILDING THE PRESENT: DEMYTHOLOGIZING

The missionary myth—not entirely new in the 19th century, but present in embryo even in St. Paul's writings, especially 2 Corinthians—can still be sensed as underlying missionary training and activity well past the middle of the present century. It is not so very long since "saving black babies" was an undertaking for all good Catholic children and promoted by missionary bodies in need of funds and fund-raising ideas. But there were already signs that the myth was not as persuasive or watertight as it once was. And when, from the heights of the mid-eighties we look back, it seems as alien as to be almost prehistoric, and as extinct as the great elk. We need to look at what had been happening.

BRAVE NEW WORLD?

As the 19th century gave way to the 20th and the 20th came of age and passed its zenith, it seems clear that the missionary myth had lost its power to sustain, rally, and encourage. "Missionary" had become a pejorative word, and the notion of mission was tarnished from its association with conversion and coercion, prose-lytism and paternalism, imperialism and ideology. The image of a monolithic Church with its centralizing and universalizing tendencies was not as attractive to Christians of the later 20th century as it might have appeared to earlier generations. The new mood, chasing away the dogmatism and discipline of Popes Pius, from IX to XII, was perceptible and would gather momentum through the late sixties and early seventies. It led away from "benighted" peoples heading for "perdition" and towards a respect for traditional religious forms and an acknowledgement of the presence of God therein; away from denominational rivalry and universalism towards ecumenism and localization; away from uniformity and the transplantation of the Church towards pluralism and inculturation. The missionary myth, which initially projected such unequivocal signs of missionary solidarity, both to mission-aries and to the Church at large, appeared more like the Emperor with no clothes, standing before men and women embarrassed and disillusioned by the posing of the previous century and angered at the petulance of a Church which refused to countenance the place of the laity, the need for new ministries, and the urgency of disciplinary reforms.

It is easy to say that the world changed in the century after the middle of the 19th. It did, of course. But we can certainly be more specific in accounting for the demise of the missionary myth than simply noting social change. There had been profound changes in the lives and perceptions of missionaries too, and of other people, looking at missionaries. To these we now turn.

A View of the Church, Now

Missionary policy and lifestyles follow—sooner or later, closely or loosely—eccle-siology (and more recently have been seen to threaten the priorities), and the missionary myth of the 19th century was predicated on an ecclesiology and sacramentology and Christology that have seen radical reinterpretation over the past twenty-five years or so. When missionaries were seen as involved in a massive rescue mission, they were regarded as important people who helped shape destinies and civilize cultures. Mis-sionaries had little reason to be plagued by doubts when their work was so evidently God's work. How could they be expected not to become paternalistic? How could baptism-bringers not see themselves as quasi-saviours when baptism was understood as so central to salvation? Even though they did try to regard themselves as "unworthy servants" (Lk 17:10), it was extremely difficult; individual missionaries occupied a central role within the current articulation of ecclesiology.

As unremarkable as it was that the missionary myth flourished in that ethos, so it is unremarkable that with the breakdown of that ethos there follows the undermining of the myth. Vatican II happens. Ecclesiology changes. "Evangelization" now shares the stage with "Development," and "Ecumenism" waits impatiently in the wings. Eternal life is no longer seen to be dependent on baptism and water, priest or missionary. Attitudes to obedience change, too. People are no longer convinced of the value of following the dictates or the pious whims—nonaccountable judgments—of Superiors, when psychology emphasizes the importance of personal integrity and the lives of those broken by "blind obedience" stand in accusation of an unfeeling and often incompetent organization. Things that may once have been accepted even though they appeared to outsiders as insufferable, discouraging, or just plain stupid, were now being repudiated by "insiders" as insufferable, discouraging, or just plain stupid! Not only was missionary work being affected by changes in ecclesiology and perceptions about authority, but the very identity of the missionary was undergoing a profound crisis. "What is a missionary?" was a question which, like "What is a giraffe?" could at one time have been answered declaratively, descriptively, and clearly. But the same question no longer seemed as easy to answer: the giraffe had become a chameleon or an unclassified hybrid.

A View of the Community, Now

The notion of "missionary policy" or "missionary ideas" was, as I said, a unitary notion in a climate in which individualism was subordinated to the common good and the goal of mission was clear and undisputed. When individualism refused to be cowed—in the secular city and in the city of God—when decision-making and hierarchial authority were scrutinized, and when the pluriformity of missionary enterprises could no longer be subsumed or rationalized under a simple view of mission, then the missionary myth would fail the test of credibility, "missionary policy" and "missionary ideas" would represent only vagueness or velleities, and the fragmentation of missionary work into elements as disparate as doctrinaire evangelism or social development would occur. By the time Vatican II was ten years old and Paul VI had written *Evangelii Nuntiandi*, the meaning of mission was very unclear and many of its practitioners had ceased to practice. "The community," which had been the repository of orthodoxy and the haven of missionaries everywhere, tried to accommodate the demands of self-determination and responsible decision-making, and struggled mightily. "The community," which was expected to be adequate to meet all the legitimate demands of its members, was found to be incapable of this kind of role. As a result, struggles ensued both on the community level and within each individual, in an attempt to rediscover authenticity and freedom as well as interdependence and the partial surrender of freedom.

Members of communities may feel trapped between the old and the new, loyalties to the group and loyalties to self, the certain and the uncertain. Clearly the identity of the community today is not what it was, or the relationships between individuals and communities have changed. Perhaps the most noticeable and notable fact over the past twenty years has been the huge numbers of missionaries leaving their communities. Whatever other reasons, the combination of loneliness, inability to accept the traditional missionary myth, and the need to grow personally in freedom, seem to have played a very large part. Increasingly one finds missionaries, deeply committed individuals, acknowledging and facing, coming to terms with and balancing their commitment to community and their need for personal growth, respect for their community's view of Church or mission but also loyalty to their own evolving view; those who cannot hold the two in balance seem destined to withdraw.

Martyrs and Others, Now

And what of martyrdom? Are there no martyrs today, and cannot their witness bind missionaries together and inject them with a rediscovered sense of pride and purpose? Yes indeed, it seems that martyrs will always be needed in the Church, with certain provisos: martyrs, who will always tend to be individualists giving a very personal witness, will not be feckless and irresponsible people, since life today is too serious and precious (when formerly it was both cheaper and less manageable); and martyrs will not be the "martyred" who, tight-lipped and passively, are determined to resist change and contrive to be martyrs to their unswerving dedication to an irretrievable past. Martyrs must be real exemplars, people of deep conviction and faith, pointing to a better way and a more hope-filled future, people who love life but who love justice more. No one is likely to undertake a course of action that might lead to death if such a person has "no confidence" in the prevailing paradigms or the value of witness. Who could "sacrifice" to reach people who do not need or do not want to be reached? And if the reaching out to people is a gesture evoking no danger at all, but simply representing good manners, would the romantic, idealistic, maverick souls who are perennially drawn to accept real challenges, find the prospect remotely enticing or attractive? No, martyrs will arise whenever there is a univocal rallying call. The problem is not with the martyrs but with the call. If modern missionaries are not attracted to martyrdom perhaps it is because they see no overwhelming need; latterly in Latin America and elsewhere, where a focus for martyrdom has become identifiable, women and men have not shirked their responsibility and martyrs have arisen. But if, in general, there are few mortal dangers or missionary-eating tribes today, what do missionaries do when faced with long years of unrewarding or unsung work? How can a missionary myth, so successful at maintaining clear lines of demarcation and dealing with anomalies and paradoxes, survive in a world where lines of demarcation have given way to lines of communication, and the exotic aspects of mission—climatic and theological—which bred such inconsistencies, have been all but domesticated and demystified? The short answer is that, in those terms, it cannot. For mission to continue, there must be an identifiable apostolate which people can freely choose to espouse. If sufficient people come forward and seek each other out, then a new missionary myth may come to be formulated. If not, mission will, I suggest, continue to be embraced by a dwindling number of people, or the enterprise will cease for a time, as a widespread social reality, in order to be superseded by a more appropriate form of missionary activity.

There will always be, surely, fools for Christ's sake, people who will put the good news above personal comfort, and find new ways to undertake the great commission. In our day—of changes in theology and social conditions, and disillusion with some past missionary methods or Roman interference—the term "liberation" is, partly at least, filling the vacuum left by the all-pervasive missionary myth. The cry is not a cry in justification of a style of mission but in hope and determination of an approaching reality, the freeing for Christ and the freeing by Christ of all who want to be free. Liberation theology, as anyone who reads Gutiérrez, Segundo, and others carefully will know, is not a dry ideology and still less doctrinaire Marxism, but an attempt to meet the fullness of the challenge of Christ expressed in the great commission. Its spirit is less and less limited to South America or Peru; increasingly it is coming to be seen as an authentic expression of Christian mission, in spite of the concentration of Roman documents such as the 1984 "Instruction on Certain Aspects of Liberation Theology" on its dubious kinship with Karl Marx. And the fruit of liberation theology? Some would see a witch hunt by Rome, others a coming to birth of a new level of Christian awareness. Some would try to reduce the reality to the Church-and-politics confrontation. But it is not about politics in any partisan sense; it is about the structures of society and the liberating power of Christ. It is about mission. When an Oscar Romero or a Jean Donovan, or a less well-known figure, male or female, lay or clerical, is "killed in combat," there is a tendency to cry "martyr!" and to indulge in ecclesiastical jingoism or myth-making—perhaps by the very people who need a palpable myth to provide them with identity and a sense of worth. But this is not to decry what is really happening; generous people are steadfastly announcing the good news in trying circumstances with little thought for personal safety. They are balanced and sane. They love life and are passionate. They are capable of turning away but are inspired to remain in position. And they die as they live—convinced of the authenticity of the mission they share with Christ.

BUILDING THE FUTURE: TOWARDS RENEWAL

Is it not then otiose to hope that the missionary myth will be reactivated? Or cannot "mission" survive without it? Does the demise of the myth imply the demise of the mission, or does it simply indicate a necessary deromanticizing and demythologizing of the missionary movement, such that it can adequately mirror the will of Christ and more effectively "come of age" in the late 20th century? Is there anything we can say, perhaps in broader sociological perspective, that would help clarify and rationalize some of the events in the history of Christian missions over the past century and a half?

In his book, New Heaven, New Earth (New York: Schocken, 1969), Burridge analyses revival movements, millenarianism, and cargo cults from such a sociological perspective and produces a scheme that can be helpful for anyone trying to understand the ebb and flow, the past and future of mission. He identifies three phases in the process of social change or (r)evolution: first, the situation which, in retrospect, can be characterized as the status quo, the rule of "old law"; second, the situation which replaces it, the "new law"; and third, the important intermediate stage of "no law." From our present perspective I think we can characterize the 19th-century mission movement as representing the "old law" phase. And I believe that the future will discern that we have already entered the "new law" phase. The "no law" is represented by the traumatic, challenging, exciting, depressing, hopeful, and confused days between the Second World War and the present.

CONSTRUCTION

Models of the traditional Church projected it as invincible and impregnable, a firm but fleshly juggernaut moving forward inexorably, an ark of salvation onto which survivors in a sea of troubles were rescued and revived, a "perfect society," hierarchically arranged, with Pope and Christ doubling for each other at the apex, Pope often upstaging Christ, an infallible authority whose practical exercise of authority was sometimes a far cry from that of Christ who came not to be served but to serve. The characteristics of the "old law" phase of the missionary Church derived from the characteristics of the universal Church, microcosm reflecting macrocosm in singlemindedness of purpose, seriousness of vision, imperviousness to criticism, certainty of leadership role, unquestioning exercise of authority, self-evidence of righteousness, and so on. Such a missionary movement, like such a Church, reacted to paradoxes and contradictions either by dissolving them through a rather vague appeal to "Providence," or by "solving" the anomalies or recalcitrant cases by fiat.

DESTRUCTION

It is possible, with the perspective of hindsight, to discern cracks in the stern façade of the missionary myth a century before the "swinging sixties." Only slowly did they spread and widen, but they would ultimately prove to have been not insignificant but structural.

In the 1870s an attempt was made to start a Mission in Monrovia, Liberia, with priests from Sierra Leone. It was a failure, and in less than a decade the attempt was abandoned with massive recriminations and very unchristian behavior towards the "Free Masons," who were accused of being the devil in disguise. This rationale was necessary, for who but Satan could turn back the mighty Church of Rome? Examples like this could be multiplied as missionaries, strung out around the globe, faced and dealt more or less successfully with reversals, and with the ever-present denominationalism of the time. Indeed denominational rivalry was not only rife but sometimes the very stuff of missionary work, for where the local people proved "resistant" or "apathetic," as in Freetown, Sierra Leone, missionaries would, without compunction, proselytize and "poach" from the flock of other Christians, and all the while undermining and belittling the efforts of "the heretics."

The façade of missionary "success" could only be maintained by some skillful cosmetic surgery or by denial of the less palatable realities; a sense of failure and discontent surfaced gradually as missions were compared and relative "failure" was sensed, or as the advance of Islam appeared to be more widespread than that of Christianity. This advance was frequently more apparent than real, however; yet missionaries, perhaps subconsciously, so as to make their little "successes" appear bigger, were quite explicit that in Sierra Leone 80% of the population were Muslim, when it was arguably less than half of that figure.

The Ecumenical Movement, planted in Scotland in 1910 and growing over half a century, flowered at Vatican II, and another theme or thread was thereby removed from the missionary myth. No longer should one close ranks against the enemy, for the enemy was now declared a friend! And by the end of Vatican II Islam, that clearly identifiable and unequivocal enemy for over a millennium, was likewise, along with the classical religions of the East, identified as *hors de combat* for Catholics. Not only were missionaries deprived of a cause, they were faced with the unlikely and unpalatable proposition that the battles of the past had been unnecessary and in vain, that God was on both sides! This shift in ecclesiology had profound effects on the missionary myth and the morale of missionaries, I believe. No longer were they expected to keep a tally of personal baptisms performed; this was now deemed—apart from the legitimate demands of official record-keeping—inappropriate and wrong. No longer could they see themselves as quasi-saviours, if baptism was not absolutely necessary.

So, in the interregnum between the "old law" and "new law" phase, we can trace the increasing undermining of the foundations of previous missionary work, both by critics from outside the Churches and, perhaps more significant, by critics from within. Positions that had previously been unquestioned and inviolate were now questioned and judged untenable. In the climate of an intellectual movement toward clear lines and principles but also toward situationalism and freedom of choice, the "no law" phase was characterized by ambivalence towards dogmas, tentativeness with regard to new solutions, and pluriformity of expression. Thus, paradoxes that had never daunted a previous generation (the need of baptism for salvation, and its unavailability; the immorality of polygamy, and its de facto existence in stable contemporary families as well as among Patriarchs and Prophets; the evil of slavery, and the use made by Christians, such as the Jesuits in Paraguay, of a slave-based economy) cried out stridently for attention. People now questioned, not just the necessity of baptism or the morality of polygamy, not just the idea of celibacy and the nature of the Christian community, but the credentials of a Church that simply could not offer baptism to all, which demanded that a man put away wives who would then be destitute, which was losing large numbers of clergy who refused to remain celibate, and which left thousands of communities without the Eucharist for long periods. Such a mood of questioning precipitated large numbers of cherished certainties into a kind of metaphysical limbo, and then transmitted them into blatant uncertainties or palpable injustices. The old myth had to go, if a new and helpful paradigm was to be brought to birth.

It almost seems that not a stone was left on a stone, after the "no law" phase passed its high water mark and the face of mission—and of missionaries—was radically changed. Yet insofar as mission is of God and a defining characteristic of the Church, the rubble must contain some, at least, of the elements of reconstruction. A new design may be required. Some materials may have to be replaced. But mission, like the phoenix, is contained in its own ashes.

RECONSTRUCTION

When we look, then, at the pre-dawn of a new day—the landscape just now being differentiated, as the "no law" phase gives place to the "new law"—what can be seen in the East? We can discern that all people are called to be saved, and that implies the real hope of their salvation, not a salvation contingent upon a missionary-with-water. We can discern that the Church is not the ark of salvation, alone on the sea, but a sign—a signpost, a beacon—of salvation, which some may discover but which others may not. We can discern that baptism too, is a sign—of incorporation into a visible community—and not a magical rite conferring salvation. And as the full dawn approaches, we can discern more and more: that all cultures have some saving graces; that God is present in cultures before missionaries arrive; that people have a *real* right to be left alone; that God is a forgiving God and a God who calls gently (not a vindictive God who abandons the weak); that structures must be evangelized; that the Church must listen as well as preach; and a great deal more.

Now the world is a global village, or a globe of villages, few of which are very remote any more. What goes on in Ethiopia or the Trobriand Islands can be screened "live" in Chicago or Sheffield. Now the exotic is shown tinged with the pathetic and the remote is trampled by tourists. Now the "noble savage" of the South seems to be not too savage, and his Northern counterpart seems not too noble. Not surprisingly, then, the missionary self-image and the missionary myth have changed quite radically.

WHITHER THE MISSIONARY MYTH?

The "new law" phase can, I believe be characterized by the primacy of the law of Christ over the law of the Church, the law of love over the law of justice. Not that the Church and justice have no place. Far from it. But those who explicitly seek the lordship and the love of Christ will surely be led along the right paths, perhaps even leading the official Church and refining ideas of what is demanded by justice on the way! A new age needs prophets, as the present age needs martyrs. Martyrs witness to something worth living for, and prophets tell forth the unpalatable for consumption and digestion by the sated.

SIGNS, SYMBOLS, AND CYMBALS

A sign that nobody heeds is useless. A sign that confuses has become a countersign. A sign that nobody understands has become an enigma. The missionary myth founded in the 19th century spoke a vernacular, and as such was understood. It spoke of winning souls for Christ and of saving them, lest they be lost and fall into perdition. It spoke of light and darkness, an ark on an ocean, rescue from Satan.

The world changes. The community and language change. Social worlds as well as linguistic forms change. And the missionary myth now represents an archaic, not to say alien reality. Whatever may be said about the need for a charter, a common point of reference, or a rationale for contemporary mission, it can hardly be the classical missionary myth that will be wheeled out to do service. It is too redolent of another time, another place.

MISSIONARY BY NATURE

If the aim of mission is "something new," then who would be rash enough to predict the future? Mission in any case is both an existential and an eschatological reality, a sign of contradiction and a beacon of light, an imperative of the Christ who redeems the world without our help. Mission, then, is something of a paradox, not so much to be understood as to be pondered and learned from. Certainly, styles of mission, like styles of government or ritual, will vary with time and in response to perceived needs and imperatives. And the style of mission in the future will not have repudiated the past, but will have learned from it.

A future missionary style will not fail to be fashioned by laity, single and married, formally or informally dedicated, temporarily or permanently engaged, as well as by religious with their own particularly but not exclusive or superior gifts. And the new phase of mission should provide opportunity for a new authentication of mission through careful discernment of Gospel values.

Assuming attention is paid to Christ, to the evangelizers, and to the real needs of the evangelized and the local Church, then there can be a permanent uncertainty about the details of missionary work without a demoralizing of missionaries and a pusillanimous reaction to the demands of mission. Perhaps the most important single ingredient in the mission of the future will be simple commitment—never really absent in the "no law" phase but sometimes lacking a focus and sometimes eclipsed. It will be commitment—not to structures or to plans, but to Christ. This was the orientation of Saint Paul, who had his own understanding of the demands of mission (2 Cor 4:7–12; 6:4–10)—tentative, Christ-centered, pessimistic, but hopeful. And why did Paul undertake and suffer all this? And why should we? Not to increase numbers, not to colonize the earth, but "so that the more grace is multiplied among people, the more thanksgiving there will be to the glory of God" (2 Cor 4:15). What a superb justification of mission: a clearly stated "missionary myth," one that transcends time and place.

13

Seeing Mission through Images

Stephen B. Bevans *

We do not so much see images as see through images, writes theologian John Shea. Taking this insight as a point of departure, the following article explores eight images of the missionary and through them comes to an understanding of mission itself. Images explored are those of treasure hunter, teacher, prophet, guest, stranger, partner, migrant worker, and ghost. Mission is understood not as a mere communication of a content, but as an invitation to search for what is already hidden in a culture. It has the courage to preach God's good, though sometimes challenging, news in season and out of season. It works through the gratefulness of a guest, the challenge of the stranger, the encouragement of the equal partner. It is concerned not with rights and prestige and recognition, but with the good of human beings. Ultimately, mission prolongs God's incarnation by continuing to make visible God's consoling and transforming love.

In November of 1897 two German missionaries to China, Richard Henle and Francis Nies, were brutally murdered by bandits in the Province of South Shantung. These two men were the first members of the young German missionary society, the Society of the Divine Word, to die a violent death in the mission fields; they were seen as heroes and martyrs, both by their confreres in China and by the whole Society of the Divine Word at large. They were regarded as two men who had given their lives heroically for Christ and for the gospel.

When the officials of the German government heard about the murders, however, they greeted the news with great joy. Now, they realized, they had an excuse to pressure China into giving Germany a naval base on the Chinese coast! In fact, there is even a story that the Admiral of the German Navy and Kaiser Wilhelm II drank a toast to the fallen missionaries—not so much because they were fallen "soldiers of Christ," but because now Germany had found a way to expand its efforts at colonization in Asia.

* Taken from *Missiology* 19 (January 1991), pp. 45–57 and reprinted with the permission of the publisher. Stephen Bevans, SVD, a former missionary to the Philippines, is Associate Professor of Doctrinal Theology at Catholic Theological Union in Chicago, Illinois. He is also associate editor of *Missiology* and author of *Models of Contextual Theology* (Orbis, 1992) and *John Oman and his Doctrine of God* (Cambridge, 1992).

The point of relating this incident at the start of an article about the nature of mission is that, whether they liked it or not and whether they were aware of it or not, missionaries in the past regarded themselves or were regarded by their governments through various explicit or implicit images. In this case, and throughout the 19th century, missionaries were highly regarded or criticized as the religious arm of colonial powers. French and German missionaries flew the French and German flags over their mission compounds, and in these compounds the culture of Europe was taught in European-designed buildings and in European languages. British missionaries saw themselves as carrying the "white man's burden," bringing civilization (read: British culture and British rule) to all parts of the world. And U.S. missionaries saw themselves as helping further the "manifest destiny" of the United States, thereby spreading the gospel of "truth, justice, and the American way" to a world they thought sorely needed it. After World War II especially, U.S. missionaries saw themselves as extensions of a country that had saved the world, a country that was morally superior to all other countries and could do no wrong.

Missionaries have always seen themselves through various images. They saw themselves as bringing salvation to a sinful, depraved, and wicked world. They saw themselves as men and women who would help to establish the church, outside of which there was no hope of saving one's soul. They saw themselves, and were seen as well by others, as apostles, as martyrs, as heroes, or—in a favorite image of at least Catholic recruiters in the 1950s and 1960s—as the "shock troops" or marines of the church.

While today, as we look forward to the year 2000, some of these former images remain valid if properly understood, times and attitudes have changed. As the U.S. Catholic Bishops pointed out in their 1986 pastoral statement, "To the Ends of the Earth," since Vatican II we have been living in a world that provides a new context for missionary activity (U.S. Catholic Bishops 1986:#9–21). Today, if the missionary activity of the church and the church's mission to the ends of the earth are still valid, missionaries need to go about mission work differently, and they have to understand themselves and be understood by others through different images.

"Images," says theologian John Shea (1987:107), "are not so much what we see as what we see through." The various images of the missionary are really not just interesting picture words; they are really concentrated theologies of mission, ways of understanding the church, ministry, the significance of Jesus Christ, and the salvation that he offers. As we move into a new missionary context, we need adequate images.

What I would like to do in the following pages is to reflect on some images of the missionary—eight in all—that are suggested by the new missionary context that the U.S. Bishops speak about in their pastoral. By reflecting on these images, I hope that we can begin to speak in a more adequate way about who missionaries are and what they are supposed to do. And by these reflections as well, I hope that we can begin to understand the nature of mission more clearly in the light of today's challenges and concerns. Accordingly, then, we will reflect on the missionary as (1) treasure hunter, (2) teacher, (3) prophet, (4) guest, (5) stranger, (6) partner, (7) migrant worker, and (8) ghost. Some of what I have to say will be more developed; some will be sketchier and suggestive. Nevertheless, every one of these images is important and bears the need for serious reflection.

1. THE MISSIONARY AS TREASURE HUNTER

My first image was proposed several years ago in the now defunct Jesuit periodical *The Catholic Mind* (Rush 1978). The article maintains that if missionaries used to be seen as "pearl merchants," now they might best be viewed as "treasure hunters."

Missionaries, in other words, do not just come to a country or culture with something to sell. They do have something very precious—the good news (gospel) of God's incredible love and mercy. However, this news most likely does not mean much to the people to whom they come because it is not expressed in their language and in their cultural forms. In their role as treasure hunters, therefore, the missionaries might see their function as looking for the treasure they have already unearthed in the context of the culture to which they have been sent. In order to find the treasure that is hidden there, they have to dig deep into the soil of the new culture that they are encountering. And since the missionaries cannot really do the digging alone, they have to enlist the help of the people of that culture and trust them to do most of the digging.

On the other hand, however, the missionaries as treasure hunters are not just looking for what they know is already hidden in a culture or a history of a people. They have some idea of the worth of the treasure buried in the soil of another people; they know that it has some similarity to the treasure that they have found in their own culture. But they know too that there is more, both for the people of their adopted culture and for themselves as well.

In the final analysis, the complete treasure is buried in all cultures and all peoples and all histories, and no person or culture or tradition will ever know what the whole treasure is until every culture, every tradition, every people is mined to its full richness. Missionaries come on one level to help the people to whom they are sent discover the treasure of the gospel and the hidden treasures of the new culture which knowledge of the gospel unearths. But they come as well to help discover that aspect of the treasure which will contribute to the good of all humankind and all cultures. Pope John Paul II expressed this idea well when he said, in a Christmas message to the College of Cardinals in 1984: "The Church is a communion of Churches, and indirectly a communion of nations, languages and cultures. Each of these brings its gifts to the whole" (U.S. Catholic Bishops 1986:#36).

Viewing the missionary as a treasure hunter discloses that the missionary does not bring a ready-made gospel message; rather the missionary brings a hope and a promise: if people dig deep into their own culture and history, if people really work hard at it, they will find a treasure that can transform their lives. The good news is not so much a detailed description of what the treasure is, but a declaration that the treasure is there. But the good news says even more: missionaries come into a new culture or people confident that the treasure that they have found in their own culture will help unearth the treasure of the new culture; they are also confident that the new treasure will enhance the one that they already have. Even further, missionaries witness to the fact that both treasures together—joined with the treasure unearthed by the gospel in all cultures—can help the world become a saner, more peaceful, and more loving place. The full treasure will be manifest when the true God is fully revealed and the reign of God is fully inaugurated.

2. THE MISSIONARY AS TEACHER

In his now famous work *The Pedagogy of the Oppressed*, Brazilian educator Paolo Freire (1968:57-74) says that teaching is often done with an analogy to a bank account. According to the analogy, the teacher approaches teaching with the attitude that he or she knows what needs to be known, and that the students know nothing. Teaching, then, is like making a deposit in a bank account. The teacher has all the money and deposits it in the heads of the students, who, like a bank account, grow accordingly.

But, as Freire and many other writers on education have insisted, this is not necessarily the best description of what teaching (or for that matter, learning) is or can be. A real teacher is one who certainly realizes that he or she knows things and has a vision that his or her students probably do not have; but a teacher also knows that students do not really learn by being treated as if they know nothing. Rather than teaching according to a mechanical model of depositing a sum in a bank account, or according to what Henri Nouwen calls the "violent" method of pouring knowledge into people's heads, the true teacher teaches according to a personalist model which aims to open up the students' minds so that they can fill their own minds with what they consider important, and at their own pace. In Nouwen's words again, teaching (and learning) is a deeply "redemptive" process by which the teacher helps the students come to know in a conscious way both how much they already know and how much more they still need to know to be adult, responsible persons in the world (Nouwen 1978:3–20).

In addition to this, a good teacher is one who learns from his or her students. In class discussion, by reading student papers carefully and judiciously, and especially through the challenges and insights that students present in class, the real teacher never ceases to be a learner. If a teacher is not somehow a companion with his or her students on the way to wisdom, if he or she cannot "infect" the student with contagious enthusiasm for truth, he or she can only instruct students with rather sterile facts and never really involve the student in the adventure of education.

It seems to me that the analogy of the missionary with the real teacher is rather obvious in this light. As missionaries we do bring something more when we bring our faith in Jesus Christ, our Christian world view, and our own particular expertise into another country and another culture. We definitely have something to teach. But if we teach according to the "banking method," we choose merely to instruct rather than to educate. Rather than trying to pour our knowledge into people's heads, we need to stimulate them to begin or to carry on their own search more passionately. Our own faith and style of life should stimulate those to whom we have been sent to examine their own commitments and to help them to revise those commitments when necessary. And as good teachers we do this with the hope that our "students" will one day surpass the teacher in both faith and wisdom. Rather than imposing our expertise on a particular culture, perhaps we need to think of our teaching in terms of offering people an alternative, supplemental way of doing or viewing things. Rather than our medicine taking the place of folk remedies and faith healings, rather than our technology replacing time-honored techniques, we might work to show how our ways of doing things are useful and helpful, *alongside* more traditional ways. Perhaps our ways are better, but—given the ecology of a particular region or a particular social structure—perhaps they are not. Or, perhaps a combination of traditional ways and Western approaches will best serve a society. And maybe even our own methods and approaches can be improved by taking in the wisdom of our "student."

"Good news," said the English Presbyterian theologian John Oman, "by its very nature, cannot be forced upon the mind, but must sing its way into the heart" (1921:273). Oman often contrasted the teaching method of Jesus, who spoke with *authority*, with the teaching method of the scribes and Pharisees, who taught only by quoting *authorities* (1936:83). While Jesus spoke right to the heart, and appealed to men's and women's experiences and deepest longings, the official teachers of Jesus' day were content simply to impose what was often a rote knowledge of past wisdom. Unless we can excite and stimulate the men and women of other cultures and other faiths to see the vision that we have seen and by which we have been transformed and more deeply humanized, our own missionary efforts can only be the peddling of authoritative truths. But if we can capture imaginations and open up to others the incredible possibilities that God in Christ so graciously offers, our teaching will possess the power and the authority of the Teacher himself, and we will be the vehicles of his truth.

3. THE MISSIONARY AS PROPHET

Once when I was in Boston and riding on the rapid transit system Bostonians call the "T," a young woman boarded the train I was on and walked up and down the aisle, chanting over and over again an appeal to save the whales, to safeguard the environment, to treat the earth and all its creatures with responsibility and love. After apparently walking through all the cars on the train, the woman got off and waited for the train going in the opposite direction so she could continue proclaiming her important and urgent message. The people on the train that I was riding seemed rather embarrassed or, in more cases, indifferent, but that did not bother the woman at all. Probably, for several hours or for the whole day she simply repeated her message about ecological responsibility to the passengers of every train she rode.

I was one of the embarrassed ones, probably because I had never encountered anything like this before, but all at once I realized that what the woman was doing in the Boston "T" was not all that different—in form at least—from what the prophets did in Israel. I particularly thought of Jeremiah walking through Jerusalem wearing a yoke (Jeremiah 27–28), entreating Judah to submit to Yahweh's will by accepting defeat by Babylon. Although this action was hardly popular with the king or with the people in general, nevertheless Jeremiah spoke the "word of the Lord." In season, out of season, despite opposition, derision, and persecution, the prophet is the one who discerns the meaning of daily events and speaks God's word to God's people. Such were Jeremiah and Amos and Isaiah and Hosea; such was the

Lord Jesus; and such must be the church, missionary by its very nature (AG 1965:#2). Perhaps missionaries do not need always to be as dramatic as the woman on the "T" or as Jeremiah in Jerusalem, but they do need to be faithful to God's good news in Jesus, despite the fact that it will often be resisted. Even though missionaries look for a treasure that is hidden among the people to whom they are sent, and even though missionaries help evoke a people's deepest aspirations, the good news of Jesus inevitably calls for transformation and change; this is something that no one embraces spontaneously.

The good news that missionaries might be faithfully presenting could be that a people needs to be responsible to itself, and not to a foreign mission board or religious order. The gospel is clear on the fact that the Spirit is lavished on the church in its local manifestation, and not limited to its missionary parent. But responsibility is often a heavy burden personnel-wise, financially, even socially (what prestige and stability, for instance, a United States missionary can give to a struggling, Third World seminary), and it might seem a lot more desirable for a local church to forfeit its freedom for some kind of easy security. Such resistance from the local church might tempt missionaries to stay on even when they are not really needed, but the true missionary will persist in prophesying the truth: the local church needs to be responsible for itself.

Or the annunciation of the good news might involve, as Gustavo Gutiérrez (1973:265–72) puts it, the denunciation of structures and conditions that thwart Jesus' lordship, structures and conditions that make genuine human existence impossible. In this case it might seem that the good news is something negative, but it is really only the other side of the coin of the announcement of God's universal love and mercy: since God loves all and calls all to life, anything that works against true human life can in no way be tolerated. We have all seen how faithful women and men have prophesied in this way and have been faithful even to the point of imprisonment and death. The witness of a Desmond Tutu or an Oscar Romero, of the five United States women and the six Jesuits murdered in El Salvador, of women and men deported from or murdered in the Philippines—such witness is a model for the missionary, who must always be a prophet of God's purposes and of God's gospel.

4. THE MISSIONARY AS GUEST

In a certain sense, this fourth image of the missionary as guest is rather obvious. Missionaries are not in their own lands; they are not in their own cultures. It makes perfect sense that they must not, like good guests must not, take things for granted, take liberties with the host's hospitality, or abuse the host's sensibilities.

But the missionary's role as guest has not always been recognized as such. In the colonial past, for instance, missionaries often behaved in many ways like ungrateful and obnoxious guests. Instead of gratefully trying to accommodate to their hosts, missionaries often forced the hosts to speak a foreign language. Instead of trying to appreciate their hosts' values, they either ignored them or ridiculed them. And instead of learning their hosts' culture and broadening themselves with it, missionaries often insulted it by forcing the hosts to dress like them and follow their customs.

It seems to me that if there is one basic attitude that missionaries must cultivate as part of their missionary activity and spirituality, it is this attitude of being a guest. Rather than arrogant visitors demanding that everything be done according to their tastes, missionaries are those who appreciate whatever hospitality the hosts can provide. And, above all, missionaries will be respectful of the hosts, realizing always that they have no real rights before their hosts.

On the other hand, there is another aspect of being a guest that also must be attended to: when one is a guest, one puts oneself in a position of being honored and served. From this angle, missionaries who have come to serve must allow others to serve them as well.

This is not easy. The whole reason for missionaries going to another culture or another country is to do things for that culture or country. This sounds like a reverse of all that is Christian, for to give is better than to receive, and to serve is to reign. Very often, however, the best way to give and to serve is to allow others to serve us, to allow others the dignity—and we could even say the privilege—of giving hospitality and friendship. We do not go to another culture or country to be hosts; we go there as guests, accepting the richness of the culture, the delicacies of the cuisine (often the most difficult thing to appreciate), the beauty of the language, and most of all, the friendship of the people.

Probably some of the most effective missionary work that I have done has been in homes of people, both rich and poor, trying to accept with graciousness their own gratitude for my being there. Not doing anything, not rendering any service, but just being relaxed and enjoying conversation and food is a very effective way of preaching the joy and peace of God's reign. And no less example can we have than Jesus himself, for whom acceptance of hospitality and table fellowship were such a large part of his own mission.

5. THE MISSIONARY AS STRANGER

A guest, no matter how welcome, is always a stranger, and missionaries are strangers in at least three senses of the term.

In the first place, missionaries will always be strangers in the other culture or country to which they have been sent. The other culture or country will always be "other;" missionaries will never be completely at home. If missionaries think they are, they should be careful. There certainly are bicultural persons, but they are very rare. Much more important, I think, is that missionaries recognize their strangeness and accept it—not as a failure or a weakness, but simply as a fact. It is almost impossible to "get inside" another culture completely.

This fact was brought home to me a few weeks after I arrived in the Philippines. One of my colleagues at the seminary where I had begun to teach told me about an old Spanish missionary that he had met years before. The Spaniard had been in the Philippines for something like forty years, and so my colleague—then a young missionary himself—asked the old priest if he really understood Filipinos. The priest answered only by saying: *"El alma del Filipino es un misterio."* But not just the Filipino soul is a mystery. To one who is a stranger, the soul of every person in another culture is equally a mystery, and no amount of linguistic, anthropological, or sociological knowledge can change this.

The fact is, however, that there is really nothing wrong with being a stranger in another culture. It is certainly something painful, but is never something bad. I believe that people do not really *want* us to be like them—to respect them, yes; to appreciate their culture, certainly; to value their language and their art, by all means; but this does not mean leaving our own differences behind. My own sense is that as long as we acknowledge our strangeness, sometimes sadly perhaps, and sometimes even humorously, we strangers will be accepted and listened to as honored and valued guests.

This frank acknowledgement of our difference and strangeness leads to a second sense of being a stranger: often this strangeness is one of a missionary's most valuable contributions to the church's mission. Very often a person's strangeness can function both to help a people understand their own culture better—somehow by seeing what it is *not* in very clear relief—and very often as well this strangeness can help to challenge a particular culture's preconceptions about itself, resulting in a strengthening and a purification.

My own experience of living for the past year with a person who has worked with the poor in Brazil has helped me understand from a fresh perspective what it means to be a U.S. American with all its power and privileges, while oftentimes shocking me into realizing how bourgeois are many of what I have considered my dearest values. I hope my own difference in the Philippines has helped some of my students define who they are against my U.S. American frankness and informality, and has helped them see some of the weaknesses in their own culture of indirectness and hierarchy. Being different and strange is not comfortable, but it can make a valuable contribution to a people's often fragile identity and can open their eyes to previously unrealized possibilities.

A third aspect of the image of the missionary as stranger is that not only are missionaries strangers in their adopted culture; missionaries become strangers in all cultures, including their own. Even if missionaries return to their own culture, they cannot just pick up where they left off several years before. An honest attempt to adapt to another culture and a genuine effort at being worthy guests in another country means that men and women who once have been missionaries can never be the same. Missionaries are never able totally to identify with another culture, but they have enriched their lives so much and have widened their horizons so greatly that any one culture will from now on seem too narrow, and any one set of values will seem too limiting. As so many returned missionaries testify, they become strangers even in their own lands.

But this strangeness only means that the missionaries can continue their missionary work in their home country. Today we speak about the importance of "reverse mission," whereby returned missionaries become agents for helping their home countries to see the world more broadly and to be concerned more fully about situations in other cultures and other countries. Returned missionaries, by sharing their experiences abroad and their continuing strangeness in their home culture, can perhaps help their brothers and sisters contribute more actively to the church's mission to the ends of the earth (U.S. Catholic Bishops 1986:#74).

6. THE MISSIONARY AS PARTNER

A friend of mine who was ministering in a heavily Hispanic area in Chicago once dropped by my office for a visit. It was clear from his enthusiasm about his work that what he was doing was something deeply meaningful to him, and his apparent love for the men and women to whom he ministered was making him a worthy ambassador of God's reconciliation. Of all the things he said that afternoon, however, one thing stood out as particularly inspiring and particularly illustrative of his work as a missionary: "The more we work," he said, "the more we see things that the people can do."

Notice that my friend said that the more he and the other priest working with him worked, the more they found for others to do. So often ministry is conceived as doing things for others—presiding over services, being available for counseling, organizing support groups, leading protest marches against housing conditions and raises in rent. What my friend was saying, though, was that it was his job not to do everything or to be the leader of everything, but to call forth the whole church community to ministry, to call every member to partnership in ministry.

Pope Paul VI in *Evangelii Nuntiandi* (1976) spoke of the fact that the goal of true evangelization is not simply the Christianization of a particular people. As I mentioned just above, evangelization begins with the silent witness of Christian men and women and then moves to a stage where the evangelizers specifically proclaim Christ and his vision of God's reign. But evangelization only reaches its completion when, after those who have received the message have been incorporated into the community of faith, they are themselves sent out as evangelizers (Paul VI 1976:#24). The whole goal of the church's mission, in other words, is to bring men and women into partnership in ministry, to make them "fellow workers in Christ Jesus" (Romans 16:3; cf. also 1 Corinthians 3:9; Colossians 4:11; Philippians 4:3).

Such a goal of mission means that missionaries need to have a strong sense of the fundamental equality of the church they are forming. Roland Allen's and, more recently, Vincent Donovan's challenges to trust the Spirit which is given in baptism and to allow the new church and new Christians to participate fully in the development of its and their communities' structures need perhaps to be taken with some caution, but all too often the problem is with *too much* caution and *too little* trust. It is only when new Christians are entrusted with ministry that they can really participate in the fullness of Christianity—for being Christian is not so much about knowing and believing particular doctrines, but about giving oneself over to loving service.

In particular, where missionary work is being done among men and women who are already Christian—and I am thinking in terms of work in the Philippines or among Blacks and Hispanics in the United States—another barrier to the missionary's becoming a partner with the people is the barrier of clericalism. Again relying on that fundamental equality and call to mission that is the birthright of every Christian (cf. LG 1981:#32), missionaries need constantly to work at developing nonhierarchical and nonclerical styles of ministry. This is not always easy, particularly in societies and cultures where the priest or minister enjoys an automatic prestige, but it is something that must be done—perhaps gradually but never hesitantly—if the church is to be the church and missionaries are to be true to their vocation of true evangelization. If the fullness of being a Christian means to be involved in ministry and responsibility for the church, one of the priorities of the missionary is learning how to be not just a servant, but a partner in service.

7. THE MISSIONARY AS MIGRANT WORKER

"I come with the dust and I go with the wind." This is how the U.S. singer-song-writer Woody Guthrie described the life of migrant farm workers of the 1930s in his song "Pastures of Plenty." The line remains an accurate description of migrant workers today, as they move from harvesting citrus fruit in the southwest United States in the winter to harvesting vegetables in the North in late summer. For a good number of U.S. Americans and legal and illegal Mexicans, keeping a job means traveling to where the work is and being ready to do whatever the job demands. It is a hard life, often filled with injustices, but it supports a family and provides a living.

This rather brutal image is not totally applicable to missionaries, but it does provide some striking and thought-provoking parallels. In times past, foreign or cross-cultural missionaries were at the center of the church's life and activity in their adopted countries or cultures. Missionaries were the church leaders, the bishops, the college presidents, the seminary rectors, the heads of nursing services in the hospital, the honored speakers at school graduations. Today, however, at least in many countries, almost the opposite is the case: missionaries have trouble even getting into a country, they are looked at with suspicion by members of the culture, and they are often regarded as usurpers of power or as outmoded fixtures that probably should be replaced. While once they were fully accepted, now missionaries are often seen as invaders—not at all unlike the way many U.S. Americans view Latin American and Asian immigrants today.

The point is not to condone the immorality of this U.S. attitude—or to justify the attitude of various mission situations—but to highlight a parallel. Just as migrant workers have to go where the work is, doing what U.S. Americans are unable or unwilling to do, so missionaries might see themselves as workers who do what the local church cannot yet or will not do itself. In the missionary context, this might be something humble, like caring for the most primitive and difficult parish, or it might be something highly specialized, like developing a complex irrigation system and training local people to administer it. In any case, whatever it is, missionaries will be willing to do it, so strong and deep is their commitment to the developing local community. Despite hostility and lack of understanding, the missionary is willing to continue working, as long as he or she is convinced that it is what the local church needs and really wants.

And in the same way as the migrant worker's task is a thankless but quite necessary one in the life of an affluent nation, so the missionary's task may be thankless but ultimately essential. He or she would not be the first preacher of God's reign to have no roots, no security, and—perhaps figuratively—nowhere to lay his or her head.

8. THE MISSIONARY AS GHOST

In her presidential address to the Catholic Theological Society of America in 1987, Monika Hellwig (1987:99-100) spoke of various images of the theologian and ended by describing the "theologian as ghost." Her point was that often a particular theologian does not get credit for a particular idea or line of thought because, even though it originated with him or her, it has become so much a part of the currency of theological discourse that people forget its source. In that case, Hellwig said, theologians should be content to let themselves be nameless, realizing that their presence will always "haunt" the idea. Hopefully, theologians would be friendly ghosts, whose best service is not to make their presence known, but to serve the theological enterprise of giving speech to faith. To give an idea to the world of theology, and to let it flourish there, might be the most wonderful thing theologians can do for the discipline and for the community they serve.

It is hard to build up a parish or a school or a hospital or an organization—and simply withdraw and leave it to another. I have known many missionaries who felt quite bitter about the fact that after so many years of service their work was not fully appreciated; then as soon as a local Christian took over the position or institution, he or she changed it according to his or her own vision. It seems to me, however, that this is part and parcel of being a missionary, and that at a certain point, missionaries must move on and the local Christian must take over. If the missionary tries to hang on, or is bitter because he or she cannot, something is wrong. In many circumstances the best thing missionaries can do is to let go of their work, to die to it so to speak, and to be present only as friendly ghosts. Perhaps it is this most difficult sacrifice of all that is required for the real fruitfulness of one's labors.

CONCLUSION

We do not so much see images as see through images, and this article has been an attempt to see through several images of the missionary with a view to coming to an understanding of mission itself. The images I have reflected upon are only representative, and can in no way be taken as an exhaustive list, but I think that our reflections have yielded what might be called a coherent way of understanding mission today. Mission, while still needing to be understood as bringing something *more* into a culture, needs to be supplemented with the idea that that *more* is often not the possession of the missionary, but the invitation to an adventure in which the missionary is an active participant. Mission is not really about transplanting the church from one culture to another, but about searching for the seeds of that church that are already hidden in another culture's soil. Mission is the prophetic preaching by word and deed alike that the God who is present in every culture is also the God who calls every culture to perfection in the light of the incarnate Divine Word; often that prophetic task is carried out by being a grateful guest and a respectful stranger. Mission is making it clear as well that God's cause is the cause of men and women, and that God calls men and women to the peace and justice of God's reign. Mission is calling forth the best in a culture and a people and involves the generosity of an offering of partnership and the humility of doing whatever it takes to get the job done. It is letting go—of one's own culture, of one's own certainties, and of one's own achievements. It works with the wisdom of Apollos and the enthusiasm of Paul, but always knowing that God gives the growth (1 Corinthians 3:7). Mission, in sum, is nothing less than the continuation of God's incarnation by the people who live as Christ's body. It is the continuing revelation of the God who saves—not by destroying what was created as good but imperfect, but by transforming a creation capable of becoming more and more reflective of God's love.

REFERENCES CITED

AG. 1981 (1965) *Ad Gentes*. Vatican Council II, "Decree on Missionary Activity." In *Vatican Council II: The Conciliar and Post-Conciliar Documents*. A. Flannery, ed. Pp. 813–62. Collegeville, MN: The Liturgical Press.

Allen, Roland. 1962 (1912) *Missionary Methods: St. Paul's or Ours?* Grand Rapids, MI: Eerdmans.

Donovan, Vincent. 1982 *Christianity Rediscovered*. Maryknoll, NY: Orbis Books.

Freire, Paolo. 1968 *The Pedagogy of the Oppressed*. New York: Seabury.

Gutiérrez, Gustavo. 1973 *A Theology of Liberation*. Maryknoll, NY: Orbis Books.

Hellwig, Monika. 1987 "Who is Truly a Catholic Theologian?" In CTSA *Proceedings* (Catholic Theological Society of America). G. Kilcourse, ed. Pp. 91–100.

LG. 1981 (1964) *Lumen Gentium*. Vatican Council II. "Dogmatic Constitution on the Church." In *Vatican Council II: The Conciliar and Post-Conciliar Documents*. A. Flannery, ed. Pp. 350–426. Collegeville, MN: The Liturgical Press.

Nouwen, Henri. 1978 *Creative Ministry*. Garden City, NY: Doubleday Image Books.

Oman, John. 1921 *The Paradox of the World*. Cambridge: Cambridge University Press.

_____. 1936 *Concerning the Ministry*. London: SCM.

Paul VI. 1976 *Evangelii Nuntiandi*. Washington, DC: U.S. Catholic Conference.

Rush, R. T. 1978 "From Pearl Merchant to Treasure Hunter: The Missionary Yesterday and Today." *Catholic Mind 76* (1325): 6–10.

Shea, John. 1987 "Theological Assumptions and Ministerial Style." In *Alternative Futures for Worship*, Vol. 6. *Leadership Ministry in Community*. Pp. 105–28 M.A. Cowan, ed. Collegeville, MN: Liturgical Press.

U.S. Catholic Bishops. 1986 *To the Ends of the Earth*. New York: Society for the Propagation of the Faith.

Part IV

THE STUDY OF MISSION

14

Missiology as a Discipline
and What It Includes

James A. Scherer *

This article was originally presented at the 1987 annual meeting of the Association of Professors of Mission in Pittsburgh, Pennsylvania. Although precise and inclusive definition of missiology is impossible, Scherer maintains that it needs above all to be rooted in the biblical faith and theological conviction that God is at work in our world, inviting all to participate in the healing and wholeness that communion with God promises. The theological meaning of mission, therefore, is both prior to and constitutive of missiology as a discipline, even though its concrete starting point might be interpreted— for example, as expressly theological (Verkuyl), or descriptive and analytical in the manner of the social sciences (Tippett).

Although an academic discipline in its own right, according to Scherer, missiology must also remain in constant dialogue with the wisdom of other disciplines—biblical studies, history, systematic theology, world religions studies, and such social sciences as anthropology and sociology. Thus the mission of the church is to be understood in all its biblical, historical, theological, and human dimensions, and these disciplines are enriched by an understanding of the total scope and goal of God's saving plan.

This article provides an introduction to missiology and points to the importance of the theological foundations of mission.

In his splendid account of the founding and first fifteen years of history of the American Society of Missiology (ASM), Wilbert Shenk concludes that "the ASM has devoted relatively little formal attention to clarification of the definition of 'missiology' as a discipline. In a real sense," he continues, "this comprises an important part of the 'unfinished task' before the ASM" (Shenk 1987:30). It will be the purpose of this essay to work toward the clarification of the definition of missiology, to identify its major components, and to indicate what it ought to include.

* Taken from *Missiology* 15 (October 1987), pp 507–22, and reprinted with the permission of the publisher. James A. Scherer is Professor Emeritus of World Mission and Church History at Lutheran School of Theology in Chicago. He is the author of numerous articles and books, including *Gospel, Church, and Kingdom: Comparative Studies in World Mission Theology* (Augsburg, 1987) and is co-editor of the Orbis series *New Directions in Mission and Evangelization*.

The new *Webster's Collegiate Dictionary* defines "missiology' as "the study of the church's mission especially with respect to missionary activity" and indicates that the first use of the term was in 1924 (*Webster's Ninth New Collegiate Dictionary*, 1986). This is surely one of the first definitions of "missiology" to be attempted by a general dictionary of the English language.

The *Concise Dictionary of the Christian World Mission* (Glazik 1971: 387f), is more tentative, offering no definition of missiology, as such, but paraphrasing it as "the science of mission," the "doctrine of mission," or "mission as a complex whole . . . systematically and comprehensively treated as a theological subject." The *Concise Dictionary* includes a range of other entries under "mission studies" and "mission studies in theological education," but it stops short of offering a more precise definition.

My own earlier but sporadic attempts to clarify some of the questions underlying this inquiry (Scherer 1971), heavily based on O. G. Myklebust's comprehensive and pioneering study on mission in theological education (Myklebust 1955 & 1957), led me to conclude that instruction in "world missions" (as I referred to it at that time) in American theological education was "plagued by a certain imma- turity and obscurity with regard to definition, methodological basis and objectives" (Scherer 1971:145). I noted then that the credibility of world missions within theological education was being weakened by a failure to think through the nature and requirements of our still fledgling discipline, which in turn was becoming a problem both for the practitioners of the discipline and for theological education in general. I think that these observations were basically true for that time.

In my more recent study, prepared for the 1985 APM Annual Meeting, signifi- cantly entitled "The Future of Missiology as an Academic Discipline in Seminary Education" (Scherer 1985), and based on a survey at ATS-related schools in the United States, I cited Louis Luzbetak's optimistic declaration of October 4, 1975, at the time of the admission of the American Society of Missiology into the Council on the Study of Religion, to the effect that "on this day missiology becomes a fully recognized academic discipline in North America" (Scherer 1985:455). I also noted a qualitative improvement in the climate for the teaching of missions, and a quantitative increase in teaching programs related to missiology, particularly in evangelical seminaries and schools of world mission, and especially between 1975 and 1985.

In the same study I reflected on continuing polarities in viewpoints between conciliar, Roman Catholic, and independent schools, and pointed to some matters for further study: (1) the need for standard nomenclature when referring to "mis- sion," "missions," and "missiology"; (2) the desirability of working toward agree- ment with regard to what I called the "normative content" in courses in missiology, especially in institutions where a single required or recommended course represents the student's sole exposure to the subject; and (3) further clarification of the partner relationship between instruction in mission and evangelism, which are increasingly viewed not as "distant cousins or potential rivals for the church's affections, but as fellow workers within the Lord's vineyard" (Scherer 1985:458–59). My 1985 appeal to the APM to address the need for standard definitions and nomenclature may be partly responsible for the topics addressed at this 1987 meeting.

WHY A NEW QUEST
FOR A DEFINITION OF MISSIOLOGY?

The quest for an agreed definition of *missiology* remains elusive, and neither the ASM, nor the teaching fraternity represented by the APM, has been able to come up with one. The reasons, I would suggest, are partly attributable to *internal* differences in aims and viewpoints between those who teach the discipline, and partly to *external* factors such as unresolved relationships between missiology and the goals of theological education in general, as well as profound changes in theological trends and attitudes in the past 25 years which have had their impact on thinking about both mission and missiology. Indeed, the most serious for *missiology*, which I shall address in more detail in a later section, is current indecision, or at least divergence of opinion, about what *mission* fundamentally is.

The history of the teaching of missiology as a discipline is being competently treated by my colleague, Richey Hogg, and I am confident that his historical overview will shed much light on the elusive character of the pursuit of an agreed definition. Why this new quest for a definition just at this time? My hunch is that those of us who teach and do research in this area need closer agreement on *what missiology* is to be able to pursue our goals in a collegial manner, given both the interdisciplinary nature of our subject, and the interconfessional stance we have purposely adopted (conciliar, Roman Catholic, independent) since the formation of the ASM in 1973.

The original reason for giving academic attention to "missiology" and claiming for it a scientific character, especially in European universities in the half century between 1869 and 1910, was to gain public recognition and theological respectability for the new discipline, and to secure its place in institutions of higher education through regular lectureships and required university examinations (Scherer 1971:145). That strategy succeeded fairly well in Europe, but it created its own problems, and has only limited relevance to the American situation.

What is still pertinent about the 19th-century European quest for missiological recognition is that European missiological scholars from the time of Gustav Warneck (1834–1910) have been obliged to present their findings in a systematic, "scientific," and comprehensive way, giving full attention to theological foundations and goals of world mission, and delineating their relationships with other fields of learning, with the life of the church, and with culture in general. More recently, Johannes Bavinck has gone to great pains to set forth the theory, foundations, aims, and approaches of the "science of missions" (Bavinck 1960) in a way that has never been attempted by more pragmatic American missiologists. This kind of thorough attention to issues of *methodology* may be useful in gaining recognition for missiology in American institutions of theological education today.

The American approach to the teaching of world missions, particularly as the appointment of mission professorships in American seminaries and in mission training schools increased following the formation of the Student Volunteer Movement for Foreign Missions (1886), and in the wake of the call from the Edinburgh World Missionary Conference (1910) for the provision of greater knowledge, training, and information about the world missionary movement, was based on different goals and expectations from those of European missiologists (Scherer 1971:146).

Missionary education in American Protestant seminaries, especially after 1910, was dominated by two goals: (1) to provide a modicum of prefield training for would-be missionary candidates, and (2) to foster missionary support at the local level by encouraging future pastors to take the lead in missionary support and promotion. The motivational and promotional aspects of missionary education clearly took precedence over the scholarly scientific aspects. This led to important practical benefits for missionaries and mission agencies, and measurably helped to overcome existing gaps between mission activity and the churches. But except in isolated cases it did not lead to serious reflection on what mission is—mostly because it did not appear at the time that much was required—and it produced no agreed definition of missiology.

My 1975 APM study reported on the travail of the APM in search of new foundations and in the attempt, in R. Pierce Beaver's memorable words (1950), "to build a lifeboat for floundering brothers and sisters" (Scherer 1985:448). J. Leslie Dunstan's striking evocation of the "lost sheep" syndrome—"lost sheep . . . scattered among the folds of history, theology, comparative religions, and education, wandering from the theological field to the practical and back again"—rather accurately described the identity problem of missiology in the 1960s. In Dunstan's view (1962), missiologists had failed to analyze the changes required in their own teaching, had not yet proposed a "clear and defensible justification" for the regular teaching of missiology in seminaries, and had generally allowed the subject to become peripheral in theological curricula (Scherer 1985:448).

The formation of the ASM (1973) and the direction taken in several recent APM meetings, this one included, suggest that a serious effort is now under way on the part of American missiologists to grapple with the systematic rationale, scope, and application of their discipline. It is to be hoped that the APM, in collaboration with the ASM and other mission institutes, will pursue this quest to its logical conclusion.

WHAT IS MISSIOLOGY?

My question should be understood as an *interrogative in search of an indicative*. We could probably all readily agree on a bland, bare-bones definition of *missiology* such as that offered by *Webster's Ninth New Collegiate Dictionary* (1986): "the study of the church's mission especially with respect to missionary activity." That definition accurately recognizes an important distinction between the *mission of the church* and the church's *missionary activity*, but it offers no clue as to the scope and comprehensiveness of the discipline, or how to relate *mission* to *missionary activity*.

By 1973, when the ASM was formed and the inaugural issue of *Missiology: An International Review* was published, there was still no agreement on a definition of what missiology is, though the term was then in current use. Gerald H. Anderson, writing in a lead editorial in that issue, commented:

The scope of concerns and participation both for the ASM and for this journal (*Missiology*) includes the pooling of knowledge, understanding, skills, and techniques provided by the social and behavioral sciences, regional area studies, and by a wide range of practical professions such as agriculture, education, medicine, and public health, as well as theological studies and devoted Christian witness in all its forms. Missiology embraces all these various elements and brings them into united service of the church (Anderson 1973).

Anderson's view of the nature of missiology was remarkably inclusive and accommodationist, "embracing all these various elements," and significantly not giving priority to theological foundations.

The spirit reflected in the comments of *Missiology*'s able first editor, Alan R. Tippett, also reflected the new attitude of inclusivity and accommodation. Tippett announced his intention of creating in each quarterly issue a "synthesis of material that speaks to an entirely new world situation," and noted the frightening task of producing a synthesis out of a "hodge-podge of diversity"—ethnic, theological, denominational, disciplinary, and sociological—and yet stressing unity without undercutting diversity of viewpoints. Tippett invited contributions from liberals and conservatives, Catholics and Protestants, theologians and anthropologists, and promised to publish material of worth whether he personally agreed with it or not (Tippett 1973:18–19).

In this infancy period, both the journal *Missiology* in its articles and the practitioners of missiology, as reflected in discussions in APM and ASM meetings, have demonstrated a continuing reticence about tackling the central issue of "what missiology is." In posing our subject as a question in search of an indicative, we can probably do no better than to look at two contrasting models of missiological method, one proposed by a European and the other by an Australian, in search of a better grasp of what missiology is and what it includes.

The Dutch Reformed missiologist, Johannes Verkuyl, in his thorough study entitled *Contemporary Missiology: An Introduction* (English translation, 1978), defines missiology as follows:

the study of the salvation activities of Father, Son, and Holy Spirit throughout the world geared toward bringing the kingdom of God into existence. . . . [M]issiology is the study of the worldwide church's divine mandate to be ready to serve this God who is aiming his saving acts toward this world. In dependence on the Holy Spirit and by word and deed the church is to communicate the total gospel and the total divine law to all mankind. . . . Missiology's task in every age is to investigate scientifically and critically the presuppositions, motives, structures, methods, patterns of cooperation, and leadership which the churches bring to their mandate. In addition, missiology must examine every type of human activity which combats the various evils to see if it fits the criteria and goals of God's kingdom which has both already come and is yet coming (Verkuyl 1978:5).

Verkuyl adds that missiology as a scientific discipline can never become a substitute for action and participation. If study does not lead to participation, missiology serves no purpose. Verkuyl affirms a close relationship between missiology and other theological disciplines—e.g., practical theology, church history, and dogmatics. He notes the difficulty of placing missiology exclusively into any of the major theological disciplines, because "it is involved with all the theological disciplines." He does not hesitate to describe missiology as playing a *complementary* role in relation to other disciplines in terms of its special responsibility for calling the church to missionary obedience (Verkuyl 1978:8–9).

A contrasting model and definition is offered by the Australian missionary anthropologist, Alan R. Tippett, author of *Solomon Islands Christianity*, and first editor of *Missiology*. Tippett calls for a "simple biblical theology on a soundly anthropological base"—a task that can be paraphrased as presenting God's message to human beings, by human beings, "in precise human contexts."

The simplest definition of missiology is "the study of man [sic] being brought to God in history" . . . "historical but not a history" . . . "theological but not a theology." . . . [M]issiology belong[s] to an interdisciplinary realm, with a vocabulary of its own that somehow needs to be related to the theory and research of each of the related disciplines. . . . Missiology is defined as the academic discipline or science which researches, records and applies data relating to the biblical origin, the history (including the use of documentary materials), the anthropological principles and techniques, and the theological base of the Christian mission. The theory, method, and data bank are particularly directed towards:

1. the processes by which the Christian message is communicated,

2. the encounters brought about by its proclamation to non-Christians, and

3. the planting of the Church and organization of congregations, the incorporation of converts into those congregations, and the growth and relevance of their structures and fellowship, internally to maturity, externally in outreach as the Body of Christ in local situations and beyond, in a variety of culture patterns (Tippett 1974:26–27).

Tippett adds that such research requires familiarity with the tools and techniques of anthropology, theology and history, plus linguistics and psychology. He does not hesitate to describe missiology as "a discipline in its own rights, not a mere borrower from other fields," with various dimensions interacting, influencing, and modifying each other in dynamic fashion, "like a field of chemical interaction, combination, and recombination, reproducing new substances by what I believe is called 'the transmutation of elements.' " . . . Missiology is a new thing with its own autonomous entity" (Tippett 1974:28).

Let me suggest that each of these diffuse and comprehensive, but also contrasting models of missiological reflection, each embodying its own definition of the central theme of missiology, is excellent and useful as a basis for our own consideration. Careful study of these and other approaches will probably dissuade us from any premature tendency to settle on an agreed definition of "what missiology is." They remind us of the current diversity and plurality of approaches; there appears to be more than one valid way of doing missiology, yet the very plurality of approaches may sometimes be seen as necessarily complementing or supplementing each other.

Verkuyl's definition focuses on the universal mandate for the church's participation in the mission of God, with special emphasis on its foundations and goals. It is theocentric and explicitly Trinitarian in nature, but replaces the 19th century's church-centric mission paradigm with the now preferred orientation to the "kingdom of God," in which the church plays a servant or instrumental role. Missiology is the "study of the salvation activities" of the Triune God throughout the world, and these activities are to be investigated "scientifically and critically" in every age with regard to presuppositions, motives, structures, methods, patterns, etc. Verkuyl does not precisely indicate a methodology for carrying out such scientific and critical investigations, but his introductory text offers many illustrations. A feature of Verkuyl's approach is its messianic emphasis on examining all activities that combat the evils that oppose and obstruct the movement of God's kingdom.

If Verkuyl's approach seems mainly oriented toward theological foundations and goals, Tippett's is by contrast more oriented to process, context, and well-defined research methods. Tippett's starting point is "God's message to humans"—a simple biblical theology on a soundly anthropological base—delivered to humans by humans "in precise human contexts." Understanding, defining, and carefully describing the *precise human contexts* in which the biblical message is communicated, and bringing to bear the latest tools of social-science investigation, present a greater challenge than delving deeply into the theological motives and principles of missiology today. Tippett sees missiology as a still-developing science, empirical and descriptive in nature, "a discipline in its own rights," "a new thing" interacting with a wide range of behavioral disciplines, but endeavoring to express "its own autonomous entity."

These two contrasting models of missiological reflection have more in common than might first appear, despite their differences. Both appeal to a common heritage of biblical and evangelical Christianity which requires that the divine apostolic mandate be honored and the biblical message of salvation be shared with the whole world. Both are comprehensive in scope, seeking to describe a sweeping picture of God's actions in human history. Both are scientific and critical in method, preferring careful criteria and guidelines for analysis and research. Verkuyl seeks to investigate the worldwide church's response to the divine mandate primarily in terms of its faithfulness to defined theological categories. Tippett wishes to enrich our understanding of how new churches in various contexts come into being and grow to maturity by utilizing the descriptive techniques of the social sciences, and by compiling data banks that illuminate the processes of communication, cross-cultural encounter, church planting, and inculturation. The two aspects offered here present a massive challenge to both the theory and practice of missiology.

WHAT DOES MISSIOLOGY INCLUDE?

Recognizing the obvious complexity of saying precisely "what missiology is," we shall be similarly wary of too-neat answers to the question of "what missiology

includes." The designers of this APM program have already tipped their hands by
providing that this presentation be followed by discussions in four disciplinary
groups, each discussing the advantages and limitations of teaching missiology
within a particular field: church history, systematic theology, social sciences, and
world religions. This is already a clear acknowledgment of the necessarily interdisciplinary nature of missiological reflection, and of the implied weaknesses in
any unitary approach. But we must be careful not to suggest "these four and no
more." Could there not be other disciplines with equally pressing and legitimate
claims? Why the exclusion of biblical studies? Why no reference to pastoral care
and Christian education? Where are ideological conflicts and encounters dealt
with? What about international ethical issues? Are social, political, and economic
systems included under the social sciences?

An encyclopedic approach which tries to correlate missiology in a comprehensive way to every discipline in the theological encyclopedia, not to mention the
social sciences, would be *a priori* self-defeating and doomed to failure. The
principal goals of missiology—"to study the church's mission especially with
respect to missionary activity"—would be lost sight of in a maze of peripheral
studies. Missiology must find a way to be holistic, integrative, inclusive, and
complementary to human learning without becoming *exhaustive*. Quantification of
knowledge and data will be of little use unless a clearer rationale—i.e., a set of
underlying controlling principles for the discipline as a whole—can be demonstrated. In the nature of the case, these missiological controlling principles should
be qualitative, goal-oriented, and specific. In order to say "what missiology is" and
to specify "what it includes," we shall need to pose specific criteria questions about
the relation of missiology to each discipline in question. Only a few illustrations
can be given.

Biblical Studies. The "Biblical Studies and Missiology" (BISAMI) project of
the International Association of Mission Studies (IAMS) has clearly demonstrated
that fundamental exegetical and hermeneutical issues are now much more at stake
in developing valid biblical models or paradigms for mission today. Biblical
scholars are reticent to focus on a single biblical "key word" or motif, such as
"witness," "sending," or the great commission as the all-sufficient justification for
the church's continuing participation in missionary activity. They prefer to work
with a range of complementary models (Bosch 1986). Some excellent studies, such
as those by J. Blauw (1962) and by Senior and Stuhlmueller (1983), have paved
the way, but the essential questions must be raised again and again in a timely way
in the light of both changing modes of mission and changing views of biblical
interpretation.

If biblical scholars do not normally focus on missiological issues, and if
missiologists are not by training equipped to handle hermeneutical matters with
depth and expertise, where will the task of correlation be done? Are the members
of the missiological fraternity not obliged to seek out and challenge their biblical
colleagues?

Church History. This discipline, under the inspiration of K. S. Latourette, John
Foster, Stephen Neill, and others, has yielded precious examples of how missiological concerns can be taken up synthetically within the larger framework of church

history. As between missiology and church history there is an extensive overlap—church history can be written from a missiological perspective—though it is also manifestly true that much church historical writing seems oblivious of the concerns of missiology. Certainly, church historical research, writing, and teaching can be permeated by missiological reflection—even enriched by it—without doing violence to either discipline. But this observation does not answer all the questions.

If one elects a historical model of inquiry to raise missiological issues, where do the related theoretical and practical issues get answered? Surely fundamental theological issues of mission cannot be ignored, even when they are not taken up in a systematically theological way, nor can the descriptive criteria developed by the social sciences for studying the processes of church growth in a local context be neglected. The whole question of "meaning in history" poses a range of related philosophical and ideological questions about the kingdom of God. Can historians handle this increasing load of interdisciplinary responsibility and if not, can they find colleagues in other disciplines who are willing to dialogue and team-teach?

Systematic Theology. Questions of mission theology appear to surpass all others in the dominating interest they hold for our generation, in marked contrast to the period before 1950 when theological issues shared the scene with matters of strategy and church relationships. Since Willingen 1952, both the "why?" of mission—can it be fundamentally justified?—and the "what?" of mission—what, after all, is mission today?—have continued until now as burning issues.

An entire range of questions touching on the starting point and goals of mission activity, God's mission and the church's, the meaning of Jesus Christ for mission, eschatology, soteriology, the relation of church and kingdom, the nature of evangelization, Christ and culture, Christianity and world religions, mission and social justice, liberation, baptism, conversion, church planting, inculturation, and mission and unity insistently demand answers. Mission planning, motivation, and practice will be seriously impeded if the church loses clarity about its fundamental principles. The missionary malaise of our present day surely owes much to disturbing change in global structures and relationships, but one suspects that the search for satisfying theological answers holds the ultimate key to genuine missionary renewal.

Missiology today is fortunately blessed with a growing wealth of study material isolating trends and developments in mission theology (Anderson 1961), comparing ecumenical, evangelical, and Roman Catholic emphases (Bassham 1979), or drawing upon the personal or collective contributions of "third-world theologians." The *Lausanne Covenant* (1974), *Evangelii Nuntiandi* (1975), the Report of the WCC-CWME Conference, "Your Kingdom Come" (1980), and the WCC *Ecumenical Affirmations on Mission and Evangelism* (1982) are all crucial efforts to restate the biblical and theological basis of world mission. Missiology today is more than the "theology of mission," narrowly understood, but it is surely not less, for mission cannot dispense with theological criticism and analysis.

But here again, as in the case of church history, questions of integration arise. Missiology is more than theological "head games"; Verkuyl reminds us that theoretical reflection must not become a substitute for missionary action and participation. Theology of mission is in danger of becoming an arid enterprise when speculation and analysis do not lead to missionary discipleship and participation. Moreover, analysis of motives, ends, and goals cannot be separated from study of the processes by which the gospel is proclaimed, the church planted, and the kingdom extended.

When the mode of missiological reflection employed is primarily that of systematic theology, what guarantees that the holistic treatment of other issues will not be slighted? Systematicians have generally shown but slight interest in, or acquaintance with, missiological issues. But missiologists who eschew the theological fray put themselves in peril of abandoning the vital center of mission today. Again, the question of interdisciplinary overload arises, prompting attention to questions of basic method in this approach.

Social Sciences. This group, actually a family of related disciplines, stands as the newest adjunct to our extended family of missiological relatives. Here, even more than in the traditional theological disciplines, questions of integration must be pressed to ensure that missiology remains holistic and that biblical, historical, and theological issues are not marginalized. Reflection on mission through the social sciences must demonstrate that such approaches are truly complementary, for they can in no sense be allowed to become *substitutional*. And when they are viewed as complementary or supplementary, can the secular value orientations of these sciences be tamed and made serviceable to missiology without robbing them of their own credibility and autonomy?

A host of questions follows. If we are talking of the "social science" group, which disciplines in particular? Are cultural anthropology, applied linguistics, and communication theory preferred over the study of global economics, international political tensions, corporate structures of injustice, ideological encounters, and competing value-systems? Why the preference for certain disciplines over others?

When the well-known philosophy of "church growth" is adopted as the leading motif, crucial questions of integration also arise. What relationship does the *quantified* study of growth bear to other *qualitative* factors, such as growth in faith maturity, ability to witness contextually, inculturation, and the relation of the local church to the church universal? Is the "homogeneous unit" principle theologically valid? Does the church-centric bias of church growth thinking do justice to theological concerns about eschatology and the kingdom? Such questions as these must be put when the social sciences are utilized as the primary mode for missiological reflection.

World Religions. Missiology and the study of world religions ("comparative religion," "history of religions," etc.) have often been bracketed as companion disciplines, and sometimes joined in a single academic appointment. Without disputing a very close relationship, it must be added that the pairing is not unambiguous or trouble-free. Missiology can in no sense be equated with the History of Religion(s). Still, the study of and response to human religions, especially in the light of divine revelation, plays an enduring central role in missiological reflection. Missiological teaching can and should only be done out of an interreligious mode when fully integrated with other biblical, historical, and theological approaches.

A primary conflict arises over the point that while history of religion ordinarily prides itself on being "value-free" and theologically "neutral," missiology is theologically committed and goal-oriented. Taken together, the two form an "odd couple" of bedmates, though the tension in the relationship can, properly handled, become the source of great productivity and originality. Disputes about the precise nature and purpose of interreligious dialogue continue to swirl about this question.

There are four or more complementary dimensions: the need to view the world of religions (including traditional and folk religions) as belonging to the same context of evangelization as culture, society, language, and ethnicity, and therefore having an intrinsic relationship to local theologies and spiritualities; the urgency of developing a theological position on religion and revelation that applies Christian categories to other living faiths; the closely related question of restating the Christian hope for the eschaton, and the Christian claim for "finality" or ultimacy in Christ (we need no longer use the pejorative "superiority"!) in the light of today's pluralistic worldwide religious encounter; and finally, actual preparation for the practice of interreligious dialogue as an aspect of mission.

Paul Knitter has recently surveyed and compared evangelical, mainline Protestant and Roman Catholic theological models for evaluating other faiths and entering into interreligious dialogue (Knitter 1985); his conclusions will probably not satisfy most members of this missiological fraternity. Meanwhile, Hans Küng and a group of Tübingen colleagues have recently completed a very impressive preliminary survey of Christianity's relationships with Islam, Hinduism, and Buddhism in which they undertake "Christian self-criticism in the light of other religions," and "Christian criticism of the other religions in the light of the gospel" (Küng 1985:xvii). Such studies as these are valuable interim aids but they are still far from definitive. The search for proper missiological integration—above all at the levels of accurate description, theological criticism, and clarity with regard to the goals of dialogue—must be persistently pushed when interreligious studies are lifted up as the primary mode of missiological reflection. The service that the study of world religions renders to the mission of God must be clearly stated.

Essential or Normative Missiology. A case must still be made for an essential treatment of missiological themes which sets the norms for all the complementary approaches we have just considered. When everything is complementary to something else in the encyclopedia of theological disciplines, the arcade of social sciences, or the world of religious studies, just what then is *normative* missiologically? Can the various complementary approaches function in the absence of an enduring awareness of what constitutes the integrating missiological center?

The basic traditions and conceptual principles embodied in the works of Warneck, Bavinck, and Verkuyl will still be needed for the guidance of those who work in the complementary areas. Does it follow that every practicing missiologist who works from a historical, theological, social science, or world religions perspective also needs to be an "essential missiologist" in touch with the roots, motives, classical foundations, and goals of the discipline—i.e., God's glory, "conversion of the Gentiles," planting of the church, hastening and preparing for the kingdom? At least it seems so to us.

WHAT MISSION IS, AND
WHAT THIS HAS TO SAY ABOUT MISSIOLOGY

Mention was made above about the elusiveness of the quest for an agreed definition of missiology, and the probable reason for this. We must now come back to this point. No less an authority than O. G. Myklebust has recently stated his view as follows:

> As I see it, the question, primarily and fundamentally, is not "what missiology is" but "what mission is." The present uncertainty is in no small degree accounted for by the failure of many missiologists to make the *text* rather than the *context* the point of orientation. Far too much attention, to mention just one example, is paid to religious pluralism and far too little to God's revelation and saving acts in Jesus as recorded in Holy Scriptures (Myklebust 1987 [emphasis added]).

David Bosch, commenting on failure of nerve and "mission in crisis," reflects the same question when he notes that "in many circles there is a great deal of uncertainty about what mission really is . . . people are grappling in a new way with the question about the essence of mission. . . . The picture is one of change and complexity, tension and unity, and no small measure of confusion exists over the very nature of mission itself" (Bosch 1980:8–9).

What does this say about our discipline? Missiology, reflecting the status of mission itself, is in a state of flux and ferment. No single definition of "what missiology is" will satisfy all stripes of missiologist in the absence of prior agreement on "what mission is." Search for an agreed definition must continue, though in the nature of the case it will probably continue to elude us. Myklebust's *text* and *context*—foundations and processes—define the parameters within which the new theoretical-empirical discipline is taking shape. No missiologist is excused from working on both fronts simultaneously. Here also a continuing dialogue among the various positions represented in our teaching fraternity will be useful.

AN INDEPENDENT OR AN INTEGRATIVE DISCIPLINE?

Our survey has already conclusively shown that a "both/and" answer must be given to this question. Missiology cannot function in independence of other theological disciplines, the world of social sciences, and world religions. Yet integration with these very disciplines can hardly take place unless there continues to be an "essential missiology" which sets the norms and raises the criteria for integration. Experience teaches that missiological learning is not likely to be extracted from other disciplines without some coaxing and prompting. Thus every missiologist should be prepared to "integrate" but without losing a sense of ultimate independence. Myklebust himself opts for a synthesis of the two approaches (Myklebust 1961:338).

As Mylkebust's studies have shown, early continental missiology was set up largely on the "independent model," designed to give status and recognition to the autonomy and worth of the then unproved discipline alongside the more venerable and recognized fields of theological instruction (Myklebust 1955). Recent continental missiology, by contrast, has taken a decidedly more integrative and interdisciplinary approach. Missiology in the United Kingdom, to the extent that it was done, showed a preference for complete integration into the field of church historical studies (Myklebust 1961), the assumption being that ecclesiology properly understood would generate missiological reflection. Here the discipline was never really established at the university level, and only in training colleges such as those at Selly Oak is missiology taken seriously. Missiological reflection in the U.K. was mainly done in mission executive offices by able administrators such as Max Warren and John V. Taylor. Some Americans have preferred this British model.

A brief comment may be appropriate with regard to the long-term effects of church-mission integration on missiological perspectives. It may be surmised that the much heralded integration of the former International Missionary Council (IMC) into the life of the World Council of Churches (WCC) at the New Delhi Assembly (1961) would probably also foster the notion that mission should be understood and done mainly from within the context of the church's institutional life—as an ongoing aspect of the total life and mission of the church. The event of integration did in fact raise all of the old questions about the "special charism" of voluntary mission societies, and the unique preparation needed for cross-cultural witness. Yet precisely at the time when the ecumenical mission enterprise was being "churchified," mission theology began to move away from a "church-centric" understanding of mission toward one more oriented toward the coming of the kingdom. In our view, missiology needs freedom from a too tight embrace by ecclesiastical structures so as to be unimpeded in fulfilling its primary task of permeating the entire *world* with the knowledge of God's saving acts. In this way it will also render its best service to the churches.

MISSIOLOGY'S RELATION TO THE MISSION OF GOD, GLOBAL MISSION, RE-EVANGELIZATION, AND THEOLOGICAL EDUCATION

Large questions deserve adequate answers, but here only a few hints can be given. Missiology's primary task is the study of the mission of the Triune God, and within that of the mission of Jesus, the apostles, the church(es), and mission-sending bodies. This means that missiology is the study of God's mission everywhere—in all six continents, "from everywhere to everywhere"—certainly no longer concentrated on sending from the West. It goes without saying that God's mission is more inclusive than that of the church, though we cannot here spell out the scope of *Missio Dei*. World mission in today's understanding is global, even cosmic, in scope. The question of the re-evangelization of the post-Christian lands of the West, the U.S.A. among them, can no longer be excluded from our global missiological agenda. Tools and conceptual criteria must be developed for analyzing the West as a "mission field." Once again we pose a question about the desirability of developing a closer linkage between missiology and the task of evangelization.

A certain faddishness now seems to be attached in theological schools to programs that foster internationalization, globalization, and cross-cultural encounters on a world scale. As valuable and liberating as such exchanges are in terms of rescuing churches and theological education from institutional myopia and parochialism, they should not be confused with the aims of missiology. These programs build to a large extent on the missionary fruits of the past and the ecumenical networks of the present, but they appear at first glance to surrender the crucial theological goals of missiology—above all its concern with the "unfinished task" and the priority of world evangelization—for the experience of ecumenical and cross-cultural togetherness. In that sense, they represent a secularized end-product of the age-old mission experience. Missiology can render a real service to programs designed to "globalize" or "internationalize" theological education by helping to infuse them with a deeper awareness of the theological significance of global travel and interchurch contact. The sending of academics and theological students into the world should emulate God's sending of Jesus into the world as a witness to the dawning of its eschatological healing and salvation.

REFERENCES

Anderson, Gerald H. 1961 "The Theology of Mission Among Protestants in the Twentieth Century," *The Theology of the Christian Mission*, ed. G. H. Anderson. New York/Toronto/London: McGraw-Hill.

_____. 1973 "Introducing Missiology," a guest editorial in the inaugural issue of *Missiology*: 1 (Jan. 1973), 3–4.

Bavinck, H. H. 1960 *An Introduction to the Science of Missions*, tr. D. H. Freeman. Philadelphia: Presbyterian and Reformed Publishing Co.

Blauw, Johannes. 1962 *The Missionary Nature of the Church: A Survey of the Biblical Theology of Mission*. Grand Rapids: Eerdmans.

Bosch, David J. 1980 *Witness to the World: The Christian Mission in Theological Perspective*. London: Marshall, Morgan, Scott.

_____. 1986 "Toward a Hermeneutic for 'Biblical Studies and Mission,' " *Mission Studies* III-2 (1986), 65–79.

Buerkle, Horst. 1979 *Missionstheologie*. Stuttgart/Berlin/Köln/Mainz: W. Kohlhammer .

Gensichen, Hans-Werner. 1971 *Glaube für die Welt: Theologische Aspeckte der Mission*. Guetersloh: Gerd Mohn.

Glazik, Jozef. 1971 "Missiology," *Concise Dictionary of the Christian World Mission*, Ed. S. Neill, G. H. Anderson, and J. Goodwin, pp. 387–389. Nashville and New York: Abingdon Press.

Myklebust, Olav Guttorm. 1955 *The Study of Mission in Theological Education*, Vol. I. Oslo: Egede Instituttet.

_____. 1957 *The Study of Missions in Theological Education*, Vol. II. Oslo: Egede Instituttet.

_____. 1961 "Integration or Independence? Some Reflections on the Status of the Study of Missions in the Theological Curriculum," *Basileia: Walter Freytag zum 60. Geburtstag*, ed. J. Hermelink & H. J. Margull. Second Edition. Stuttgart: Evang. Missionsverlag.

_____. 1987 Letter to the author, dated Oslo, March 6, 1987. Used with permission.

Scherer, James A. 1971 "Mission in Theological Education," *The Future of the Christian*

World Mission: Studies in Honor of R. Pierce Beaver, ed. W. J. Danker and Wi Jo Kang. Grand Rapids: Eerdmans Publishing Co.

_____. 1985 "The Future of Missiology as an Academic Discipline in Seminary Education: An Attempt at Reinterpretation and Clarification," *Missiology* 13 (Oct. 1985), 445–60.

Senior, Donald C. P. and Carroll Stuhlmueller, C. P. 1983 *The Biblical Foundations for Mission*, Maryknoll: Orbis Books.

Seumois, Andrew V., O.M.I. 1961 "The Evolution of Mission Theology among Roman Catholics," *The Theology of the Christian Mission*, ed. G. H. Anderson, New York/Toronto/London: McGraw-Hill.

Shenk, Wilbert R. 1987 *The American Society of Missiology 1972-87*. Elkhart, Ind.: The American Society of Missiology.

Tippett, Alan R. 1973 "Missiology: 'For Such a Time as This,' " *Missiology* 1 (Jan. 1973), 15–22.

_____. 1974 "Missiology, A New Discipline," *The Means of World Evangelization: Missiological Education at the Fuller School of World Mission*, ed., Alvin Martin. South Pasadena, Calif.: William Carey Library.

Verkuyl, Johannes. 1978 *Contemporary Missiology: An Introduction*, tr. and ed. by Dale Cooper. Grand Rapids: Eerdmans Publishing Co.

Part V

DOCUMENTATION

15

The Whole Gospel from Latin America for All Peoples

Third Latin American Congress on Evangelism *

The Third Latin American Congress on Evangelism (CLADE III) took place in Quito, Ecuador, August 24–September 4, 1992. It attracted more than one thousand evangelical Christians from twenty-six countries. Convened by the Latin American Theological Fraternity, CLADE III sought to commemorate 1492, to recognize the growing missionary vitality of evangelical churches in Latin America, to face the challenge of the present, to contribute to the unity of God's people, and "to encourage the development of a missionary vision and a wholistic evangelization all over the Latin American continent and beyond it." The Quito congress was a significant missiological event, both because it demonstrated that Latin American Protestants are taking seriously their role in world evangelization, and because it attempted to deal critically with crucial missiological issues facing the Latin American evangelical movement.

Five hundred years after the arrival of Europeans in the Americas, as we gather in Quito, Ecuador, for the Third Latin American Congress on Evangelism (CLADE III, August 24–September 4, 1992), we wish to express our gratitude to God for this assembly of evangelical[1] Christians from 24 countries with their rich variety of cultures, ethnic groups, and languages. We meet to reflect on the theme "The Whole Gospel from Latin America for All Peoples" at a time of great global changes which pose serious questions regarding the situation of the peoples of our continent.

We confess our faith in the whole gospel of Jesus Christ according to the Holy Scriptures, united as a family with all the evangelical churches of Latin America, and in the same spirit as that of CLADE I and CLADE II. We have reflected upon different aspects of the gospel in relation to our context and the challenge that it presents for our participation in world mission. We commit ourselves to put into missionary practice the consequences which result from the reflection and testimonies presented in this assembly.

---

* Reprinted from *Report of CLADE III*, Latin American Theological Fraternity. September 1992.

I. THE WHOLE GOSPEL

1. THE GOSPEL AND THE WORD OF GOD

The whole counsel of God and the manifestation of his kingdom have been made known to us through the gospel. The Scriptures record the revelation of God in concrete acts in history. They converge on Jesus Christ, the full and definitive expression of God's revelation. Thus the Word of God is the basis and the starting point for the life, theology, and mission of the church.

2. THE GOSPEL OF CREATION

God is the Creator of all, and what he created is good. He created the human being, man and woman, in his image, as beings called to live in a harmonious relationship with him, with their neighbors, and with nature. God placed them as stewards responsible for the whole creation for the benefit of all humankind. But human beings fell into sin and the whole creation suffered the effects of this fall, remaining captive to sin and death. God, however, in his sovereignty has taken the initiative in establishing a covenant to reconcile human beings and everything created to himself, through the person and work of Jesus Christ. In Christ, God is restoring human dignity, transforming cultures and leading his creation to final redemption.

3. THE GOSPEL OF FORGIVENESS AND RECONCILIATION

Jesus Christ is the incarnate Word, the gift of God and the only way to him. Through the life, death, and resurrection of Jesus Christ, forgiveness is offered to human beings, and reconciliation and redemption for all creation. In order to receive salvation, repentance and faith are essential as an expression of total dependence upon God. Those who receive forgiveness become children of God and this new filial relationship enables them to obey him. The new life involves maintaining and developing this relationship with their Creator. It produces a new relationship with their neighbors and with all creation, mediated by an alliance with the Lord and based on the practice of love, truth, and justice. God in Christ creates a forgiven and reconciled community, called to be an agent of forgiveness and reconciliation in a context of hatred and discrimination.

4. THE GOSPEL AND THE COMMUNITY OF THE SPIRIT

The person of the Holy Spirit acts with power in the world primarily through the church, granting life, power, and gifts for its development, maturity, and mission. The church, the community of those reconciled to God, is sent into the world by Jesus Christ. In the church a radical change takes place, demonstrating the divine purpose to eliminate all injustice, oppression, and signs of death. As the community of the Spirit, the church should proclaim liberty to all those oppressed by the devil and promote a pastoral ministry of restoration which brings consolation to those who suffer discrimination, margination, and dehumanization.

5. THE GOSPEL AND THE KINGDOM OF GOD

With the coming of Jesus Christ, the kingdom of God became present among us, full of grace and truth. The kingdom stands in constant conflict with the power of darkness; the struggle occurs in heavenly places and is manifest in the entire creation and personal, collective, and structural levels. The community of the kingdom, however, lives, sustained by the confidence that the victory has already been won and that the kingdom of God will be fully manifest at the end of the ages. With divinely delegated power and authority, the community assumes its mission in this conflict to become God's agent for the redemption of all creation. The King Jesus Christ became incarnate and calls his community to do the same in the world. To follow him as his disciples means to appropriate Christ's life and mission.

6. THE GOSPEL OF JUSTICE AND POWER

The gospel reveals a God who is holy, just, and powerful in both character and action. Therefore, the church is called to live in accordance with the justice of the kingdom, by the power of the Spirit. In a world characterized by the abuse of power and the predominance of injustice, the testimony of the church confronts the powers that dominate the present order. Thus the proclamation of the kingdom announces Jesus Christ and denounces the forces of evil.

II. FROM LATIN AMERICA

1. THE EVANGELICAL CHURCH
FROM A HISTORICAL PERSPECTIVE

In the Latin American evangelical community a missionary concern for other continents has been awakened. New generations of evangelicals, however, generally do not know their own historical roots and Protestant heritage. The knowledge of our own history is essential in order to avoid the errors of the past, to recuperate distinctive characteristics of our heritage, and to fulfill our missionary mandate.

In Latin America and in the Caribbean, Protestantism has historical roots that date from the 16th century. It is an integral part of the history of Latin America, not simply an alienating foreign element at the service of the advance of present-day imperialism. This affirmation does not excuse the evangelical church for its historical errors and for the deformations of the gospel as it was introduced and established on this continent. It is essential, therefore, to examine the positive and negative contributions of European and North American missiology as well as those of Latin American missiology.

2. GOSPEL AND CULTURE

The gospel is relevant to all of human reality, including culture through which humankind transforms creation. The capacity for cultural creation is a gift granted by God, in whose image human beings were created. Thus, it is important that culture occupy the place it deserves in our logical reflection and practice.

During these 500 years, our continent has witnessed contempt for the autochthonous cultures and their systematic destruction in the name of evangelization. The subjection and the abuse which the indigenous peoples suffered must be condemned. Thus it is absolutely essential to seek reconciliation between our peoples. At the same time we must recognize that every culture can be an adequate vehicle for the faithful communication of the gospel. From this perspective every culture should be understood, respected and promoted without presupposing the superiority of one culture over others. It should be pointed out as well that every culture is affected by sin, which introduced corruption, conflicts, egotism, and the breaking of relations between God and all of creation. Therefore, all cultures are under the judgment of the Word. The Creator may not be identified with his creation nor with any particular culture. The revelation of God in Christ transcends both and at the same time enters into a relationship with both creation and culture to redeem them.

Evangelical missiology should function in two ways. First, it should recognize, respect and dignify peoples and their cultures; second, it should evaluate them in the light of the judgment of the Word, offering the hope of the gospel for their transformation. The faithfulness of the church to the purposes of God demands a contextual hermeneutic which permits the faithful communication of the gospel in open dialogue with culture. The church should fulfill its mission of announcing integral salvation to the whole human being in the reality in which he or she is rooted.

3. EVANGELICAL IDENTITY

As evangelicals, we need to reevaluate our indigenous, African, mestizo, European, Asian, and creole roots, and consider the plurality of cultures and races that have contributed to our enrichment. As the Latin American church, we confess that we have identified more with foreign cultural values than with those authentically our own. By God's grace, because of our cultural identity and our evangelical identity we can face the world without a sense of inferiority or shame.

The affirmation of our evangelical identity involves reaffirming our commitment to our Reformation heritage. It does not mean assuming a noncritical position with respect to our tradition, doctrines, or missiology. As a church we are called to consistent reformation in the light of the Scriptures as our final authority.

We must evaluate the models of mission we inherited from the past or import in the present, and seek new models. This requires forging a missiology from Latin America that takes into account the experiences and contributions of the churches from the different ethnic and cultural groups of the continent. Nevertheless, the search for new models must not lead us to make concessions with respect to the truth of Jesus Christ.

We thank God for progress in the unity of the evangelical church in Latin America and for the new forms of cooperation which have arisen in the fulfillment of its mission. However, we must recognize that individualism and denominationalism have created divisions in the Latin American church. To confess the unity of the church in Christ means to overcome ideological, cultural, social, economic, and denominational barriers. We need to open ourselves to constructive dialogue, to value each contribution, to strengthen communion, and to cooperate in mission. It is not honest on our part to proclaim a gospel that reconciles the world if we still have not become reconciled among ourselves.

4. THE SOCIAL-POLITICAL CONTEXT

Latin America at present can be characterized as a continent in crisis. Various countries have suffered under repressive military regimes which committed grave violations of human rights. In others, many years of civil war have caused enormous human and economic loss. The persistence of male dominance in our culture has made women the victims of different kinds of discrimination which limit their full participation in social and civil roles. Profound social and racial divisions in the country and in the city place millions of men, women, youth, and children in conditions of extreme poverty, denying them the employment, adequate food, housing, health, and education that make possible equality of life that is truly human.

Purely formal democracy, corruption of state institutions, and inadequate neo-liberal economic measures show that power does not serve the whole of society, least of all the impoverished majority. The problems of corruption, the external debt, drug traffic, terrorism, moral degradation in its different forms, and the disintegration of the family also lacerate our peoples.

5. THE RESPONSIBILITY OF THE CHURCH

In the face of this situation, our Christian conscience cannot close its eyes. The gospel of the kingdom of God exhorts us to practice justice, which is the essential consequence of forgiveness and reconciliation in Jesus Christ. Our faithfulness to the call of the gospel demands that we assume Christian responsibility in the conflictive situations of our continent. The church must affirm and promise the life denied by all sin, by unjust structures, and by avaricious interest groups. Within its community, the different forms of discrimination predominant in society on the basis of sex, educational level, age, nationality, and race must be ended. The church fulfills its mission as it follows Jesus' example and takes seriously God's question to Cain, "Where is your brother?"

We recognize that the Latin American evangelical church generally has not assumed this responsibility faithfully. It has confused the world, into which it was sent to serve, with worldliness and sin and has isolated itself from social and political processes. In some cases, it even justified violent dictatorial regimes. This explains why some evangelicals who have participated in the public arena have achieved little or nothing in favor of the majority of the people; on the contrary, they have limited their political participation to satisfying personal interests and to obtaining certain privileges for the evangelical church.

At the same time, we celebrate the growing awareness of the evangelical church with respect to its social and political responsibility and its increasing participation in society. Different evangelical entities, churches, and individual believers participate in development projects, in public administration, and in institutions that defend human rights.

6. THE RESPONSIBILITY OF THE CHRISTIAN

The proclamation of the whole gospel commits us to the creative work of developing more and better ways of participation in society. The certainty of the final triumph of Jesus Christ, guaranteed by his resurrection, impels us to make constructive contributions, even though they may not achieve definite results. Our commitment to Jesus Christ as the only mediator of the peace of God provides the foundation for the conviction that his redemptive work is relevant for every conflict and for all human suffering.

Responsible participation in civil life requires the preparation of leaders motivated by the Christian call to service. The church should affirm that every aspect of national life is an area of legitimate action for Christian service. It must provide formative help and pastoral accompaniment for those who have a political calling. At the same time it is necessary that the church assume its prophetic function to denounce, among other matters, the abuse of sex, the manipulation of the communications media, and the deification of the state, money, and violence, whatever its origin. It does so legitimately when it manifests in its own existence the life of love, justice, and peace which is possible through obedience to the Word and the power of the Spirit of God. The exercise of leadership in the life of the local churches should be marked by the model of the suffering servant and show a contrast with the political demagoguery and other deformations caused by the abuse of power.

Practice is demonstrating that local churches can respond to the needs of their communities according to the extent of their resources. They are developing projects that show the possibility of transformation, beginning with local initiatives and resources that promote appreciation for the dignity of persons and of peoples; we see here a challenge that should be taken seriously by the entire evangelical community. The power of the gospel and consistent action on the part of evangelical churches can permeate and transform the conditions of injustice and inequality that prevail today in Latin America.

III. FOR ALL PEOPLES

1. THE UNIVERSALITY OF MISSION

God fulfilled his promise to provide a redeemer for the whole world. The purpose of God is that all human beings be saved through faith in Jesus Christ. The sufficiency and the universality of Jesus Christ are of the essence of the gospel. The universal character of the Christian faith and the confession of the sovereignty of Christ confer on the church its missionary nature. Consequently, the church is sent into the world to live and to be the messenger of the universality of the gospel.

The divine purpose and the universality of the gospel do not mean that all pathways and options are valid in order to obtain God's salvation. The sacramentalistic and ritualistic practices which express the intention to achieve justification by works are foreign to the purpose revealed by God in the Scriptures. The unique truth of the gospel and its resultant ethic oppose all universalism and relativism that consider every religious experience as equally valid.

2. THE WHOLE CHURCH IS MISSIONARY

The whole church is responsible for the evangelization of all peoples, races, and tongues. A faith that considers itself universal but which is not missionary becomes sterile rhetoric lacking authority. The affirmation that the whole church is missionary is based upon the priesthood of all believers. For the fulfillment of this mission, Jesus Christ has provided his church with the gifts and the power of the Holy Spirit.

3. INTEGRAL MISSION

The vision, action, and missionary reflection of the Church should be based upon the gospel which, when it is comprehended in all its fullness, is proclaimed in word and deed and is directed to the entire human person. We must do our missiology on the basis of the Word, from our Latin American reality, and in dialogue with other missiologies, seeking to overcome the deformations or dichotomies that may have affected the gospel we received. This also demands a comprehension of the new challenges posed by the world today, such as globalization, postmodernity, the resurgence of racism, esoteric religions, and growing ecological deterioration.

4. THE NEW MISSIONARY CONSCIOUSNESS IN LATIN AMERICA

The Holy Spirit has brought to life in Latin America a new missionary consciousness. To the missionary practice of the past is added a growing willingness to assume the responsibility of the church, in obedience to the Word, from within Latin America. Opportunities for the preparation and sending of missionaries to other continents and contexts have increased during these last years. However, the new possibilities provided by this missionary activity should lead us to a continuous evaluation and correction of models and experiences in the light of the Word of God.

5. THE INCARNATIONAL PATTERN FOR MISSION

The incarnation is the model for the mission of the church. In his incarnation Jesus identified himself with sinful people, shared their aspirations, anguish, and weaknesses, and dignified them as creatures made in the image of God. The church is called to approach its mission in Jesus' way. To accomplish this demands the crossing of geographical, cultural, social, linguistic, and spiritual frontiers, with all that this entails. In all the world, the growth of great cities and their impoverished masses constitutes an especially urgent challenge. To respond to all of these needs it is necessary to reconsider the New Testament model, adequately use the social and human sciences, and reflect on this practice. Also indispensable is the spiritual discipline that equips the missionary with the holiness and the humility that make possible a real respect for and appreciation of other languages and cultures and faithfulness to the gospel.

6. THE URGENCY OF THE MISSION

The church in Latin America must fully and without delay assume its responsibility in world evangelization. It should create and promote training centers in every country, with adequate programs of preparation for local and transcultural missions. The structure of all theological education should be revised in light of the missionary imperative. Missionary advance has always arisen from the spiritual vitality during periods of renewal. To be a missionary church, the church in Latin America must renew its dependence upon the Spirit and give itself to prayer. In this way it can respond to the challenge to proclaim the whole gospel from Latin America to all peoples of the earth.

CONCLUSION

We praise God for the privilege he has given us to attend the Third Latin American Congress on Evangelism at this critical moment in the history of our peoples. Such a privilege moves us to renew our commitment to our Lord Jesus Christ and to his church as the bearer of the Good News of the kingdom of love and justice he came to establish. With humility we commend ourselves to God so that he, through his Holy Spirit, may instill in us the determination to please him in everything according to his good will. "Now to the King eternal, immortal, invisible, the only God, be honor and glory forever and ever. Amen."

NOTE

1. The term "evangelical" in this document, according to the usage in Latin America, refers to all Protestant churches and Christians.

16

The Verdun Proclamation

Caribbean/African American Dialogue
and the Caribbean Council of Churches *

Meeting at St. John, Barbados, from 1–3 May 1992, the Caribbean/African American Dialogue (CAAD) and the Caribbean Council of Churches (CCA) held a consultation to reflect on the meaning and challenge of the year 1492 and to search for a common vision for strategies of people's liberation, "lest we endure another 500 years of racism and dispossession." The consultation agreed that the event should not be a backward-looking exercise of self-pity but a sharpening of consciousness regarding historical conditions," thereby to understand better our present realities and to be able to chart a course for our total liberation and self-realization." The continuance of racism and economic domination from outside the region were seen as determining factors, the question being: how to escape the throes of helplessness, hopelessness, alienation, and dehumanization that beset the Caribbean? Among recommendations from the consultation was one calling on the churches to work for the creation of a Caribbean theology—one that will liberate Caribbean people from a Eurocentric worldview.

PREAMBLE

The Caribbean/African American Dialogue (CAAD) and the Caribbean Council of Churches (CCC) brought together representatives from throughout the Caribbean (including Surinam and Cayenne) and from North America and the United Kingdom in a consultation held at the Marian Retreat Center, St John, Barbados, 1-3 May, 1992. This consultation was the first Caribbean activity in the implementation of decisions taken at the first Inter-Continental Consultation of Indigenous, African-American and African-Caribbean Peoples on Racism in the Americas, convened by the World Council (WCC) in Rio de Janeiro in September 1990.

The Rio de Janeiro consultation reflected on the meaning and challenge of 1992, the year of the fifth centennial of the arrival of Columbus in the Americas and the Caribbean, in the context of the search for a common vision for future strategies of peoples' liberation "lest we endure another 500 years of racism and dispossession."

---

* Taken from *International Review of Mission* 82 (January 1993), pp. 63–71, and reprinted with permission of the publisher.

The Caribbean-African dialogue does not separate itself from the challenge that confronts all dispossessed peoples of the hemisphere—indigenous, black, East Indian, "poor whites"—nor indeed from its responsibility to join the struggles of all oppressed peoples of the world, dramatically highlighted by the deeper significance of the 1992 anniversary, as we seek to reverse the course of our marginalization, which both symbolically and realistically may be considered to have begun in 1492.

The consultation paused to reflect on these five hundred years and agreed that looking back should not be an exercise in self-pity, nor the pathological discarding of our responsibility for our own salvation at the present time, when political independence has been achieved in the majority of the Caribbean countries and political power is in the hands of the people. We look back in order to sharpen our consciousness of our historical condition, thereby to understand better our present realities and to be able to chart a course for our total liberation and self-realization.

The consultation looked at the dominant factors that make up the Caribbean's historical condition. For example, racism and imperialistic economic domination entered into a symbiotic relationship in the founding of new world societies, and has assumed grotesque proportions. They continue to underlie the contemporary realities of the Caribbean and the third world in general, although they have acquired a new complex set of dimensions, with class, for example, coming to intersect with race as the focus of economic exploitation.

The consultation also recognized the positive aspect of the resourcefulness and resilience of Caribbean peoples as they created cultural systems of religion, world view, and language, not only to put order into their daily lives, but also as instruments of resistance, rebellion, and survival. The Haitian revolution is seen in particular as an important act, but it is one among many others of self-liberation that have abounded in the post-Columbian Caribbean historical experience. These acts of self-liberation gave freedom to a greater number of persons than those who were freed by colonial edict. The consultation observed that the Caribbean would do well to consider whether at the present time, rather than the quincentenary of Columbus' adventure, it is the bicentennial of the Haitian revolution that should be the significant anniversary.

As we face the prospect of the emergence of a monolithic capitalist global village, it becomes even more urgent for the dialogue to continue among Caribbean peoples (and indeed among third world peoples in general) to determine our own place, on our negotiated terms, in the new dispensation. We want to continue to deepen our knowledge and understanding of our condition, refocussing the role that racism and capitalism have played historically in genocide, economic deprivation and marginalization, family disruptions, personal and cultural alienation, and prepare ourselves to withstand the continuing dehumanization that we may expect from the unbridled, neoliberal free-market systems that Caribbean governments seem poised to adopt.

This leads to the question: How do we escape the throes of helplessness, hopelessness, alienation, and dehumanization now besetting the Caribbean? Without pretending to have definitive answers, the consultation examined a number of issues and defined a modest set of actions and measures to which participants committed themselves.

CONCERNS

RACISM

Xenophobia and racism seem to be inherent in human nature. Throughout the history of humanity, human beings, as individuals or as groups, have always resented, feared, or resisted the presence of, or the intrusion of, other people or groups, just because they were foreigners, or "different."

It was in the 16th century, when the development of the mercantile system was to give birth to capitalism, that racism really took on new dimensions as a concept whereby one ethnic group (namely the black Africans) were labelled genetically inferior on the basis of their different origins and skin color.

Within the decade that followed the intrusion of Columbus into this part of the world, most of the indigenous populations had been exterminated by the European conquistadors in their ravenous lust for gold.

From their viewpoint, it then became a "vital necessity" to capitalize on an availability of cheap labor to improve and increase production. In order to mitigate the plight of the "Indians," the church endorsed the trade in Africans as slaves.

Measures were deliberately and methodically taken by legislative authorities of the political powers to perpetuate this exploitation and oppression.

The black African was classified as subhuman—just above the animal, "a tabula rasa" — devoid of intellect and soul, who therefore could be sold as chattel. The Christian churches played their part in this dehumanizing process. The colour of the African's skin was interpreted by religious authorities as living proof that he was cursed by God. To put a seal on the matter, neither the intellectual capacity nor the spiritual life of the African was recognized. As a consequence, both the so-called superior race and the so-called inferior one came to internalize these beliefs about themselves, designed by the white European.

When the European powers invaded Asia and Africa in the 19th century, although the driving force behind them was their desire to acquire wealth and assert supremacy, they professed that the white man's burden was to civilize.

Today, five centuries after the intrusion, new peoples have come, slavery has been abolished—at least physically—and most of the region is enjoying political independence.

Still, racism is never far away. Its hideous face shows itself more and more openly; the alter ego of human greed and lust for power by the few who have capital over the many. The dehumanizing process takes so many forms: we keep repeating the same self-debasing sayings and proverbs about ourselves and our skin colour; we keep on having the same self-destructive attitudes towards ourselves and our people, persistently seeking the European's seal before accepting recognition of ourselves as able and talented people, and endorsing and perpetuating the same evils against our resident minorities. Our women are overworked and underpaid in the world of commerce; our Haitian brothers and sisters endure seemingly endless suffering; worst of all, we make ourselves guilty of initiating among or against our oppressed fellow human beings the same patterns of racial hostility from which we ourselves have so direly suffered.

Even if European civilization in dealing with other civilizations does not—as it should— rid itself of the prejudices that have dehumanized Europeans as much as their ex-slaves, surely it is high time we ourselves broke away from a eurocentric framework and moved into a humane design of civilization, as subjects of our own destiny, with pride in our past and in the achievements of our resistance, with pride in our survival and in the great contributions we have made to humanity.

Indeed it is time we put into practice the call of this Creole poem:

> Yo lire tannou
> Yo bannou ta yo
> Nou ka tire ta yo
> No ka pwan tannou
> Nou ka libere nou.

> (They took what was ours
> They gave us theirs
> We are removing theirs
> We are taking ours back
> We are liberating ourselves.)

CARIBBEAN CULTURAL IDENTITY

A people's culture is their way of life as formed by their own historical experience in their own geographical environment. It therefore becomes immediately clear that a Caribbean cultural identity is an indisputable reality. Born of displacement, resistance, and survival, it is a cultural identity attested to this, such as our creolization of both the languages and lifestyles adopted from Europe and our (too often) ready adaptability to their models—attested to in the significantly open-air aspects of our lifestyle, the percussive character and notable folk-rhythm of our music, in the catching sensuality of our dancing, in our pervasive religiosity, and so on.

Most of these characteristics are markedly underpinned by a black-African ethos, which spreads across all the euro-determined national and linguistic boundaries of the Caribbean and which has established a certain unity, definable as Caribbean, in the diversity of territorial or insular subcultures of the region. To that basic unifying design have been added significant Asiatic elements, mostly East Indian, and to a lesser degree Chinese, together with—mostly on the rimland continental territories—remainder elements of our aboriginal predecessors— Arawak, Carib and Maya—the only truly indigenous Caribbean peoples.

Caribbean culture therefore has developed out of the dynamic cross-fertilization of all the world's major races—Amerindian, Caucasian, African, Indian, Chinese—each today a recognizable limb of an egalitarian stock that is unmatched anywhere else on earth. It has provided a conglomerate heritage that in some ways leads the world, as in the historically unsurpassed Amerindian respect for the environment, or in present-day musical inventiveness as shown by the Trinidadian steel band, or in flashes of sporting supremacy, as on the cricket field; in other ways, benefitting from the natural gift of perennial sunshine, it has created its own kind of colorful festivals—carnival, kadooment, jonkonnu, mashramani, etc.—that each have a peculiar power to galvanize cooperative communities of friendship out of the ranks of strangers, so much so that this Caribbean cultural skill has become a welcome import in the friendless megacities of Britain and North America.

There is a heritage, too, of vital skills and of values developed through a long Caribbean history of enforced adversity, skills of harnessing the environment for survival, whether it be flavouring and preserving foods, or using medicinal herbs from the bush; values of respect anxiously sought but morally earned among one's peers and then keenly cherished, and values of responsibility to the extended family.

Caribbean culture has emerged creatively as an identifiable entity, even if a loose one, out of a harshly repressive past. The CARIFESTA experiences since 1972 have shown the immense potential that culture has for bringing and binding together Caribbean peoples of every race and nationality. If for that reason alone, we must proudly preserve it. If for that reason alone, we must strongly defend it from being penetrated and damaged by mass media and other forces from external cultures, some simply uncaring but some purposefully programmed to distract and destroy or to dissolve and absorb, but by whichever means ultimately to control us without choice or chance of resistance.

In order to strengthen ourselves for such defense we need to address and discard some of the aspects of our historical heritage that are negative: a ready self-efface-ment before a Euro-American product or model, a propensity for skin-shade preferences or rationalized racism, mistaken notions of self-preservation in the form of parochialism or insularity, and perhaps worst of all, the fostering of paramountcy and rajaship by or around those we entrust with the authority of leadership.

We must agree and then resolve to attack and remove those deep-rooted diseases from our present condition, while at the same time nurturing that conglomerate Caribbean stock which is our basic culture so as to make it flourish even if civilization does become a global village, vitally lighting up our own corner of it and contributing as much rich color as it chooses to receive from the whole.

ECONOMIC DEMOCRACY

The question of economic democracy is a question of justice. It has to do with people being able to reproduce the conditions of their existence in ways that bring security and rising standards of living; it means progress and dignity. The historical condition of Caribbean and African-American people has been one rooted in the contradiction between the economic and political spheres of social existence. On the one hand, the arbitrary separation of economics from politics and, on the other, the acceptance of economic equality in coexistence with claims of formal political equality. This artificial separation has given rise to economic injustice and political oppression and regression.

Injustice associated with hunger, want, deprivation, and economic insecurity result not from economic shortage per se, but from a lack of justice. The absence of freedom and justice result from social systems that elevate greed and possessive individualism to the status of values while devaluing the needs of the collective community. This has been the result of making the state into the servant, not of individual interests, but of powerful and privileged factions that come to dominate society. Economic democracy rests on the idea of reordering the priorities of the state and society. It calls for decentralizing decision-making and allowing for the creation and development of institutions in society through which groups at the community level are free to develop their potential, not merely for survival but for full living. It means conditions under which economic insecurity, injustice, deprivation, scarcity, and terminal poverty are overcome and where justice, freedom, and human dignity become the norm. It means treating the resources of society as patrimony, as a trust of the people in perpetuity. It means gender equality, not merely in law, but also in the structures through which the roles of women in economic production, biological reproduction, sexuality, and socialization are transformed through the abolition of patriarchal domination of society's resources and of women's lives. It means sensitivity to the environment and an end to environmental degradation, a new compact between human beings and nature. Economic democracy is impossible under discrimination based on racial, ethnic, or national origin; it is incompatible with religious intolerance or any form of national chauvinism.

Therefore, for Caribbean peoples who have suffered these many centuries and whose descendants still bear the mark of oppression and exploitation, economic democracy demands nothing less than land reform so that appropriate strategies may be implemented with a design to feed the people. It demands popular participation in decision-making, with a view toward industrial development strategies that result in meaningful employment. The objective is to develop skills and to harness the productive energies of the people. Economic democracy for Caribbean peoples requires educational programs geared to the needs of the modern world economy. This calls for curriculum development. Economic democracy in the Caribbean must take into account the tenuousness in the relationship between sovereignty as a legal factor and autonomy as the capacity not only to design but to effectively implement strategies deemed appropriate for the survival of the nation. Given the small economic scale of Caribbean economy and society, the pursuit of economic democracy demands nothing less than the effective integration of the fragmented Caribbean nation and the building of appropriate linkages across the diaspora, for we are a nation without borders.

TOWARDS A CARIBBEAN THEOLOGY

The encounter of the two worlds, which began with Columbus' entry into the Caribbean, was the beginning of a struggle for survival that continues to this day. The European colonization of the Caribbean and the Americas has led to the near annihilation of the original peoples who inhabited these islands, the enslavement of millions of Africans to replace the indigenous population, and the arrival of thousands of Asians from India, and to a lesser extent China. All these persons were important for one thing, and that was to provide the labor force necessary for creating wealth for the colonizers.

The one factor that allowed the peoples of the Caribbean to survive was their belief system, or religion. Their religious beliefs and practices gave these people, especially the African population, the fortitude they needed to withstand the dehumanizing practices of the Europeans. This does not mean, however, that our people have come out unscathed. The peoples of the Caribbean continue to suffer the trauma of that wretched system.

The religious mosaic of the Caribbean presents the world with the most interesting feature to be found anywhere. Here we have a very curious blending of African and European religious practices. What is so interesting about this meeting of religions is the fact that although the Europeans used all sorts of force—physical and psychological—to wipe out the beliefs and practices of Africans, they have not succeeded, and these beliefs and practices continue to live on (even if not in their pure forms) and have altered Christianity, the religion of the Europeans.

In spite of the unique character of the Caribbean, the world view that dominates the region is still very much eurocentric. The existence of many religious beliefs and practices does not mean the acceptance of all of them. Those that are accepted are the ones the Europeans have approved. Afrocentric religious beliefs are still considered evil and even where there is religious tolerance there is still a great deal of suspicion. Except for students of anthropology, sociology, and history, little effort has been made to understand the religious beliefs and practices with an African base. The officials of the Christian churches do not recognize a need for dialogue with these religious beliefs even when there is conflict between what the churches teach and what the people believe.

The fact that the Christian churches, which by and large are led by clergy who are the descendants of Africans, do not see any value in dialoguing with the religious beliefs and practices found among African peoples goes to show the extent to which prejudice against Africans has been instilled within the peoples of the Caribbean. It also confirms how very eurocentric the churches are in their thinking.

Today one witnesses an even more aggressive attack on the religious practices of African Caribbean peoples, and to some extent the religious practices of the peoples of Indian origin. These religious practices are termed cults and are said to be of satanic origin. This new wave of attack comes from biblical fundamentalists originating in the Bible belt of the USA, some of whom have political agendas.

With the advent of modern means of communication, especially the electronic media, we witness a set of values that can be considered foreign to the region. Caribbean peoples are now being exposed to lifestyles that are unsuitable and unaffordable. These newly found ways of living are destroying the very fabric of the society and are causing governments to turn to international lending agencies to pay wages and balance budgets. These agencies then impose measures on the countries that then deprive poor people of the necessities for comfortable living.

What the people of the Caribbean need, if they are to progress in a meaningful way, is a shift in focus. The eurocentric world view has done untold harm to the Caribbean psyche and continues to undermine their self-confidence; when they are constantly seeking the approval of others, Caribbean people do not have the confidence in themselves that would enable them to seek solutions to Caribbean problems in the Caribbean itself. That self-confidence will come about when they are able to reject a eurocentric world view.

The role of the churches in assisting in the bringing about of a eurocentric world view has not been a minor one. The churches have contributed and continue to contribute to such a view. If the churches are to break with eurocentrism then they must be prepared to question their theology, which is the foundation for eurocentrism.

When we look at the theological thinking behind slavery—and even emancipation—it was not to liberate the African but to "civilize" him, which really meant getting him to be totally submissive to the colonizers. The movements for liberation were not led by the religious thinkers, and in many instances came under heavy criticism from the churches. Today the churches cannot claim to be at the forefront in the quest for total liberation; most of those at the center are persons who either do not adhere to the churches' teachings or are marginalized by church authorities.

During this year of the quincentenary, when some are preparing to celebrate Columbus' entry into the Caribbean, one can see subtle ways in which the eurocentric world view is being confirmed. Even the churches, by observing five hundred years of evangelization while ignoring what those five hundred years have meant for indigenous American and African peoples, are knowingly, or possibly unknowingly, contributing to such a view.

If the churches in the Caribbean felt that they should in some way mark the quincentenary, they should use a totally different approach. The churches should be calling on the theologians in the region to start a process of theological reflection that would enable the peoples of the region to reject totally the suggestion that the world is eurocentric. Today, when there is a call for a new world order, it is imperative that Caribbean theologians come to realize that any idea of a new world order is incomplete if it excludes the views of non-European peoples, particularly if Caribbean thinking is excluded.

CALLS

1. We call upon the churches in the Caribbean to work for the eradication of all forms of racism and to campaign vigorously for the liberation of indigenous peoples in Caribbean states.

2. We call upon the churches of the Caribbean to work for the creation of a Caribbean theology, one that will liberate Caribbean people from a eurocentric world view.

3. We call upon the governments and peoples of the Caribbean to express solidarity with the peoples of Cuba as an economic war is being waged in that country.

4. We call upon the people, churches, and governments of the Caribbean to pursue actions to secure the implementation of the OAS accord and the return of the legitimate government of Haiti.

5. We call upon the Caribbean community to recognize the right of Puerto Rico to self-determination.

6. We call upon the Caribbean community to work for a multilingual community that would make it easier for Caribbean people to communicate with one another.

7. We call upon the governments of nations of the Caribbean to make it easier to travel around the region by providing cheaper air fares and removing visa requirements.

As Caribbean peoples, we reject the attempt to glorify 1492 without asking pardon of indigenous Caribbean and American peoples and peoples of African and Asian origin who have been brutally treated as a result of the encounter, and who to this day continue to suffer the effects of it.

As a Caribbean people who have survived the middle passage, we affirm all the positive things that have survived, such as our rich cultural heritage, our religious traditions, our deep sense of family, and our respect for other peoples. We will work to bring about changes in the economic order that would lead to the proper development of our people, as well as working to recover those elements of our culture that are being eroded by deliberate design of external forces through the use of the powerful electronic media and politically motivated religious groups.

We are committed to the building of a new Caribbean, a Caribbean that does not exclude any nation or state, nor any language group. We embrace all the members of our Caribbean family.

We are totally committed to working with African Americans in North America, Central America, and South America, as well as with Africans in mother Africa and the diaspora for the eradication of racism, and to building bridges of friendship with indigenous Caribbean and American peoples, peoples from the subcontinent of Asia, and indeed all oppressed people in the world.

We are committed to the building of a new world, a world built on justice and peace, and we demand that we be given every opportunity to assist in the creation of this new world.

Index

DATE DUE